There is often a waiting list for this book.

Please return it to
The Adult Mental Health Resource Centre
22554 Lougheed Hwy   Ridge

 **W9-BGY-837**

Kids Are Worth It!

Giving Your Child the
Gift of Inner Discipline

Barbara Coloroso

Somerville House Publishing
Toronto

Canadian Cataloguing in Publication Data

Coloroso, Barbara
     Kids are worth it : giving your child the gift
of inner discipline

ISBN 0-921051-74-3 HC

1. Child rearing. 2. Self-control in children
I. Title.

HQ770.4.C4C65 1994   649'.6   C94-930178-7

Cover Design: Andrew Smith Graphics
Cover Photography: Monty Nuss

Printed in Canada

Published by Somerville House Publishing,
a division of Somerville House Books Limited,
3080 Yonge Street, Suite 5000, Toronto, Ontario M4N 3N1

Somerville House Publishing acknowledges the financial assistance of the Ontario Publishing Centre, the Ontario Arts Council, the Ontario Development Corporation, and the Department of Communications.

20   19   18   17   16   15   14   13   12   11   10   9   8

To Anna, Maria, and Joseph,
I wish for each one of you
the gentle joy that comes with justice seeking and peacemaking

Acknowledgments

My heartfelt thanks to

Jane Somerville and Adrian Zackheim for saying yes to my work, and giving me support, encouragement and guidance throughout these last three years.

Patrick Crean for insisting that the metaphorical axe be taken to my first, second, and third drafts of this book.

Jennifer Glossop and Michael Goodman for providing, through their editing expertise, the necessary axes.

Meg Blackstone for writing all over my manuscript and reminding me again and again of the issues facing parents of young children.

My friends and colleagues, Jim Coombs, Dave Cummins, Connie Dembrowsky, Steve Jackson, Elizabeth Loescher, Patricia Hauck, George Saunders, Ronald Sloan and Judith Timson for their gentle criticisms and helpful suggestions.

Nancy Samolin and Dr. Peter Marshall for their advice and encouragement as they wrote two books and started a third while I labored on this one.

My friend from childhood, writer and editor, Michael McNierney, for showing me how to turn my hand gestures, facial expressions, and spoken words into a coherent written text.

The authors I have quoted throughout this book, whose writings have greatly influenced my work.

My husband, Don, for teaching me how to turn on the computer, fix syntax errors, recover whole chapters lost on the hard drive; and for laughing, crying, and celebrating with me as we give to, grow with, and learn from our three children.

Contents

Introduction

... because they are children
and for no other reason
they have dignity and worth
simply because they are...
—BARBARA COLOROSO

My road to parenting was anything but a direct route. In the late 1960s, at the age of seventeen, I entered a Franciscan convent to become a nun, and began my freshman year at university to become a special education teacher. Little did I know then that the path to these two goals would radically influence my parenting skills years later. The special education courses I took during my first year were based on a behaviorist model, full of rewards and punishments, charts, stickers, stars, threats, and bribes. The model worked with rats; surely it would work with kids. Something didn't seem right about manipulating rats and kids with rewards and punishments, threats and bribes, but I couldn't put into words the discomfort I was feeling, and besides, I didn't know what to use in their place.

The following year, entering the canonical novitiate, also known as a year of silence and reflection, I immersed myself in the study of philosophy and theology. It was during this time that I began to challenge what I had learned in my education courses. I carried on long arguments in my head, similar to the arguments I find myself in now with my three teenagers. And the arguments in my head then were as futile as the arguments with my teenagers now. Since there was no decisive winner or loser, when I began my teaching career I tried to reconcile the teaching methods with my philosophical tenets, but that didn't work either. Believing kids were worth it simply because they were, not because they produced or behaved in a way I wanted them to, didn't match with rewarding "appropriate behavior" and ignoring or punishing "inappropriate behavior." Not treating them in a way I myself would not want to be treated conflicted with "making them mind for their own good." And using techniques that left their dignity and my dignity intact didn't connect with withholding food from rats or kids. What did all of this have to do with the Latin roots of disciplining with authority, that is, giving life to a child's learning? Could children become responsible, resourceful, and resilient if they were controlled, manipulated, and made to mind? Could they develop a sense of inner discipline if all of the control came from outside?

Kids are worth it! Giving your child the gift of inner discipline is my answer to those questions. The answer is more an approach to parenting than a collection of techniques. Believing kids are worth it, not treating them in a way I would not want to be treated, and behaving in a way that leaves our dignity intact are not themselves specific tools; rather, they provide an attitude and an environment that helps me help my children develop a sense of self-discipline.

With a husband and three kids, I am obviously no longer a nun. I am also not a perfect parent. In the midst of the many trials and errors I have had in raising them, I have often told my three kids how lucky they were not to have a perfect parent. Anna has just as often replied, "You are so lucky; you don't have perfect kids either." Maria has been known to ask, "How come you don't always do what you tell other people to do?" And Joseph once asked a group of teachers, who had just attended one of my lectures, if they would like him to be "good" or "bad." They laughed, I groaned, and with an innocent look on his face, Joseph remarked, "Well, they want to see what you would do either way." The following pages are what I do, have done, would have done, wished I had done, and plan to do next time.

These are only hints and guesses,
Hints followed by guesses; and the rest
Is prayer, observance, discipline, thought and action.
                                    —T. S. ELIOT, FROM *FOUR QUARTETS*

Chapter 1

Kids Are Worth It!

Believe nothing merely because you have been told it...
Do not believe what your teacher tells you merely out of
respect for the teacher. But whatsoever, after due
examination and analysis, you find to be kind, conducive
to the good, the benefit, the welfare of all beings—that
doctrine believe and cling to and take it as your guide.
                                        —BUDDHIST APHORISM

You have come here to find what you already have.
                                        —BUDDHIST APHORISM

There are no quick fixes, easy answers, or recipes for parenting,
but I believe most of us have the tools we need to be good parents if only we could find them. Our problem is that these tools
are often covered over at the bottom of our mental toolboxes.
The tools that come first to hand do not serve us well. These
tools were given to us, often unintentionally and without malice,
by our parents, grandparents, siblings, and extended family, as
well as by our society. Often, when a hammer would best serve
our needs, we reach into the toolbox and come out with a hatchet
without realizing it. It is no wonder that some of our parenting
carpentry is such a mess.

To get the tools we need, we must first become aware of the
inappropriate, ineffective, or destructive tools that we are using.
Then we must be willing to let go of the old tools and begin
using those that can serve us and our children better.

In this book we will look closely at a few of these inappropriate tools. Some you may never have used or even thought of; others you'll swear were at your dinner table last night. Look them over and decide which ones you need to change.

Talk to your kids about them and ask your kids to help you. It's unnerving to be in a crowd at the city park and have my son tell me I'm giving him a minilecture when I am right in the middle of a good one, or to have one of my daughters tell me, rightfully so, that the question I just asked was really dumb. But in both situations the kids were right, and I got the opportunity to stop and start over using more appropriate tools. Are you uncomfortable with the way you handled your teenager last night? Did you "lose it" when your toddler decorated the walls with permanent marker? Are you angry, hurt, or embarrassed? Questioning and exploring are the first steps toward change. It's a two-way street; when you talk to your children about helping you stop using inappropriate tools or doing things that get in the way of their growth, you can also show them that the temper tantrum they are throwing in the grocery store just isn't going to get them the cereal they want.

As you begin to identify the ineffective tools that are a part of your parenting toolbox, you will also realize that you have the opportunity to unpack them and replace them with lighter, more responsible, constructive tools that do not weigh you down.

Before identifying and sorting the tools, it helps to know what kind of mental toolbox we are using to carry them around. The toolbox is defined by the answers to two basic questions:

1. What is my parenting philosophy?
2. What is my goal in parenting—to influence and empower my children or to control them and make them mind?

WHAT IS MY PARENTING PHILOSOPHY?

Few of us explore our philosophy of parenting *before* we become parents. Then, after we have our children, when we are tired and worn out, we tend to parent the way we were parented. Our mother's words roll off our tongue even though we swore we'd never talk like her. Our hand swings to hit our child just as our father's hand swung to hit us, and yet we swore we'd never hit our children. In a panic we frantically read parenting books and attend every lecture on parenting offered in our community.

Yet a lot of crazy, unproductive, or unhealthy techniques in parenting are advocated by so-called experts. If we haven't looked at our own parenting philosophy, we won't be able to separate the good from the bad; we won't be able to challenge with conviction "the way it has always been done," or to reject such invalid premises as "if it was good enough for me, it's good enough for my children." However, if we know our own philosophy, we can examine various parenting tools including those we are using right now. If a tool doesn't fit with our philosophy, regardless of who said it or what kind of research is behind it, we can choose not to use it. I have found three tenets to be the most useful in evaluating my own and other people's recommended parenting techniques:

1. **Kids are worth it.** I'm sure you believe this, too, because I know you're not in parenting for the money.
2. **I will not treat a child in a way I myself would not want to be treated.** If I wouldn't want it done to me, I have no business doing it to my child.
3. **If it works and leaves a child's and my own dignity intact, do it.** Just because it works doesn't make it good; it must work and leave the child's *and* my own dignity intact.

KIDS ARE WORTH IT!

They are worth it *because* they are children and for no other reason. They have dignity and worth simply because they are. They don't need to prove their value as human beings; they don't have to prove their worthiness to us; nor do they need to earn our affection. Our love for them cannot be conditional, although our likes and dislikes can be. We don't have to like their hairdos, the earring in the nose, or their strange-looking shoes. Our love for them does have to be something they can count on, something they know will always be there, even when they are in trouble and we'd probably rather not be there. Being there when they are resting comfortably in our arms, smiling up at us for the first time, is easy; being there when they are cutting teeth, colicky, and crying through the night is not. Being there when they learn to ride a two-wheeler is easy; being there when they have wrecked the family car is not. Being there when they are performing in the school play is easy; being there when they call from the police station is not.

Niyimpa kor ntsetse ba—"It takes an entire village to raise a child."

—AFRICAN PROVERB

Believing that kids are worth it also means believing that our neighbor's kids are worth it. As adults we need to be willing to make the sacrifices necessary to ensure that all children in our community will be able to have what they need: proper medical treatment; food, clothing, and shelter; opportunities to explore, grow, and be nurtured in a safe environment. This is too much for one individual to do, but it is definitely possible if as a society we believe that our kids are worth it, worth the time, energy, resources, and commitment necessary. Just saying we believe it is not enough; we must be willing to act on that belief. If we say we are committed to the well-being of our children, then we need to reconsider how as a society we spend our money.

A Lebanese citizen, weary of the continuous shelling in his homeland, told a *New York Times* correspondent, "There will be peace when we begin to love our children more than we hate our enemies." If we are going to say our kids are worth it, we must be willing to put our money where our mouth is. We must be willing to put our child-rearing practices there as well.

I WILL NOT TREAT A CHILD IN A WAY I MYSELF WOULD NOT WANT TO BE TREATED

The ethic that we should treat others as we ourselves want to be treated and not in a way we ourselves would not want to be treated is found in all the great religions of the world:

1. Baha'i:
"It is Our wish and desire that every one of you may become a source of all goodness unto men, and an example of uprightness

to mankind. Beware lest you prefer yourself above your neighbours."
—Baha u llah, Gleanings, 315

2. Buddhism:
"Hurt not others in ways that you yourself would find hurtful."
—Undana-varqa: 518

3. Christianity:
"As ye would that men should do to you, do ye also to them likewise."
 —Luke 6:31

4. Confucianism:
"Surely it is the maxim of loving-kindness: Do not unto others that you would not have them do unto you."
—Analects, XV, 23

5. Hinduism:
"This is the sum of all true righteousness: deal with others as thou wouldst thyself be dealt by. Do nothing to thy neighbour which thou wouldst not have him do to thee after."
—The Mahabharata

6. Islam:
"No one of you is a believer until he desires for his brother that which he desires for himself."
—Sunnah

7. Judaism:
"What is hateful to you, do not to your fellow men. That is the entire Law, all the rest is commentary."
 —The Talmud, Shabbat 31a

8. Taoism:
"The good man ought to pity the malignant tendencies of others; to rejoice over their excellence; to help them in their straits; to regard their gains as if they were his own, and their losses in the same way."
—The Thai-shang, 3

9. **Zoroastrianism:**
"That nature only is good when it shall not do unto another whatever is not good for its own self."
—Dadistan-I Dinik, 94:5

The Golden Rule, as it is called, can serve us well when applied to our relations with our children. If we are not sure whether what we are doing with children is right, we need only put ourselves in their place and ask if we would want it done to us—not *was* it done to us, but would we *want* it done to us? If the answer is no, then we have to ask ourselves why we would ever want to do it to our children.

If I wouldn't want to be slapped across the face, why would I slap my son? If I wouldn't want to be screamed at when I made a mistake, why would I scream at my daughter when she dropped the cake I had decorated for my mother-in-law? If I wouldn't want to be ridiculed when I attempted to learn to roller-blade at forty-three, why would I ridicule my daughter as she jerked the car out of first gear into second after being shown ten times how to do it smoothly? If I wouldn't want my gardening skills to be compared with my neighbor's, why would I compare my son's math performance with his older sisters'?

We don't have to look only at the here and now to see that it is best not to treat kids in a way we would not want to be treated. If we use techniques today that control our children in an attempt to make them mind, we will be in trouble when we got old and this next generation has learned (because we spent years teaching them) how to control those weaker than themselves. I'll guarantee you, when we are old, those weaker than them will be us. I won't do to a child at seven something I wouldn't want done to me at seventy. It's hard to imagine my grown child putting me on a sticker contract for getting out of bed, dressed, and to breakfast on time in the morning when I am seventy years old. "Come on, Mom. Remember, if you get up on the first call, get dressed by yourself, and show up for breakfast on time, I will give you five stars. You can put those five stars on the chart we put up on your bedroom wall. If you get twenty-five stars by Friday, you can redeem those stars for a trip to the bingo hall with your friends." It would be even harder to imagine being hit for speaking my own mind—in other words, for talking back—when I am seventy years old. It might appear to work, but it would be at the expense of my sense of dignity and self-worth.

A good check of a parenting tool is "Would I want it done to me?" As simple a question as it appears to be, it can make the difference in how we parent this next generation. I believe that for the first time in our history we have the tools necessary to break the cycles of dysfunction, abuse, and neglect. We now have the individual and collective awareness of the damages that physical and emotional abuse can cause a child, a family, and a society. I am not naive enough to believe that it will be simple to make the necessary changes. There will be strong opposition from those who believe children are property to be owned and controlled. Some will fight to the bitter end to assert their "right" to abuse their children physically, emotionally, and sexually. I also know that those of us committed to making a change must also fight the demons from within, for we carry in our mental toolboxes destructive tools that are well-worn family heirlooms, passed on from generation to generation.

Too often children are treated as the property of adults, to be used or abused by those bigger than themselves. In the late 1800s Elizabeth Barrett Browning wrote about children being abused in factories:

> Do you hear the children weeping, O my brothers,
> Ere the sorrow comes with years...
> They are weeping in the playtime of the others,
> In the country of the free.
> —FROM "THE CRY OF THE CHILDREN"

Have we not yet learned to hear their cry? Apparently not. In 1978, James Dobson wrote in his book, *Temper Your Child's Temper Tantrums*:

> For the strong-willed toddler, mild spankings can begin between fifteen and eighteen months of age.... Administer spankings with a neutral object—that is, a small switch or belt—but rarely with the hand.... A spanking should hurt or else it will have no influence.... Some strong-willed children absolutely demand to be spanked and their wishes should be granted. However, the compliant youngster should

have experienced his last woodshed episode by the end of his first decade.

He still recommends these practices today when speaking to parents on his internationally syndicated radio talk shows.

Under the guise of discipline, physical and emotional violence toward children is legitimized and sanctioned. ("No kid of mine is going to talk to me like that. I'll wash your mouth out with soap." "A good spanking never hurt anyone." "You're so stupid. Even a three-year-old could do better than that.")

Philip Grevin, a historian, states the problem and offers a positive solution in his book, *Spare the Child:*

> The past holds a powerful grip upon the future by shaping feelings, actions, and beliefs in the present. The pain and suffering experienced by children who have been physically punished resonate through time, first during the seemingly endless days and nights of childhood and adolescence, and later through the lives we lead as adults. The feelings generated by the pain caused by adults' assaults against children are mostly repressed, forgotten or denied, but they actually never disappear. Everything remains recorded in our innermost beings, and the effects of punishment permeate our lives, our thought, our culture and our world.

> The evidence is everywhere—surrounding us, engulfing us—yet, like the air we breathe, usually invisible to us. Once it becomes visible, surely we will begin to see our world and ourselves differently. Then we will be in a better position to consider alternatives to coercion, hitting and painful discipline and to make the choice that will be more nurturing, loving, and life-enhancing than those associated, generation after generation, with physical punishment.

Physical punishment is an obvious form of abuse. Not-so-obvious and often-overlooked forms of abuse are emotional battering and neglect. When children hear constant criticism and putdowns, they begin to see themselves as not good enough or just plain bad. ("Can't you do anything right?" "You were an accident. I wish you had never been born." "Why can't you be like your brother?")

Other children are neglected by their parents. They may have all the material possessions they could want, but no nurturing, cuddling, or warm words of encouragement—only coldness. The deep sense of loss and grief doesn't show up in bruises or broken bones but in a broken heart—a hopelessness and despair that affect their marriages, their connections as family, their work, and their play.

Once we are committed to the idea that we will not treat our children in a way we ourselves would not want to be treated, we can begin to find responsible, effective alternatives to the punitive tools of threatening, hitting, psychologically or verbally abusing, neglecting, or abandoning our children.

IF IT WORKS AND LEAVES A CHILD'S AND MY OWN DIGNITY INTACT, DO IT

Just because a technique works or appears to work doesn't make it a good one. A serious problem with the many parenting tools that control kids and make them mind is that both parents' and children's dignity and sense of self-worth are sacrificed in the name of behavior modification or behavior management. Behavior management is based on power and control. It is a way of manipulating children through bribes, rewards, threats, and punishment. It "makes" children mind, but it emphatically does not leave their dignity intact. The "good behavior" is purchased at a terrible cost.

BRIBES, REWARDS, THREATS, AND PUNISHMENT—POWER AND CONTROL

Never rely on rewards and punishments to promote altruistic behavior. Both tactics send the wrong message: that kindness is a commodity that can be bought or

bartered. In the end, loving support and good example are a child's best lessons in the art of compassion.
—ELIZABETH NAVAR FINELY, "LITTLE BIG HEARTS," *PARENTING*

During my undergraduate studies, I saw the power of behavior modification firsthand. I saw it work—*on rodents*. It is not too hard to see the dangers of applying it to human beings. By its nature the technique keeps a child dependent and fearful—dependent on a parent for rewards given for *positive* behavior and fearful of whatever punishment that same parent would mete out for *negative* behavior.

Regardless of the fancy words it may be clothed in, these techniques are about domination, manipulation, and control—not exactly what you were thinking of when you rewarded your child with a candy bar because he went a day without hitting his sister. Or when you offered to buy your daughter a new outfit if she kept her room clean. Rather than seeing children as unique individuals with the right to express their own needs and have them respected, parents who consistently employ these techniques tend to see kids as people needing to be shaped and made to behave in the way the parents want them to behave. That this attitude is mostly unconscious makes it all the more dangerous.

Bribes, rewards, threats, and punishment leave control in the hands of the parents (sometimes literally) and give children the message that "I, as an adult, can and will make you mind," often with the rationale "for your own good."

BRIBES AND REWARDS

Do good for good is good to do.
—JAMES NACHTWAY

Dr. Alice Miller, author and psychiatrist, refers to the use of positive reinforcement bribes and rewards as "stoning a child with kisses." ("If you are good at the store, I will let you play with your friend when you get home." Note the use of the words I *will* let *you*. The relationship with the child is based on control. "If you get five As on your report card, I'll buy you that bike." "If you stop crying, you can get a cookie out of the jar.") The child may be good at the store, get five As, and stop crying, but the message is still about control and manipulation. The control is external to the child, not internal. The responsible actions are performed for the payoff, not out of a sense of self-esteem, self-control, or self-responsibility.

Kathy Tyler, a parent concerned about the abundant use of external rewards in her children's school, wrote in a letter to her school board:

> The way we choose to motivate people says a great deal about how we feel about them. When we have faith in someone and respect for the task, enticing them with treats becomes unnecessary. Faith and respect alone inspire their action. However, if the task seems distasteful to us, or the doer unworthy of our faith, then we resort to "carrot dangling." This "treat for tricks" technique may work well for animal trainers, but I doubt it serves us well in raising a future generation of thinkers and problem solvers. (Actually, even marine mammal trainers have found that whales and dolphins respond best to signs of appreciation like pats, hugs, and smiles.) ... It appears that we are operating with an attitude of fear rather than faith.

Kids who are consistently bribed and rewarded are likely to grow into adults who are overly dependent on others for approval and recognition, lacking their own self-confidence and sense of responsibility. The questions they will often ask are:

- What's in it for me?
- What's the payoff?
- Does it count for anything?
- Do you like it?
- Did you see me do it?
- Did I do it right?

THREATS AND PUNISHMENT

If you want to prevent your child from developing a normal responsible conscience which will enable him to control

himself, build your relationship with him on a punitive basis. Control his behavior primarily by spanking and scolding, especially scolding.
                —ROSS D. CAMPBELL, *HOW TO REALLY LOVE YOUR CHILD*

Threats and punishments are by their nature punitive; they are adult-oriented, are based on judgment, and impose power from without instead of acknowledging the power within children. They arouse anger and resentment and invite more conflict. Most important, they rob a child of his sense of dignity and self-worth. They can take the form of:

Isolation ("If you hit your sister again, you will stay in your room for the rest of the day.")

Embarrassment and humiliation ("If you lie, I will tape a long cardboard nose on your face and you will look like Pinocchio.")

Shaming ("Shame on you for wetting your pants.")

Emotional isolation ("Don't come to me for a hug—you were a bad boy to bite your brother.")

Grounding ("You talk like that to your mother one more time and you will be grounded for a week.")

Brute force ("Bend over, and don't you dare cry. If you cry, I will hit you harder.")

The use of such negative reinforcement degrades, humiliates, and dehumanizes children who are the objects of it. Indeed they may stop teasing their sister, not lie openly to their parents, quit biting their brother, and not cry, but they have also learned to behave "appropriately" only when they fear getting caught and punished. Their sense of self-worth, their sense of responsibility, and their sense of appropriate, responsible, caring actions are seriously compromised.

Faced with domination, manipulation, and control by someone bigger than themselves, children will experience one of three things:

1. *Fright—doing as they are told out of dependency and fear.* ("If I don't do what she tells me to do, she will make me go

to bed without supper again." "He'll beat me again if I go over to your house.") Children will obey the adult only until they are able to get what they need themselves or grow big enough to strike back or leave.

2. *Fight—attacking the adult or taking the anger out on others.* ("If he hits me one more time, I am going to kill him." "If Mom can hit me when I've done something wrong, I don't see why I can't hit my little sister.") This response often produces an equal or more severe response from the adult, and the cycle escalates.

3. *Flight—running away mentally or physically.* To escape from a controlling and manipulating parent, children stop letting the parent into their world of feelings, beliefs, and activities, or they actually remove themselves from the house—they are forced to run away to survive. ("I'm okay, just leave me alone, I can handle this myself." "I don't know what time the game is, Dad. Besides I don't want you there." "I'm out of here. I'll take my chances on the street.") Sometimes the escape is into self, and the results can be devastating. Children whose needs and feelings are dismissed, ignored, punished, or negated begin to believe that they have no value or worth and are at high risk from the perils of sexual promiscuity, drug abuse, and suicide.

CREATIVE POWER IS INFLUENCE, NOT FORCE

A man convinced against his will is of the same opinion still.
—GERMAN PROVERB

In my first year of teaching, I came into the classroom armed with all of the behavior-management tools I had been taught in my university method courses. Having left behind my year of silence and all the questions about control and manipulation raised during that time, I thought one of my main responsibilities was to get my students "to mind." A five-

and-a-half-year-old taught me differently. He simply would not sit in his seat. I tried all the management tools I had been taught: "Jeff, please sit.... Look how nicely Susie is sitting.... I'll give you five stars if you sit in your seat.... The principal is coming in, please sit! ... SIT!" Nothing worked, not even the direct approach. He looked me straight in the eye and dared, "Make me!" I walked over and forcefully sat him down; he leaped right back up. I then did something I would never do today: I grabbed him and sat down, pulling him with me. Laughing at me, he announced, "As soon as you get up, I'm getting up too." I learned from him that I really couldn't control kids and make them mind. Even with all my behavioral tools I couldn't make them do something they chose not to do. Not only did I feel foolish but Jeff was still out of his seat, and neither of us had much dignity intact.

What Jeff was helping me to learn firsthand was that really powerful teachers and parents do not attempt to control their children through threats, punishments, or rewards—all of which can backfire. In fact they don't attempt to control their children at all. Control tactics compel or prevent actions and force kids to behave in an adult-approved way. Often the result of control is either that kids become submissive, obedient, and compliant or that they go to the opposite extreme and rebel against any and all authority.

Thoroughly exhausted, I went home that evening to reevaluate my role as a teacher, my teaching techniques, and my goals. It did not happen overnight, but I came to see that to be truly effective in the classroom, I had to honor my belief that kids were worth it by treating them with the dignity and regard I wished for myself. I could, and would, use only those techniques that left both of us with our dignity intact.

A few years after my disastrous experience with Jeff, while teaching a group of troubled adolescents at a university laboratory school, I was confronted by my university adviser, who was teaching a course on behavior management. His graduate students had come into my classroom to observe, and were bothered that I had no charts on the wall, no token system of rewards, no stickers, and no stars. Also I wasn't handing out a lot of praise, using brute force or threats, and taking away privileges. I asked my adviser if he felt the students were "on task," meaning doing the work that was expected of them. Well, yes they were. Were they working independently? Yes. Were they working cooperatively? Yes. Were they solving their own problems? Yes. Were they resolving conflict together? Yes. Were they killing one another or innocent bystanders? No. The defense rested. What we were doing was working.

It didn't happen in a day. Many of these students had come from programs that were saturated with heavy-duty behavior-modification techniques. They had been on tokens from morning to night. One token for getting out of bed, two tokens for smiling when they got out of bed, and a third token for getting dressed—all of which they could redeem for breakfast. It's not surprising that, once in my class, they would ask, "What are you going to give me if I get this assignment done?" My response was much different from what they were used to: "What you get is you get done, that's what you get." It took a while to convince them that I believed in them, that I knew they were capable of doing the task they needed to do, and that they could solve their own problems. Yes, their progress was charted, but they charted it themselves. And there were no stars at the end—just the satisfaction of knowing they had accomplished a task and the opportunity to go on to another skill. And they had the faith in themselves that they could master it too.

The same method works at home. A five-year-old struggling to ride a two-wheeler needs support, literally and figuratively. She needs encouragement. ("I know, you can do it. Try it again.") She doesn't need threats. ("If you don't get up on that bike right now, I'm going to spank you." "You'll have to ride a three-wheeler all of your life.") And once she takes off on her own, she doesn't need a reward for accomplishing this difficult task. ("If you learn to ride the bike, I'll get you a new one." "I'll give you an ice-cream cone if you ride down the street without help.") Her own satisfaction and faith in herself are the best reward. She won't be able to tell you she has these things, but the sense of well-being that they give her goes so deep that she will instinctively strive for them.

The reward for a thing well done, is to have done it.
                                        —RALPH WALDO EMERSON

Influence and Empower, Not Control and Make Mind

True obedience is a matter of love, which makes it
voluntary, not by fear or force.
                    —DOROTHY DAY, PEACE ACTIVIST

Do you want to influence and empower your children or control them and make them mind? Most of us will probably say that we want to influence and empower. But often our techniques belie that answer and very forcefully demonstrate that we are out to control our children and make them mind. We might not use brute force, but we do tell our child to go stand in the corner when she has hit her brother. Obediently she goes and stands in the corner, or defiantly she refuses to stand in the corner, forcing us to resort to other punitive measures. Either way she has not learned to deal responsibly with her anger, and we still won't trust her alone with her younger brother.

INFLUENCE

One of the truly great educators of our time, Haim Ginott, commenting on the powerful influence we have on children, said:

It is my personal approach that creates the climate. It is my daily mood that makes the weather.... I possess a tremendous power to make a child's life miserable or joyous. I can be a tool of torture or an instrument of inspiration. I can humiliate or humor, hurt or heal. In all situations, it is my response that decides whether a crisis will be escalated or de-escalated and a child humanized or dehumanized.

If we believe that our goal is to influence and empower our children, then our behavior needs to flow from that belief. The first part, influence, is the easiest to do because we do it whether we make the effort to or not. The question is, Will our influence be positive, productive, and responsible, or negative, unproductive, and irresponsible?

Your habit of smoking a pack of cigarettes a day will not make your child smoke, too, but your actions will definitely influence your child's behavior. If you spend your weekends in outdoor activities with your children instead of sitting in front of the TV, the chances of your children becoming couch potatoes when they grow up are slim—possible but slim. If you take good care of yourself, your children will probably take good care of themselves.

We influence and are influenced by the people around us all of the time. If I gave a lecture and the entire audience got up and left, they would definitely influence my behavior. Note that they would not control it. I could continue to talk to an empty room if I wanted to. I could choose to give the same lecture next time, possibly sparking another mass exodus, or I could look at my lecture to see how I might improve it. I could also seek out the advice of an elder in my field of work and ask for some guidance and advice. You will be influenced—not controlled—by the information in this book. What you do with the information is your choice. Would that we could give children the same choice.

> Love is the ability and willingness to allow those that you care for to be what they choose for themselves without any insistence that they satisfy you.
> —WAYNE DYER

EMPOWER

> From a little spark may burst a mighty flame
> —DANTE

Power is like a candle with a huge flame. Our flame as parents can light up the life of every child we come in contact with and never be diminished itself. The beauty of empowering another human being is that we never lose our own power in the process. In fact we will have a greater light to see by; and in old age, when our light starts to flicker, and it will, we will have this next generation's light to guide us. (We had better hope it's a lot brighter than ours, considering what we are leaving them to deal with.)

Empowering our children involves first giving them a secure, safe, nurturing environment—offering them unconditional love, caring touch, tenderness, and concern for their physical, emotional, and spiritual well-being. With a strong, loving foundation in place we can begin to give our children the opportunity to make choices and decisions, all the while providing a structure on which they can build, increasing their responsibilities and decision-making opportunities as they grow. Teaching them to make their own decisions enables them to learn to be responsible individuals who can act in their own best interest, stand up for themselves, and exercise their own rights while respecting the rights and legitimate needs of others.

If we accept that we can influence and empower our children, we will no longer feel that we must control them and make them mind. We can then begin to look at the empowerment tools that are the alternatives to the manipulative tools of behavioral management. They are encouragement and discipline.

ENCOURAGEMENT, NOT BRIBES AND REWARDS

There is a universal truth I have found in my work.
Everybody longs to be loved. And the greatest thing we
can do is let somebody know that they are loved and
capable of loving.
    —FRED ROGERS (OF "MISTER ROGERS' NEIGHBORHOOD"),
                                              IN *PARADE*

Instead of giving them rewards and bribes, we can encourage our children. Promised bribes, rewards, stars, praise—all of these come after the deed is done the way we want it done. They are highly judgmental and say, "You have done well what I wanted you to do; you have pleased me." The emphasis is all on the parent. Encouragement, on the other hand, can come at any time, is nonjudgmental, and emphasizes the child's importance by expressing confidence and trust in the child. A child trying to walk falls flat on his face. He doesn't need praise. ("You fell well. Good fall!") He doesn't need a bribe. ("Come to me and I'll give you a cookie.") He certainly doesn't need punishment. ("You klutz, when are you going to learn to walk?") What he needs is encouragement, someone to be there to help him up if he needs it and to tell him, "I know you can do it. Try again."

Encouragement inspires. It imparts courage and confidence. It fosters and gives support. It helps a child develop a sense of self-pride and enhances internal motivation. Encouraging a child means that one or more of the following critical life messages are coming through, either by word or by action:

- I believe in you
- I trust you
- I know you can handle this
- You are listened to
- You are cared for
- You are very important to me

The ways these messages can be expressed are as various as the parents expressing them. These six critical life messages are concrete and unambiguous. They need no definition or explanation. There is no way they can be faked and no chance they won't be received if they are truly offered.

These messages are also conveyed in true discipline, the creative and life-giving alternative to punishment.

DISCIPLINE, NOT PUNISHMENT

The main source of good *discipline* is growing up in a loving family, being loved and learning to love in return.
—BENJAMIN SPOCK, *BABY AND CHILD CARE*

Instead of punishing we can discipline our children. Contrary to popular belief, discipline is not synonymous with punishment.

Punishment, by its nature, is adult-oriented, requires judgment on the part of the adult, imposes power from without, arouses anger and resentment, and invites more conflict. Punishment is doing something to a child when the child behaves in a way that the parent judges to be inappropriate or irresponsible. It involves a strong element of moral judgment and demonstrates the parent's ability to control a child by force. It also teaches the child that might makes right. I shudder when I see a parent slapping a five-year-old child while yelling, "You bad boy, don't you ever hit your little brother." What it says to the kid is that when you are bigger, you can hit someone smaller than you—which is exactly what the kid has just done.

Often the child does not know what the punishment will be, because usually there is only an arbitrary connection between what the child had done and the resulting punishment. Sometimes the attempt to control a child is more subtle than physical force. Under the guise of "logical consequences," some parents will try to make kids "feel the pain" for the wrong that they have done rather than find a way to solve the problems that were created by the kids' actions. A seemingly logical consequence ends up being nonphysical punishment, but punishment, nevertheless. A child fails a class and his dad takes away his skateboard as punishment. Another doesn't put her toys away and finds the next day that her mom, to teach her daughter a lesson, has given the toys to a local charity. A ten-year-old shows up late for dinner and is told to go to his room and not expect any food until breakfast. Two children are fighting and their parents ground them for a month. None of this really makes any sense to a child (or to a thoughtful adult).

DISCIPLINE WITH AUTHORITY

Children are extraordinarily precious members of a society; they are exquisitely alert, sensitive, and conscious of their surroundings; and they are extraordinarily vulnerable to maltreatment or emotional abuse by adults who refuse to give them the profound respect and affection to which they are unconditionally entitled.

—*WISDOM OF THE ELDERS*

Discipline is not judgmental, arbitrary, confusing, or coercive. Going back to the Latin roots, to *discipline with authority* means to *give life to learning.* Our goal as parents is to give life to our children's learning—to instruct, to teach, to help them develop self-discipline—an ordering of the self from the inside, not imposition from the outside. Any technique that does not give life to a child's learning and leaves a child's dignity intact cannot be called discipline—it is punishment, no matter what language it is clothed in. The following four steps of discipline give life to a child's learning in a way that punishment cannot. Discipline

1. Shows kids what they have done
2. Gives them ownership of the problem
3. Gives them options for solving the problem
4. Leaves their dignity intact

While on a field trip with his third-grade class, my son, Joseph, had broken a beaver bait jar at the natural-history museum. It could have been worse. It could have been an irreplaceable dinosaur leg. He was very lucky. It was a very replaceable beaver bait jar. I was pleased to learn that my son had not been punished for what he had done. He was not paddled—which is punishment, no matter how you took at it. He was not sent to the principal's office—which could have been punishment. He did not have to write five hundred times "I will not break a beaver bait jar"—which is punishment. Nor was he banned from the next field trip—which could have been punishment. Instead his teacher wisely explained to him, "Joseph, you have a serious problem, and I know you can handle it." Joe wrote a letter to the natural-history museum staff; he replaced the beaver bait jar (which was a trip unto itself); and he put in writing how he would handle his feet, hands, and mouth creatively and constructively on the next field trip. My son was not punished, he was disciplined—shown what he had done wrong, given ownership of the problem, given ways to solve it, and was left with his dignity intact.

In giving life to children's learning, discipline involves real-world consequences or intervention, or a combination of the two. It deals with the reality of the situation, not with the power and control of the adult.

Real-world consequences either happen naturally or are *reasonable* consequences that are intrinsically related to the child's actions:

- If a child puts her shoes on the wrong feet, her feet hurt (*natural*)
- If a child goes outside on a chilly day without a coat, he will get cold (*natural*)
- If a teenager wrecks the car, she may use the car as soon as she has a plan for getting it repaired (*reasonable*)
- If a twelve-year-old borrows your clothes and returns them torn, he needs to get them repaired (*reasonable*)
- If he continues to ruin things he borrows, soon no one will loan him any more clothes (*natural*)
- Coming home late for dinner might mean a child eats a cold supper (*natural*) or can heat it up (*reasonable*)

The lessons are learned without nagging, reminding, or warning from the parent. Real-world consequences teach children about the world around them and that they themselves have positive control over their lives. They can make decisions and solve problems.

If natural consequences are not life-threatening, morally threatening, or unhealthy, it is good to let a child experience them, without warnings or reminders. But if the natural consequences *are* life-threatening, morally threatening, or unhealthy, as a wise and caring parent you must intervene.

LIFE-THREATENING CONSEQUENCES

Anytime a child's life would be at risk, there is no question that a parent must intervene. This is no time to teach a child a lesson.

You wouldn't tell your eighteen-month-old that if she ran out in the street, she would get hit by a car, then say to her, "Just try it." No, you have an obligation to keep a toddler safe, to keep her in a place where you can see and prevent her from running out in the street. At eighteen months she is too young to be told,

"If you run out in the street, you will need to stay in the fenced yard."

Some parents would argue that if a child is too young to understand a reasonable consequence and the natural consequence is life-threatening, then "a good swat on the butt" is the solution. My neighbors' two-year-old showed his parents the folly of such reasoning. He understood cause and effect, only not in the same way his parents did. After getting his swat on the butt, the next time he wanted to go exploring, he ran across the street with his hands on the seat of his pants. Punishment often teaches a child that if he is going to do something he shouldn't do, what he needs to do first is "cover his butt."

If your ten-year-old threatened to jump off the roof of the house, you wouldn't say, "Go ahead and experience the real-world consequences for your irresponsible behavior. We'll discuss it after you land." No, you grab the kid and give her a second chance at life. If your teenager arrived home dead drunk and fought you for the car keys so that he could drive a friend home, you wouldn't say, "Go ahead and experience the real-world consequences. See if I care." No, you would either restrain your kid, hide the car keys, or remove the distributor cap from the car—or all three.

MORALLY THREATENING CONSEQUENCES

Lynn Leight, the author of *Raising Sexually Healthy Children*, puts moral issues in the framework of four answers to the question, Why can't I?

1. Because it is unkind. (For instance, an eight-year-old says she is not going to invite two girls in her class to a birthday party, when she is asking all of the other girls in the class.)
2. Because it is hurtful. (A four-year-old is holding the family cat by its tail.)
3. Because it is unfair. (A six-year-old keeps taking toys away from a two-year-old, does it "nicely," and leaves the two-year-old bewildered.)
4. Because it is dishonest. (A teenager tells you he is going to take a test for a friend.)

In each of these situations a parent can take the opportunity to teach the child about the virtues of kindness, compassion, fairness, and honesty and can provide guidance and options for behaving in a virtuous way. If you are a courageous and giving parent with principles and values that you are willing to stand up for, if you "walk your talk," your children will have a wonderful model to learn from and emulate.

UNHEALTHY CONSEQUENCES

If a child is behaving in a way that would put her health at serious risk, a parent or other caring adult needs to intervene. For example, if a twelve-year-old refuses to brush his teeth regularly after he gets braces, the dentist can remove the braces and suggest that the child get the braces back on when he is willing to do what is necessary to protect his teeth (*reasonable*), rather than letting him experience the natural and lifelong consequence of discolored or rotted teeth. Similarly, a bulimic teenager needs caring adults to intervene before her physical and emotional conditions become life-threatening.

If a situation is neither life-threatening, morally threatening, nor unhealthy, ask yourself if the natural consequence of what your child is doing would give life to your child's learning. If the answer is yes, stay out of it and let nature take its course. If your toddler wears her shoes on the wrong feet, she'll figure it out soon enough. I've yet to see a teenager with shoes on the wrong feet; it just doesn't happen.

RSVP—FOUR CLUES TO REASONABLE CONSEQUENCES

If the natural consequence is nonexistent or would not give life to your child's learning, it may be time to help out with reasonable consequences. Many parents struggle to come up with consequences that are appropriate and meaningful. If you have to struggle to come up with a consequence, step back and ask yourself if you are trying to punish your child or discipline him. Natural consequences just happen; reasonable ones take a bit of reasoning but not a lot of energy on your part, and certainly shouldn't be a struggle. Discipline by its nature requires more energy on the part of the child than on the part of the parent. With your guidance and support as well as the backbone of the four elements of discipline (see page 29), the issue for your child is to solve a problem she has created and to learn from the whole experience.

Just as RSVP is a request for a response, a consequence that is reasonable, simple, valuable, and practical will invite a responsible action from your child. When in doubt about a consequence, you can check if all four clues are present:

1. **R—Is it reasonable?** Does it make sense and is it appropriate? If a toddler breaks a glass, it would not be reasonable to have her pick up the pieces, but it would be reasonable to ask her to hold the bag as you picked up the shards. Sending her to her room doesn't make sense; having her help mop up after the glass is picked up does. Spanking her isn't appropriate, nor is making her drink out of a baby bottle, but asking her to pick one of two plastic glasses to use today is appropriate.

2. **S—Is it simple?** If you find yourself drawing up a ten-page legal contract with your teenager concerning the use of the family car, you are asking for trouble, arguments, and attempts at finding loopholes. ("You told me I couldn't use the car if I let it run out of gas; you didn't say anything about running out of oil.") Far better to teach your teenager that with the opportunity of using the car come certain *responsibilities*. Driving it into a post in the school parking lot might mean he gets the opportunity to ride his bike to school while the car is being fixed, and he gets to come up with a plan of paying for the damage and maybe paying for a rental car for you to use. Putting it in terms of "If you have a problem, you need to have a plan for solving it" eliminates the need to construct a consequence for every conceivable violation of a litany of rules for using the car.

3. **V—Is it valuable as a learning tool?** Buying her friend a new book to replace the one your daughter ruined while trying to read as she also removed her nail polish can

teach your daughter not to tackle both tasks at the same
time. Berating her for being so irresponsible won't, nor
will telling her she can't borrow any more books from
anyone ever again.

4. **P—Is it practical?** Telling your child he can't go to school
until all of his chores are done is not practical; letting him
know that if he doesn't do the chores before he goes to
school, he will have to do them before he goes out to play
after school is practical.

If it isn't all four of these, it probably won't be effective and it
could be punishment disguised as a reasonable consequence.
Telling your teenager that she can't drive the car for a week
because she didn't come home at the time she promised and
you had to hire a cab to get to your meeting is simple, but it
isn't reasonable, valuable, or practical. Since she is the one who
drives her brother and sister to school in the mornings, you get
punished, she gets a break, and she doesn't have to take ownership of her problem of coming in late. Grounding her for six
months is also simple but not reasonable, valuable, or practical.
Having her pay for the cab you had to hire is reasonable, simple,
valuable, and practical. If she makes a habit of being late, it
could be RSVP to tell her she will have to find another way to get
to her after-school activity next Friday because you need to know
that you have a car to get to your meeting.

Breaking a beaver bait jar provided Joseph with a wonderful
opportunity to be disciplined with the help of consequences that
were reasonable, simple, valuable, and practical. Punishment
would not have taught him anything about a solution to his problem. Discipline provided the four steps for him to flesh out his
responsibility for his own behavior.

GIVING LIFE TO LEARNING—A NEVER-ENDING STORY

Discipline is not just for kids. We can benefit from discipline at
any age. In fact, if we adults don't know real discipline, it will be
very difficult to discipline our children rather than punish them.

An old friend who is both a writer and an editor stopped over one day as I was struggling with this book and offered to help. He took my text and ripped it apart paragraph by paragraph, then asked me to explain what I was trying to say. He wrote it down and began to teach me how I could put my ideas into a new format with its own rhythm, gesture, and tone. It was painful to let go of the quick phrases that had worked so well for so long with audiences but seemed bare and incomplete on paper. He didn't do it for me; he didn't bribe me or praise me; he didn't laugh at my efforts; and he didn't threaten me. What he did was:

1. Showed me what I had done wrong. (Took the text apart.)
2. Gave me ownership of the problem. (It was my book, and he told me that he knew I could do it but that I would need to let go of a lot and trust in my own ability to write.)
3. Gave me ways of solving my problem. (He showed me how to make the leap from quick phrases to written text, first by doing it for me, then by helping me do it myself, then by watching me do it, and finally by bantering with me to make sure I was really saying what I wanted to say.)
4. Most importantly, through the whole process, he left my dignity as a person, a speaker, and a writer intact.

If we can begin to see what powerful tools encouragement and discipline are in our own lives, we can begin to empower our own children, treating them with the dignity and regard we would want to be treated with ourselves.

> Life is no brief candle to me. It is a sort of splendid torch which I've got hold of for the moment, and I want to make it burn as brightly as possible before handing it on to future generations.
>
> —GEORGE BERNARD SHAW

It is extremely difficult, if not impossible, to empower our children if we have little or no flame ourselves. If we are going to give our children the message that they are worth it, we first need to believe that we are worth it. On a recent airline trip the flight attendant giving preflight safety instructions added her own bit of wisdom to the usual announcement: "For those of you traveling with infants or children, consider your oxygen needs first before helping someone who may need your assistance. It is critical that you secure your mask before helping someone who may need your assistance. YOU WILL BE OF NO HELP TO ANYONE ELSE IF YOU ARE NOT BREATHING YOURSELF." She got a laugh from the passengers, but the message was a startling reminder that if we don't take good care of ourselves, we will not be able to give anything to anyone else. Providing a nurturing, caring, safe, loving environment for ourselves and giving ourselves opportunities to grow and learn will give us the energy we need to empower our children.

We form a circle of hope.
We pass the flame to one another.
If my candle goes out, yours will light it.
Together we make a brighter light...
And each candle promises something of its own:
That darkness is not the last word.
                    —DAVID MCCAULEY, AMERICAN FRIENDS SERVICE
                                        COMMITTEE

Chapter 2

Three Kinds of Families

Families are mini-cultures and they share language,
attitudes and behavior in common. These tend to be
acted out in each generation, and passed along.
  —CAROLYN FOSTER, M.A., *THE FAMILY PATTERNS WORKBOOK*

Who of us is mature enough for offspring before the
offspring themselves arrive? The value of marriage is not
that adults produce children but that children produce
adults.

—PETER DE VRIES

Kids are kids, simply by virtue of their age and their stage of
human development. But parents are parents only in relation to
their children. If you don't have kids, you aren't a parent. If
you do have kids, you have a family. And if you are alive and
kicking and reading this book, you have, or had, a family of some
kind, because you were born into one, even if you never knew it.

We all tend to be self-centered to some degree, to think of
relationships as how someone relates to *me*. When we think of
families, we naturally think first of individuals as they relate to us
personally—or don't relate, as the case may be, because that's the
way we experience a family—my father, my sister, my kids, my
husband, his mother, his brother, maybe his kids from a previous

marriage. But we can learn a lot about parenting by looking at the family as a whole, as an entity in itself. Just as individuals have their own natures, histories, and personality structures, so do families. We are kids or parents within the context of a family, and what kind of family it is makes all the difference in the world to how we parent and how kids grow up.

There are three basic kinds of families: brick-wall, jellyfish, and backbone. What distinguishes them is the kind of structure that holds them together. This structure affects all the relationships of the family: child to parent, parent to child, parent to parent, child to child, and even the way the family as a whole relates to the outside world. A brick wall is a nonliving thing, designed to restrict, to keep in, and to keep out. In brick-wall families, the structure is rigid and is used for control and power, both of which are in the hands of the parents. A jellyfish has no firm parts at all and reacts to every eddy and current that comes along. In jellyfish families structure is almost nonexistent; the need for it may not even be acknowledged or understood. A backbone is a living, supple spine that gives form and movement to the whole body. In backbone families structure is present and firm and flexible and functional.

The backbone family provides the support and structure necessary for children to realize fully their uniqueness and to come to know their true selves, which are suppressed in brick-wall families and ignored in jellyfish families. They are empowered by trust in themselves, in others, and in the future. Being secure in their own unique selves, they are capable of love and empathy for themselves and others. Backbone families help children develop inner discipline, and even in the face of adversity and peer pressure, they retain faith in themselves and in their own potential.

Brick-wall and jellyfish families, although at opposite extremes, tend to raise children who know what to think but not how to think or feel, and who lack a sense of a true self. They have neither faith in themselves nor hope for the future and are therefore at risk of damage or destruction from the three horsemen of the adolescent apocalypse: sexual promiscuity, drug abuse, and suicide. Neither family provides the structure a child can use as a backbone for developing mentally, physically, sexually, emotionally, and morally. Both families can produce children who as adults will believe themselves to be powerless and unable to live truly satisfying lives.

Gloria Steinem, writing about the true self in *Revolution from Within*, said:

> We do know that, like children, adults whose innermost feelings and preferences are ignored, ridiculed, punished or repressed come to believe that there is something profoundly, innately "wrong" with them. And conversely, those who are able to honor these inner promptings know what it is to feel at home with themselves.... One thing is clear: The human mind can imagine both, how to break self-esteem and how to nurture it—and imagining anything is the first step toward creating it. Believing in a true self is what allows a true self to be born.

As we look at the three kinds of families, you will probably find a bit of your own home in each. Some illustrations will make you cringe as you recognize the dinner scene in your home last night. Others will reaffirm that, as tough as it was to make it through last week's conflict with your teen, hanging in there was worth it. Your examination of the three types of families will encourage your growth as a parent. The keys to this process are recognizing the messages and tools you received from your own parents and are still carrying around; becoming conscious of the messages you are giving your own children, either directly or indirectly; and becoming aware of the emotional and physical environment you are creating for yourself and your children.

Psychiatrist Alice Miller summed up the reasons we need to acknowledge and explore our past in her book *For Your Own Good:* "I have discovered that we are less prey to ... the repetitive compulsion if we are willing to acknowledge what happened to us, if we do not claim that we were mistreated 'for our own good' and if we have not had to ward off completely our painful reactions to the past. The more we idealize the past, however, and refuse to acknowledge our childhood sufferings, the more we pass them on unconsciously to the next generation."

Are there changes you want and need to make? Has screaming at your children left you drained and scared? Are there things you can't change? Having three babies in three and a half years not only means caring for three toddlers at the same time but also dealing with three teenagers at the same time.

Are there things you are doing you feel good about? You took the time to take that trip to the park knowing that the dishes, laundry, and scattered toys would still be there when you returned—and they were, and you and your child were now refreshed, renewed, and relaxed.

THE BRICK-WALL FAMILY

> Children need parents who model self-discipline rather than preach it. They learn from what their parents actually do; not from what they say they do.... When parents rigidly discipline (and don't walk what they talk), the child becomes overdisciplined.... The overdisciplined child is rigid, obsessive, overly controlled and obedient, people pleasing, and ravished with shame and guilt.
> —JOHN BRADSHAW, *HOMECOMING*

In the brick-wall family the building blocks—the bricks— that are cemented together to make the family are an obsession with order, control, and obedience, a rigid adherence to rules, and a strict hierarchy of power. Kids are controlled, manipulated, and made to mind. Their feelings are ignored, ridiculed, or negated. Parents direct, supervise, minilecture, order, threaten, remind, and worry over. The brick-wall family is in essence a dictatorship, perhaps a benevolent one but a dictatorship nevertheless. Power in a brick-wall family equals control, and it all comes from the top.

BASIC CHARACTERISTICS OF A BRICK-WALL FAMILY

1. *Hierarchy of control.* The parent has absolute authority, enforces order, and always wins. Sometimes the techniques are obvious, blunt control tools. ("I'm in charge here, and you will obey me or else." "I don't care what the teacher or anyone else says, you'll do what I tell you to do.") Often the techniques are more subtle, though no less damaging. ("Please do this the way I say." "This is the right way.")

2. *Litany of strict rules.* Thou-shalt-nots and don't-you-dares are used to enforce desired behavior. ("You will make your bed

this way because I said so." "You will sit here all night if it takes you that long to finish your spinach." "As long as you are in my house, you will not cut your hair." "Please don't cut your hair; it upsets me to think about it.")

3. *Punctuality, cleanliness, and order.* Parents enforce unyielding time lines, unnecessary sanitary restrictions, and unbending boundaries. ("You are to be home at midnight, not one minute after." "Don't touch anything in the store. You'll get your hands full of all kinds of germs." "All of the toys need to be put back exactly as you found them. I spent two hours putting them in order.")

4. *Rigid enforcement of rules by means of actual threatened, or imagined, violence.* Brute force is often used, and failure to meet expected standards is "corrected" with severe punishment. ("I'll break your arm if I see you doing that again." "I don't care if you are sixteen, you're not too big to paddle." "Open your mouth— I told you if you said that word again, I would wash your mouth out with soap.")

5. *Attempt to break the child's will and spirit with fear and punishment.* ("Don't give me any excuses. Just give me the car keys—you're grounded." "Stop crying, or I'll give you something to cry about." "If you are going to act like a girl, you are going to dress like one.")

6. *Rigid rituals and rote learning.* Parents enforce strict procedures for sleeping, eating, dressing, playing, and religious observances. ("I don't care if the movie isn't over, it is time for bed right now." "Eat those peas with your fork." "You can't wear that shirt with those pants." "Get out there and do whatever you have to do to win." "As long as you are in this house, you will go to religious services with us." "We don't do things that way.")

7. *Use of humiliation.* Parents employ sarcasm, ridicule, and embarrassment to manipulate and control behavior. ("How could you be so stupid?" "You're such a crybaby. No wonder no one will play with you." "A turtle can run faster than you.")

8. *Extensive use of threats and bribes.* Parents alternate between the carrot and the stick. Kids never know what to expect. ("Touch that stereo and you will be in your room for the rest of the day." "If you stop crying, I will give you a candy bar. If you don't stop crying, I'll give you something to cry about.")

9. *Heavy reliance on competition.* Parents encourage or force children to compete in order to get them to perform and excel.

("Let's see who can make the best cookies." "You're my favorite son—I love you the most." "She is smarter than you." "If you try harder, you can beat him out for the part.")

10. *Learning takes place in an atmosphere of fear.* Mistakes are bad, and there is no margin for error. Perfection is the goal. ("You put so much as a dent in this car, you'll never drive it again." "If you wet in your pants, you will go back to wearing diapers, just like a baby." "Your sister got straight As. There is no excuse for this B." "You'll disappoint us if your grades aren't good enough for you to get into our alma mater.")

11. *Love is highly conditional.* In order to get affection or approval, children must do as they are told, not as they would like. ("If you are well behaved, I'll love you. If you are not, I won't." "Look what you have done to the family name. I am ashamed that you are my child." "If you ever get in that kind of trouble, don't bother to call home." "Mommy's little boy would never do that.")

12. *Separate, strictly enforced roles.* Boys learn to repress any feelings of weakness and fear appearing vulnerable. Girls learn to fear feelings of anger and to express learned helplessness. ("Boys don't cry." "Don't be such a sissy." "Good girls don't do that." "Your brother will change the tire for you. I don't want you to get your hands dirty." "You're Daddy's girl.")

13. *Teach what to think, not how to think.* If children are taught what to think, they are more easily manipulated. They come to believe that they must think of what's right for others, often at the expense of what's right for themselves. ("Put your coat on. It's cold outside." "Don't you think you should change that outfit? You look better in the red one." "Don't make your mother cry." "Make your dad proud of you.")

14. *Risk of sexual promiscuity, drug abuse, and suicide.* Because of a lack of strong self-esteem, children seek affection and approval through seduction and overt sexual activity. They have a strong sense of self-hatred, repressed anger, and rage. ("I'm no good." "I can't do anything right." "If you knew the real me, you wouldn't like me." "What would anyone see in me?" "I'm easy. Love me and I'll do anything you want." "I just want to make the pain go away." "I'd be better off dead.")

15. *Refuses to acknowledge the need to get help.* Personal problems are denied and hidden from other members of the family. Family problems are covered over by a veneer of "everything is all

right" or kept as "family secrets." Seeking help, either as an individual or as a family, is seen as a sign of weakness. ("Dad's not drunk, he just needs more sleep. He's been working so hard." "Don't tell anyone about what happened last night." "Your sister is just going to visit your aunt and uncle for a few months. Nobody needs to know where she went." "Grandma doesn't need to know about this; it would make her sick." "We don't need any help, we can get through this ourselves. Therapy is only for really crazy people.")

Brick-wall families give kids little opportunity to find out who they are, what they can do, and who they can become. The children are not allowed to express their opinions and feelings. Intimidated, coerced, threatened with physical violence or actually abused, they often become compliant and apathetic, easily led by any authority figure. As adults, some seek out partners who control and abuse them. They may even abuse their own children, perpetuating the cycle of abuse. Others swear they will never raise their children the way they were raised, and instead set up a jellyfish home for their children. Still others, while acting passively out of necessity, store up their rage and resentment until they are bigger, then let it all loose in acts of violence against themselves or others.

From the outside a brick-wall family often seems to be a close-knit unit. But it's only a facade. Underneath the surface is a volatile mixture of anger, rage, degradation, and frustration, held in place by brute force, coercion, or intimidation, and waiting to explode.

The Jellyfish Family

Children growing up in an atmosphere in which love and care are lacking or given with gross inconsistency enter adulthood with no ... sense of inner security. Rather, they have ... a feeling of 'I don't have enough' and a sense that the world is unpredictable and ungiving, as well as a sense of themselves as being questionably lovable and valuable.

—M. SCOTT PECK, *THE ROAD LESS TRAVELED*

The opposite extreme of the brick wall is the jellyfish family, one that lacks a firm structure and, like the brick wall, stifles the healthy display of feelings and emotions, albeit in different ways.

Jellyfish families can be divided into two types, though the effect on the children is the same. The first kind is created by a parent who came from a brick-wall home and promised never to raise his children the way he was raised. The problem is that he was never allowed to develop his own backbone, and as a result he doesn't know how to create structure, consistency, and safe boundaries in his own family. The second kind of jellyfish family is created by a parent who physically or psychologically abandons her children, forcing them to fend for themselves. Because of her own problems—which may also stem from a brick-wall upbringing or from a jellyfish upbringing—she has trouble caring for herself, let alone for her children.

JELLYFISH A

The first kind of jellyfish parent was taught what, when, and how to speak, act, and react; he was not taught how to think. So when it comes time to develop a backbone structure in his own home, he doesn't know how. How could he? He never learned to think or to act from his own intuition. He knows only how to act according to the rules that were pounded into him and how to react out of fear. He is frightened of repeating the abuse he knew, but doesn't know what to replace it with. So he becomes extremely lax in discipline, sets few or no limits, and tends to smother his children. Anything his child wants, his child gets, even if the child's wants are at the expense of the parent's own needs. Since he doesn't recognize his own needs, he can't tell the difference between what his child simply wants and what the child really needs. There is no structure at the critical points of a family's day-to-day life. Instead chaos surrounds bedtime, mealtime, chores, allowances, TV viewing, fighting, and problem solving.

Some typical remarks from jellyfish-A parents are the following:

"She goes to bed when she's tired. It doesn't matter to me where she sleeps or if she puts her pajamas on or not. I always had a set bedtime, and it didn't matter that I had a friend over, I had to be in bed by eight o'clock or else."

"We fix her whatever she wants to eat; there's nothing wrong with chocolate doughnuts for breakfast and lunch. I always had to eat whatever was put in front of me."

"He's only a child once. Why should he have to spend his childhood doing chores? I had to work from the time I was six years old."

"If she needs money, I want her to have it. I don't ever want her to have to worry the way I had to about money."

"He's smart enough to make his own decisions about what he watches on TV. My parents let me watch only what they wanted me to see."

"Let them duke it out; they won't hurt each other. We were never allowed to fight in our family. If we did, we got a beating. If we disagreed with our parents, we said it beneath our breath. I want her to be able to say whatever she wants to say to me."

"I have to go to the store to get a new bat for our neighbor. My daughter misplaced the bat, and the boy needs one for a game today. My parents never helped me out when I had a problem. They would have yelled at me and made me walk the twenty miles to the store myself."

When the lack of structure results in absolute chaos, major problems develop. Then the parent, in frustration or panic, tends to revert to the only parenting techniques he knows: the rigid brick wall of threats, bribes, and punishments.

"Get to bed right now. I'm tired of you being up so late. If you're not asleep in ten minutes, tomorrow you will be in bed by six."

"You will eat whatever your grandmother serves you. I don't want her to think I've raised a spoiled brat. If you eat everything, I'll get you an ice cream on the way home."

"Your room is a disaster. If it's not cleaned by noon, I'm going in there and cleaning it the way my father did it."

"Look at all the money you've wasted. You're just like your mother—you think it grows on trees. You want spending money, go earn it yourself—I had to."

"Shut that TV off. It's been on for six hours straight. No TV for the rest of the month."

"I've had it with your fighting. Both of you stop, or I'll give you something to cry about."

"I've taken care of too many of your problems. It's time you handled your own. Walk the twenty miles into town to get some school paper. I'm not getting it for you."

As the parents vacillate between brick wall and jellyfish, the children are left so disoriented and confused that they easily lose a sense of who they are. They often seek comfort, support, and recognition from any adult willing to give them some kind of security, consistency, and structure. Like their counterparts in a brick-wall family, though for opposite reasons, they are often drawn to cult or gang leaders. The child of brick-wall parents seeks warmth and security from them as well as a sense of belonging, whereas the child of jellyfish parents hopes to find some consistency and structure.

JELLYFISH B

The second kind of jellyfish parent has personal problems that keep her almost totally centered on herself. She may be incapable of caring for her children because of her own lack of self-esteem or because of drug, alcohol, or sexual addiction or a mental disorder. Or she may be simply too involved in getting her own life together really to be concerned about the welfare of her children. An example is a parent who becomes addicted to addiction-recovery groups, attending meetings night and day at the expense of her children's need to have a parent there for them. Instead of—or in addition to—these forms of self-centeredness stemming from trying to deal with her own psychological problems, she may simply be a workaholic or destructively selfish, pursuing her own social and professional goals at the expense of her children. She may just not want to care for her children. Remarks from jellyfish-B parents might be:

"I need to go to all of these meetings so that I don't start drinking again. If I keep myself busy, I won't have to think about my craving."

"But Thursday is my baseball-game night. I need the break. I can't go to the open house at school because of my game. If you are having any problems at school, your teacher will let me know."

"I'm sorry I missed your school play, soccer game, and dental appointment, but look at the award Mom worked so hard for so long to get. Someday you'll appreciate all that I've done for you kids."

Or, finally, the latchkey child, wearing the house key on his neck, picks up his younger sister from the day-care center across the street, opens the front door, and finds a note: "Fix your own dinner. I'll be home at midnight. And make sure you do the chores around here."

In the second kind of jellyfish family no one is around to provide a nurturing, caring, supportive environment for the children. They begin to believe that if anything is to get done, they must do it themselves; they can count on no one. They feel unloved and abandoned and begin to mistrust others. Out of necessity they learn to lie and to manipulate people to get their basic needs met. As adults they will be lonely and incapable of loving. Dishonesty and manipulation will become a way of life for them.

BASIC CHARACTERISTICS OF A JELLYFISH FAMILY

1. *Anarchy and chaos in the physical and emotional environment.* ("Hold on, let me find a pencil in all this mess ... Kids, keep it down ... I can't hear on this phone ... I don't know where your shoes are ... they are somewhere in the closet under the pile of clothes for the Goodwill ... I know I'm late with that report, I can't remember where I put it ... can I get back to you in a minute? I see Jill playing in traffic again. Someday she'll learn to stay in the yard. Do you have this much trouble getting it all together? Can you imagine, the neighbors had the gall to ask the Board of Health to make me clean up the front porch and the kitchen. I swear, I need six extra hours in the day. Call me again later, we only got to talk for an hour, I've got to go.")

2. *No recognizable structure, rules, or guidelines.* ("The kids eat

whenever they feel like it. If they get fat, they get fat. It's not my fault." "A curfew, what's that?" "You can wear whatever you want to wear outside. I don't care if you freeze—the choice is yours. Maybe by the time you are six years old, you'll know better than to wear shorts in the snow.")

3. *Arbitrary and instant punishments and rewards.* ("When you were fighting yesterday, I just ignored it. Well, today I'm not up to ignoring it. You so much as look at your brother with that look, and I'll beat you good." "You are such a sweet girl, I'm going to buy you that pretty dress you were looking at yesterday.")

4. *Minilectures and put-downs are tools of the trade.* ("If you hadn't spent your money on those little toys, you would have had money for this big one." "You're such a klutz. I'll set the table myself.")

5. *Second chances are arbitrarily given.* ("I know I told you if you dented the car, you'd have to pay for it. I'll pay this time, but next time you will have to pay for it yourself, trust me.")

6. *Threats and bribes are commonplace.* ("You go out in the street, the police will get you." "If you masturbate, hair will grow on your hands, and then everyone will know." "If you give me a hug, I'll give you a cookie." "If you get straight As, I'll give you five dollars."—This is often said to the kid who never had better than a C average.)

7. *Everything takes place in an environment of chaos.* ("I can't make all the other kids be quiet while you study. What do you think this is, a library?" "Just throw some beans in the pot and let everyone eat when they are hungry—there is never any time to sit down and eat together." "He'll have to tie his own shoes. Maybe if he falls on his face enough, he'll learn how to tie them.")

8. *Emotions rule the behavior of parents and children.* ("I'm too upset and tired to get off the couch and fix a meal for the kids. They will have to fend for themselves again." "He made me angry, so I hit him.")

9. *Children are taught that love is highly conditional.* In order to get affection or approval, they must please their parents; they feel an obligation to make their parents feel good. Recognition and love must be earned. ("Be a good girl for Mommy." "I'd love you more if you would cut your hair." "You made me so happy by getting on the honor roll. I want everyone to see what a smart son I have. You take after my side of the family.")

10. *Children are easily led by their peers.* ("Come on, no one's home at your house. They'll never know we were there." "If you loved me, you would do it. You won't get pregnant, trust me." "I dare you to play chicken with him." "Everybody else shaved their head.")

11. *Risk of sexual promiscuity, drug abuse, and suicide.* Because of a lack of strong self-esteem, children seek out affection and approval through sexual activity; a sense of belonging or escape through drugs; and a way out of the pain through suicide. They suffer self-hatred, repressed anger, and rage. ("I'll do whatever you want if you will just love me." "If you really knew me, you wouldn't like me." "Everyone else is using drugs." "My parents won't miss one bottle of whiskey." "My parents just don't care." "I binge and then I force myself to vomit. I hate myself when I do it." "I can't take it much longer. I feel like I'm going to explode." "The pressure in my head is killing me.")

12. *Parents are oblivious to major family problems, and fail to recognize the need to seek help.* Major problems are looked upon as minor concerns. Often, it is only when someone outside of the family recognizes a serious problem in the family that the children get the help they need. ("If we don't make a big deal of it, I'm sure it will go away on its own." "She's slow to walk or talk but I'm sure there isn't anything wrong. Besides, I don't have time to take her in to the doctor's." "He was only drunk. It could have been worse, he could have been using drugs." "The teachers just don't understand. I ditched school when I was young. It won't hurt her to miss a few classes." "Boys will be boys.")

Jellyfish families of both types have little external or internal structures. A permissive, laissez-faire atmosphere prevails. Children are smothered or abandoned, humiliated, embarrassed, and manipulated. They become obnoxious and spoiled and/or scared and vindictive. Since they receive no affirming life messages from their parents, they view themselves and the world around them with a lack of optimism. They end up being afraid of expressing themselves. They keep their feelings under guard and spontaneity in check; or they swing to the other extreme and become reckless, uncaring, uncontrollable risk takers.

Kids may survive but they cannot thrive in a brick-wall or a jellyfish environment. They need the boundaries and guidelines that a structure gives their lives, but it needs to be a flexible, open, compassionate one that is adaptable to circumstances, not the harsh, rigid, closed organization of a brick-wall family. And they need a stable environment conducive to creative, constructive, and responsible activity, not the chaos and instability of the jellyfish family. As parents we can provide our children with both stability and flexibility and the opportunity to thrive by creating an emotional, physical, and moral structure in our homes—a backbone family.

THE BACKBONE FAMILY

The ability to act in and through love, to be non-violent, to be generous, and to respect the rights and needs of others comes from having been generously and gently loved and respected.
—RITA NAKASHIMA BROCK, IN *CHRISTIANITY, PATRIARCHY AND ABUSE*

Backbone families come in many shapes, sizes, and colors. They don't come from any particular background or social strata. They don't live in special neighborhoods. They aren't necessarily headed by older parents or by younger parents. They are not necessarily religious or nonreligious, nor are they of any specific race or ethnic origin. They are characterized not so much by what they do or don't do but by how they balance the sense of self and the sense of community in all that they do. Interdependence is celebrated.

Backbone families can also be described by what they are not: They are not hierarchical, bureaucratic, or violent. Backbone parents don't *demand* respect—they demonstrate and teach it. Children learn to question and challenge authority that is not life-giving. They learn that they can say no, that they can listen and be listened to, that they can be respectful and be respected themselves. Children of backbone families are taught empathy and love for themselves and others. By being treated with compassion themselves they learn to be compassionate toward others, to recognize others' suffering, and to be willing to help relieve it. The backbone family provides the consistency, firmness, and fairness as well as the calm and peaceful structure needed for children to flesh out their own sense of a true self. Rather than being subjected to power expressed as control and growing up to control others, children are empowered and grow up to pass what they have learned of the potential of the human spirit on to others.

BASIC CHARACTERISTICS OF A BACKBONE FAMILY

1. *Parents develop for their children a network of support through six critical life messages given every day:*

- I believe in you
- I trust you
- I know you can handle life situations
- You are listened to
- You are cared for
- You are very important to me

Through love, acceptance, and encouragement, children's sense of self is recognized, valued, and esteemed.

2. *Democracy is learned through experience.* At family meetings, either formal or informal, all family members are aware of events, schedules, and problems and are invited to participate as fully as possible in planning activities, fixing schedule problems, and resolving conflicts. Children see that their feelings and ideas are respected and accepted and that it is not always easy to juggle the needs and wants of all members of the family. As the children grow in responsibility and decision-making abilities, their opportunities for both are increased. And as they grow, their parents become more flexible.

3. *An environment is created that is conducive to creative, constructive, and responsible activity.* The physical, emotional, and moral environments are not rigid or unbending, nor are they cluttered with debris, mixed messages, or poor models. Mistakes are viewed as opportunities to learn and grow.

4. *Rules are simply and clearly stated.* In establishing the rules, parents draw on their own wisdom, sense of responsibility, and perception of their children's needs, constantly increasing opportunities for their children to make their own decisions and to learn to set their own boundaries. ("The car starts when everyone's seat belt is buckled." "You can decide which bike helmet you would like to buy. If you want to ride your bike, you must wear a helmet.")

5. *Consequences for irresponsible behavior are either natural or reasonable.* They are also simple, valuable, and purposeful. There is no need for threats, bribes, or punishment. ("When you walk in puddles, your sneakers get wet [natural]." "You will need to replace your friend's jacket that you borrowed and lost [reasonable, simple, valuable, and purposeful]")

6. *Discipline is handled with authority that gives life to children's learning.* Kids are shown what they have done wrong, are given ownership of the problem, and are offered ways to solve the problem. Their dignity is left intact.

7. *Children are motivated to be all they can be.* They are accepted as they are and invited and encouraged to be more than they thought they could be. Learning takes place in an atmosphere of acceptance and high expectation. ("You can do it, I know you can." "Try to reach the next rung. I'm here to catch you if you need me.") Parents are at ease with themselves and their own ambitions, so they can be helpful when a child is struggling with a new skill. Children are given time to learn and perfect skills.

8. *Children receive lots of smiles, hugs, and humor.* All three are given freely and without conditions attached. Children learn that touch is critical to human bonding by watching parents give to each other and by receiving loving and caring touches themselves. They see their parents enjoying life and sharing laughter with them, not laughing at them.

9. *Children get second opportunities.* This is not the same as the arbitrary second chance without responsibility used in the jellyfish family. Kids are clearly given responsibility and a reasonable consequence for not following through. When they blow it, and kids will, they are given a second opportunity to try again, after they have been given the opportunity to experience the consequences for blowing it the first time. ("You can drive the car again after you have contacted the insurance company and made plans for repairing the damage done to the back fender. Until

then you will need to walk, ride your bike, or take the bus.")

10. *Children learn to accept their own feelings and to act responsibly on those feelings through a strong sense of self-awareness.* Parents are empathic and emotionally available to them, modeling appropriate ways to express the full range of emotions. ("I am sad that he is moving to a new town. I will miss him." "It's okay to cry, son. I am sad, too, that their family won't be our neighbors anymore. You and Sam had many wonderful times together. Let's think of something to do that will make the move a little easier for him.")

11. *Competency and cooperation are modeled and encouraged.* Parents demonstrate the ability to do a variety of tasks, and they help their children learn new skills. They show their children how to work and play with others. They show them how to become competent, cooperative, and decisive. ("I think you are old enough to learn to use the power mower. Watch me do this section, and you can do the other." "Let's figure out where we can bike to this weekend. I'll check the bikes this time. Who wants to fill the water bottles, make the snacks, or map out the bike-path route?")

12. *Love is unconditional.* Because they are children and for no other reason, they have dignity and worth, simply because they are. ("I love you." "You are fun to be with." "I'm here if you need me.")

13. *Children are taught how to think.* They are encouraged to listen to their own intuition, to be spontaneous, to be creative in thoughts and actions, and to reason through problems. They are spoken with, not to; listened to, not ignored. They are encouraged to challenge authority that is not lifegiving, as well as to respect the true wisdom of their elders. They are given a thirst for knowledge of the old and a spirit of curiosity to discover the new. ("When you have a gut feeling about something, trust your own intuition." "You'll figure out a way to solve that problem; I know you can do it." "Can you tell me how you feel about it and what you think we can do to fix it?" "I hear what you are saying. I hadn't thought of it that way." "If someone in a position of authority asks you to do something that is unkind, unjust, unfair, hurtful, or dishonest, you need to listen to your own conscience." "Grandpa learned from the soil. He taught me, and I'd like to teach you." "If your heart is a muscle, how come it doesn't get tired the way your leg muscles do?")

14. *Children are buffered from sexual promiscuity, drug abuse, and suicide by the daily reinforcement of the messages that foster self-esteem:*

I like myself. Parents can give this message in many ways every day, starting with liking themselves and letting kids know that they love them just because they are.

I can think for myself. ("You can do it, I know you can." "Tell me how you see it, how it will work.")

There is no problem so great, it can't be solved. Realities are accepted. Problems are solved. ("You failed math this term [reality]. I know you can do what you need to do to get the required math credit you need for graduation [problem to solve]. I'm here to help if you need me." "Your red shoes are still wet [reality]. You can pick out another pair to wear to school [problem to solve].")

15. *The family is willing to seek help.* Problems are not denied or hidden. Parents recognize when they need to seek advice from elders or trained professionals, and receive the advice with an open mind and heart. ("Grandma, I need help with my baby. This is all new to me." "We are having trouble communicating with each other. I would like to have a third party help us. I've never had a teenager before.")

Being a backbone parent isn't easy. There are no quick fixes, no sure answers, just lots of opportunities to grow. If you aren't already one, becoming a backbone parent is even more difficult. If you identified yourself in the brick-wall or jellyfish family system or a patchwork of all three, remember that you cannot change everything overnight. You might need help and support to make the changes that will be necessary. You might be able to find that help in a supportive neighbor, friend, or mentor. Sometimes a professional in the field can help you make sense of where you have been, where you are going, and what you can do to get there. And don't overlook one of your best resources: your own children. It is true that children tend to grow in a healthy, functional way if they have parents who are growing in a healthy, functional way, and it is also true that parents can gain wisdom from their children.

I can imagine that someday we will regard our children not as creatures to manipulate or to change but rather as messengers from a world we once knew but which we have long since forgotten, who can reveal to us more about the true secrets of life, and also our own lives, than our parents were ever able to. We do not need to be told whether to be strict or permissive with our children. What we do need is to have respect for their needs, their feelings, and their individuality, as well as for our own.
—RITA NAKASHIMA BROCK, IN *CHRISTIANITY, PATRIARCHY, AND ABUSE*

As my husband and I examined our own backgrounds, we discovered that he came from a basically brick-wall background and I from a basically jellyfish-A background. How often the two are attracted to each other! The problem is that a brick wall and a jellyfish do not a backbone family make. We both had to examine the parenting messages and tools we got or didn't get from our own parents, had to keep the good and get rid of the bad, seek out support and advice from other healthy adults, and look at our own family structure or lack of structure.

As we explored our own family histories, we each found a rich and colorful heritage to pass on to our children. We also have had to acknowledge and confront the alcoholism and all its nightmarish messages that were part of both our childhoods. We made a commitment to ourselves and our children to do whatever repair work was necessary to fix the holes in our own childhoods so that we would not pass on to our children the destructive legacy of alcoholism we had seen passed from one generation to the next in both our families.

As I was writing this book, I was never at a loss for examples from personal experience for the jellyfish family, and Don was just as quick to give me examples for the brick-wall family. And, as if I really needed more, our children were quick to cite things they had heard from us that they could readily classify as brick wall or jellyfish. But the backbone messages are coming more easily now. It is refreshing to see our teenagers, more often than not, reaching for their backbone tools as their first response to everyday situations.

We know that we and our children are worth the effort and pain it takes to tear down the old and establish a new backbone structure in our home. It's not a onetime decision but an ongoing commitment to ourselves and our children. If you come from either of the two family extremes, or from a patchwork of all three, you can make that same commitment. You're worth it and your kids are worth it.

> Ruminating about the past will get you nowhere. So go ahead and learn from the past whatever you can, and then put it behind you. Remember, there is nothing you can do to change it, but you can use its lessons to improve your future.
> —ABRAHAM J. TWERSKI, *WHEN DO THE GOOD THINGS START?*

> "How does one become a butterfly?" she asked pensively. "You must want to fly so much that you are willing to give up being a caterpillar."
> —TRINA PAULUS, *HOPE FOR THE FLOWERS*

Chapter 3

Three Alternatives to No and Other Plan Bs

If we don't change our direction, we are likely to end up
where we are headed.
—ANCIENT CHINESE PROVERB

Now that you know what kind of toolbox you have and the
kind of family that helped you create that toolbox, you can begin
to examine the tools in it. Some are serving you well, some are
weighing you down, and others are waiting to be used. Some
need to be unpacked and left behind, while others simply need
to be modified. If what you are doing isn't doing for you what you
need to get done, it is time to resort to a plan B.

No, Nope, No Way, Never

Ever notice how often we say no to our kids?
   "Mom, can I have a cookie?" "No, it will spoil your supper."
   "Dad, can I go over to Tracy's?" "No."
   "Mom, can I use the car?" "No."
   "Dad, can I stay out all night with my friends?" "No!!"

   Kids learn not to take us seriously on the big no because we
keep changing our minds on the little ones. The following are
three alternatives you can start using right away so that when

you really need to say no to your kids, they will believe that you mean it.

First Alternative: "Yes, Later"

"Mom, can I have a cookie?" "Yes, later."

Note that I didn't say, "No, you can have one later." The five-year-old is all ready to fight a no, but how do you fight a "Yes, later"?

"Oh, but, Mom, I'm so hungry."

"Okay, have one cookie." It's already later, at least three seconds later. But the important thing is that you have not changed a no to a yes; it was a yes all along. And don't add, "Make sure you eat your supper." What are you going to do if she doesn't, get the cookie back? The threats we make!

Second Alternative: "Give Me a Minute"

"Dad, can I go over to Tracy's?" "Give me a minute."

There is nothing wrong with asking for a minute to develop your own case. You might be thinking, *Gee, it might be nice to have some quiet for a little while.* "Yes, you can go," or *We have a lot to do before our company comes tonight.* "No, you can't go." At least when you say no, you'll know why you're saying it. How often many of us say no to our kids without the foggiest idea as to why we said it. No just sounded good. Then we have to try to defend it.

If your child wants an answer right away, a variation of "give me a minute" might work more effectively: "If you want an answer right now, it's no; if you can wait a bit, maybe."

THIRD ALTERNATIVE: "CONVINCE ME"

"Mom, can I use the car?" "Convince me."

I use this one the most with adolescents, but it can be used with any child who is verbal. Why should I spend all my energy at my age trying to convince my adolescent she can't have the car; let her spend all her youthful energy convincing me she should.

"Mom, all my friends... " "I'm not convinced."

"But you let Maria." "I'm not convinced."

"Mom, if you don't let me use the car, you'll have to drive all of us to play practice." "I'm convinced!"

If you have used these alternatives instead of repeatedly saying no to the point where it's no longer taken seriously, then, when your sixteen-year-old asks if he can stay out all night with his friends, you can say *no!* There is a time and a place for no.

I used to work with runaways, pregnant teens, and juvenile delinquents. I have yet to meet one of these troubled young people who was not begging for someone in their life to say no to them. Saying no to them can mean that they are important enough to place limits on, that someone does care about them. You and I are limited by our physical backbone. There are things we cannot do because of it—literally bending over backward, for example. But that backbone enables us to interact creatively, constructively, and responsibly with others. We are just as limited by our moral and emotional backbones. There are things we don't do, not because "it's against the law," "it's against my religion," or "we might get caught," but simply because we have internalized certain nos into our own moral backbone. They are part of what we call a conscience or, in some cases, common sense. That backbone is not fully developed in most sixteen-year-olds. Backbone parents provide both the freedom and the boundaries necessary to help their children create their own moral backbone.

So your son asks, "Can I stay out all night?" A good answer is no! He'll probably ask "Why not?" Our typical response as parents—"Because I said so"—is a dumb reason. He could go out the back window after you've locked the front door, and he still won't know why you said no. Tell him why. Basically there are four reasons: sex, jail, drugs, and personal safety.

"Son, you can't stay out all night because of sex, jail, drugs, and personal safety."

"You don't trust me!"

"Oh, yes, I do. I trust you from the moment you walk out the door in the morning until you get back in the evening. It takes less than ten minutes to get involved in sex, jail, or drugs, and I trust that you're not. See, I trust you a whole lot. But after midnight in this community, when everything else is closed down, there isn't a whole lot else left to do besides sex, jail, and drugs, and I don't want to put you in a position you can't handle yet."

"But, Mom, everybody's staying out."

"Not true; you're not."

"You don't love me."

"Yes, I do."

Your teenagers are not going to appear very impressed. Many, however, are going to be outright relieved, because they can tell their friends, "I can't go because they won't let me." You get to be the "fuddy-duddy" while their own backbone is developing.

No matter what kind of parents we are, we need to remember that our children have free will and are subject to peer pressure. No matter what we do or say, some teenagers will go out the back window after we've locked the front door. If we have taught them why instead of "Cause I said so," they will have a better chance of surviving out there. It's not enough to just say no.

Brick-wall parents are notorious for saying no simply "because I said no" or "because you will do as I tell you to." No is used as a control tool to force kids to be compliant. In a brick-wall family no meaningful explanation need ever be given. The result is that kids conform, without any thought on their own part to inflexible, externally imposed structures, or they will go to the extreme of rejecting even the valuable and healthy limits necessary to function responsibly in a society.

Jellyfish parents rarely, if ever, use the word no. Often this is because, having come from a brick-wall family themselves, they swear they will never impose such "rigidity" on their children. Other jellyfish parents simply don't have the internally developed moral spine to stand up to the demands of their children.

The kids of both types of jellyfish parents run wild and have no guidance to help them develop an internal moral structure themselves; or they will be drawn, out of a need for some sense of order and structure, to people who will impose that structure on their lives. And these people will not, I guarantee, be ones that you would have chosen to guide your children. Both brick-wall and jellyfish families run the risk of their children being easily led into cults or gangs where someone else does their thinking for them.

Backbone parents save their no for the big issues, when there is no bend, when they mean it, intend to follow through with it, and it is in the best interest of the safety and well-being of the child. With the no they give an explanation that is meaningful. Children can then begin to develop their own internal moral structure that enables them to function responsibly and crea-tively in society. These are the children who will also have the spine to stand up and speak out against injustices.

Save your no for the big issues, when you really mean No! The rest of the time, as the no begins to form on your lips, stop a moment and see if one of the alternatives might better serve both you and your kids:

1. "Yes, later."
2. "Give me a minute."
3. "Convince me."

THE MINILECTURE

Joey's outside without a coat. He's not freezing—that would be life-threatening, and I would have to intervene. In this case he's just cold. I could minilecture him: "If you had put your coat on, you wouldn't be cold." He already knows that. Minilectures contain information the kid already knows, or could easily figure out.

Some classics in the world of minilectures are: "If you hadn't hit your brother, you wouldn't be in your room." "If you hadn't eaten all of the sweets, you wouldn't be sick." "If you would have done it the way I told you to, you wouldn't be in this mess." "If you had studied, you wouldn't have failed." These messages are akin to my husband saying to me, "If you hadn't put the car in reverse, Barb, we'd have two cars." I don't need that information as I'm getting on the city bus, any more than a kid needs to hear, "If you had put your coat on, you wouldn't be cold."

Instead of minilecturing my son, I can walk outside and ask, "Joe, you look cold." Standing there shivering, he says, "I'm freezing, I'm going to get a sweatshirt." And I say, "Good thinking." The kid decides how to handle a problem he has created. You know as well as I do that if you get locked in a power struggle with a kid, you will lose; if you even suggest that he put a coat on, he would rather freeze than let you be right—especially if he is thirteen. There is no way he's going to let you win.

What kids need instead of minilectures are opportunities to solve problems they are confronted with or have created. It helps to have an adult who will support them with the belief that they can handle their own problems: "You have a problem, and I know you can handle it."

QUESTIONS THAT GET US NOWHERE FAST

There are four types of questions which have no reasonable answer and no constructive reason for being asked.

1. *Questions with no right answers.* ("Why on earth did you write all over the wall?") Have you ever gotten a good answer to that question? You may get some great and creative stories as answers, lots of excuses, or blame placed on someone else; still, you will be left having to pass judgment on the answer, since you asked the question. Instead of asking a question, make a statement. Statements are much more productive. ("Let's talk about the writing on the wall." Or "Dawn, you wrote on the wall. You need to figure out a way to get the writing off the wall before the end of the day.") Ownership of the problem and the need for a solution to the problem stays where it belongs—with the child.

2. *Questions with no options.* ("Will you please be quiet?") What if your child says no? Are you really giving him the option

to say yes or no? Questions with no options are really commands cloaked in a request. Statements, again, are more productive. ("Please be quiet for a few moments while I figure out where we are going.")

3. *Questions that punish.* ("Can't you ever do anything right?" "Do I always have to be standing next to you to keep you from getting into trouble?") These are killer questions. They serve no constructive purpose and are sure to work against a child's self-esteem. A statement of the problem is more effective. ("You didn't feed the turtle this morning, and he looks awfully hungry." "You need to figure out a way to replace the neighbors' window.")

4. *Questions that are wishy-washy.* ("That's a good idea, don't you think?" "Do you mind if I say something?") These questions take away from your own assertive stance as a parent. Again, statements are more powerful, and let your child know what you are really feeling. ("I like that." "I need to say something.")

Before asking a question, question why you are asking it. Does the question need to be asked? Am I looking for information? Could a statement work better? "I need help getting the baby to sleep" will serve you better than "Why on earth won't this kid go to sleep?" The best questions are the ones we ask ourselves before we ask someone else.

Empty Threats

"I'll break your arm, I'll wring your neck, you'll never, ever, go on another holiday with us again!" None of us are perfect parents. When we are tired, worn out, exasperated, fed up, and at our wits' end, it is easy to resort to empty threats to scare our kids into doing what they need to be doing. If you hear these words come out of your mouth, take heart, you've not totally lost it. You can come back with: "I blew it, I'm not really going to break your arm. I need five minutes to calm down and try to make sense of this before we talk about what to do. And by the way, I'm open to suggestions."

ULTIMATUMS

"If you don't stop that right now, I'm going to send you to live with your father." You've just spent $10,000 in legal fees to get custody of your child, and you're threatening to send him to live with his father. "If you don't shape up, young lady, I'm dropping you off at the orphanage." You know you won't do it, but does she know it?

Ultimatums leave no room to negotiate or maneuver. By trying to assert absolute power, you have put yourself in the position of having no freedom and have left the outcome up to the child. What if your son doesn't stop whatever it was he was doing? Are you really going to send him to his father's? If your daughter doesn't "shape up," will you really drop her off at the orphanage? More serious than your loss of power is the fear of abandonment you have put in your child by simply making either threat.

Instead of ultimatums, which are often made in the heat of anger, take time to cool off, then come back with what you need from your child. "Jim, I'm real angry right now, I'm going to take some time to cool off, then we can talk about the problem here."

PUT-DOWNS (SARCASM, RIDICULE, AND EMBARRASSMENT)

"Your sister never did anything like that." "You're just like your mother." "You'll never amount to anything." "I figured you would do something stupid like that." "Why don't you just grow up?"

Put-downs are generalizations and labels that reduce a child's sense of dignity and self-worth. Kids who have been scarred by put-downs tend to use these tools against themselves. "I'm such a klutz." "I'm no good for anything." And they use them in their relationships with others. "You call yourself a soccer player?" "You are stupid."

Turnarounds, positive alternatives, are specific and directed at the problem and not the child. "Nicki, please take your feet off the table." "Please rinse the dishes before you put them in the soapy water." "You can drive the car after you have a plan for getting the dent fixed."

BE CAREFUL!

The roads are icy, and your teenager is going to drive to the school play. Your first impulse is to tell her to "be careful." Why would you give her the car keys if you have to remind her to be careful? Plan B could be, "The roads are icy, and I know you can handle the car [or you wouldn't be giving her the car keys]. Let's go over again what to do if the car slides." To which you will probably get, "Oh, Mom!" But once she has told you how she would handle the car, you can tell her to have a good time at the play. If need be, she can come home and tell you she did a "360" on the highway. She knows problems can occur, you have faith in her ability to handle them, and she can discuss them with you without fear of being punished. If you tell her to "be careful," your neighbor will probably be the one to tell you that your daughter did a "360" on the highway.

"Be careful" is really a plea, directive, or a cloaked command aimed at the person spoken to. It may be a way of trying to tell your child you love her and that you are concerned. If that's the reason you say it, just say so: "I love you and I'm concerned." The ownership of the statement stays where it belongs, with you.

THINK FOR YOURSELF, BUT YOU BETTER LISTEN TO ME

Years ago, I went from secondary teaching to elementary-crisis teaching, and I found myself in the middle of a crisis, which is not surprising except that it was my crisis, not the kids'. I had parents on my case regularly because I refused to tell upper elementary kids in Colorado to put their coats and mittens on. These same parents had said they wanted their children to learn to think for themselves, learn to make good decisions, and not be easily led by their peers. Nevertheless, they insisted that I make their ten-year-old sons and daughters put their coats and mittens on before they went outside.

Instead, I asked my students why they thought they should wear their coats and mittens. They'd raise their hands and respond, "Cause my mom said so," or "Cause you'll catch pneumonia if you don't." The first, in itself, is not necessarily a good reason, and the second is simply not true.

If you happen to be a schoolteacher as well as a parent, I'll bet you've seen kids who never bundle up and who, much to your dismay, are never absent. They are in school every single day. They never get the flu; they never get chicken pox; they certainly never get pneumonia. Then there are the kids whose parents bundle them in layers, warm up the car, drive them directly to school, and hand the teacher a note saying, "Don't let them go outside today. It's too cold." These same kids are absent half the winter with fevers and flu and that very pneumonia the coat and mittens were supposed to guard against. Obviously, this is not the reason you wear your coat and mittens. Don't lie to kids when you are teaching them how to think.

I taught them the real reason why. I held up a piece of frozen meat and said "Kids, look at this meat; it doesn't move, does it? It's kind of cold, isn't it? Now feel your bodies. They're kind of warm, aren't they? Feel your heart, it's moving, isn't it? If you go outside with your coat all buttoned up, all the warm air stays in, and there's a good chance your heart will keep moving. If you go out with it wide open, or worse yet, with no coat at all, there is a possibility that all the warm air will go out, the cold air will come in, and your organs will freeze, heart, kidneys, liver, solid, just like this hunk of meat!" The kids said, "Yuuuck!" I didn't lie to them. That is why you wear your coat, so your organs don't freeze. "But don't worry about it, your body can take care of itself; it starts protecting itself by drawing heat from the parts it can live without, your hands will go first." I showed them pictures of white dots and black fingers and no fingers from frostbite. "And that's why you wear your mittens." Most kids left my class making the decision on a regular basis not to let their organs freeze.

If you find yourself thinking for your kids, you are probably handing down a well-worn family tool. Think about the last time you went to your own parents' home. As you were walking out the door, did your mother say, "Don't forget to bundle up?" You're now a responsible adult, and you still get "Don't forget to bundle up." Or you're walking out the door with your own children, and your dad says, "Do you think you have that kid bundled up enough?" Think for yourself, yet the underlying message is, "You better listen to me."

Richard P. Moffat tells the story of a friend who went to visit her mother one weekend. "Tired from the day's travel, she went to bed early, only to pick up a book and begin reading. Her concentration was interrupted some hours later when her mother knocked on the door and stated: 'It's almost midnight. Don't you think it's a bit late to still be reading?' 'Mother,' she replied to her ninety-seven-year-old parent. 'I'm sixty-two and can stay up as late as I like!'"

What kids need, instead of being told what to think, is lots of information about themselves and the world around them, and the opportunity to make lots of decisions, including some less-than-wise ones. As long as their decisions are not life-threatening, morally threatening, or unhealthy, let their choices and the consequences of those choices be their own to grow with and learn from.

Self-trust is one of the first steps toward becoming a responsible, resourceful, resilient human being. As Faith Baldwin has said, "Character builds slowly, but it can be torn down with incredible swiftness." Children don't need many nos, any mini-lectures, unnecessary questions, empty threats, ultimatums, put-downs, warnings, or dictates. What they do need is support, explanations, encouragement, opportunities to be responsible, and invitations to think for themselves.

Let us be kinder to one another.
—ALDOUS HUXLEY, ON HIS DEATHBED

Chapter 4

I Can Be Me

I want you to get excited about who you are, what you are, what you have, and what can still be for you. I want to inspire you to see that you can go far beyond where you are right now.

—VIRGINIA SATIR, *PEOPLEMAKING*

You smile as your baby smiles at you, clap as he takes his first step, laugh as she says *mama* for the first time—ah, parenting is such a wonderful, rewarding experience. Then you see the dreaded word form on your baby's lips: "NO." Your child has just left babyhood for the terrific twos, entering into the first age of rebellion, and you begin to look for the return policy on the birth certificate.

Kids tend to rebel at three ages: at two, at five, and at puberty. In an attempt to assert their individuality and their own independence, they distance themselves both physically and emotionally from those caregivers closest to them. Kids rebel at two against their mothers: "I can be me, apart from you." Dad can't understand why Mom can't get along with this charming, independent two-year-old; and Mom is going crazy. (This is reversed if the primary caregiver is the father.) They rebel at five against Mom and Dad: "I can be me apart from both of you." Now Dad's going crazy, and Mom reassures him, "I've been through this once, it will pass." And at puberty kids rebel against the entire older generation, of which you and I happen to be members: "I can be me, apart from all of you!" (If you happen to have a two-year-old, a five-year-old, and a kid at puberty and you wondered why you felt like you were cracking up, now you know. And if you happen to have a spouse who is reaching forty, you could have four at the age of rebellion! Hang in there; it will pass, just as all birthdays do.)

At each age of rebellion, in an attempt to establish an identity apart from their parents, kids try any number of ways to say, "I can be me." The two-year-old insists on dressing himself, buttoning the top button in the third buttonhole, pants on backward, and shoes on the wrong feet.

The five-year-old takes great glee in publicly contradicting both Mom and Dad when either of them tries to relate an incident to a friend. ("Mom, you've got that wrong. I didn't say that to my brother." "But, Dad, you've got the whole story wrong!")

For the school dance the thirteen-year-old decides not to wear a dress you traveled twenty miles through rush-hour traffic to pick up from the cleaners. She wears your slacks and her dad's favorite sweater instead. ("Nobody wears dresses to dances anymore.")

Although all three ages of rebellion can be trying as well as growing times for both parents and kids, it is at the third age of rebellion that all three families see the fruits of their labors. At this stage the teenager is saying, "I can be me, apart from the entire older generation."

A teen comes in with his hair frizzed.

Brick-wall parent: "No kid of mine is walking out of here with his hair looking like that. You get that straight right now, or you're not leaving this house." Teenager thinks, "I can't be me in this family."

A teen comes into the living room wearing makeup that matches the primary color chart. Brick-wall parent: "No kid of mine is walking out of here with that garbage on your face. You get that off right now, or I will scrub it off myself." Teen thinks, "I can't be me in this family."

A kid walks out of the bedroom wearing shoes laced from the top down. Brick-wall parent: "You get those shoes laced properly or you're not leaving this house." Teen thinks, "I can't be me in this family."

During my teen years a friend who came from a brick-wall family would frizz her hair, put on the makeup, and roll her skirt up *after* she got to school. Her parents could walk down the hall and not even recognize their own daughter! She could not be herself and express the person she was trying to become around her parents. My friend was saying, "I am who you think I am only when I am around you. I can't tell you who I really am—you wouldn't approve."

Brick-wall parents impose rigid rules and dictate thou-shalt-nots and don't-you-dares. They do not teach or bend; instead they constantly set up a contest of wills. In this clash of wills at the third age of rebellion, either the parent wins decisively and the kid represses the anger and rage or turns them inward, or the kid takes a quantum leap into serious, life-threatening, morally threatening, or unhealthy rebellion. Either way the teenager loses his sense of dignity and self-worth. Kid says, "I can't be me in this family."

When one strives to manifest self according to the standards and mores consistent with others' many expectations ... that one will gaze upon his own mirrored reflection, yet will never see himself.

—MARY SUMMER RAIN, *WHISPERED WISDOM*

The jellyfish-A parents don't want to alienate their teenagers; they want to emulate them. Kid frizzes his hair, mother frizzes hers! There isn't one teenager in the house; there are two: Mom and kid. Teenager thinks, "I can't be me in this family."

Kid comes in with a new pair of jeans; Dad asks if he can borrow them. Kid thinks, "I can't be me in this family."

A teen practices a new dance step that is not life-threatening, morally threatening, or unhealthy (there are a few of those around). Jellyfish parents say, "Teach us." The poor kid has to put up with her parents break-dancing at the school assembly. Teen thinks, "I can't be me in this family."

A teenager in a jellyfish-A family struggles to gain any kind of recognition that he exists apart from his parents, that he is different from them, a unique and capable self. The problem is he hasn't learned from his parents how to do it. "I can't be me, I don't even know who 'me' is." The inconsistencies and mixed messages in a jellyfish-A family so disorient the teenager that he loses a sense of who he is.

In a jellyfish-B family, parents provide little or no structure, supervision, or guidance; they are usually into their own rebellion and absent in body or mind. Often, in an attempt to be recognized, the teenager goes to extremes in clothing or behavior. Kid says, "I can't be me. Nobody in this family even notices I'm around. I'll get them to notice me somehow! Why isn't just being me enough? Why don't they care?"

To have one's individuality completely ignored is like being pushed quite out of life. Like being blown out as one blows out a light.

—EVELYN SCOTT

None of the kids in these kinds of families can explore the facets of who they are or who they can become. The brick-wall teenager must be what the parents want her to be, or risk serious rebellion in an attempt to show her parents that she can be the me they don't want her to be. The jellyfish teenager has no model or guide and no responsible structure to build on. With no guidance from his parents he will attach himself to others who will offer support, even if it means sacrificing his own integrity, or he will close himself up so as not to be disappointed or hurt anymore. In closing himself to the pain he also closes himself to the possibilities of joy that come from reaching out, taking risks, and embracing others.

As a backbone parent, when your teenager comes in with his hair frizzed, one thing you can do is let him know you don't like it. (If you like it, it's not rebellion. If you tell him you like it, he'll have to resort to shaving both sides and greasing the top and dying it purple to get the desired reaction of disdain from you.) Just look at him and say, "Yuck! " then add, "But it's your hair." You've just given your teenager the opportunity to say, "I can be me in this family!"

Aunt Lucy may complain. Backbone parents put up with lots of disapproval from their brick-wall relatives. ("You're going to let your kid go out the door looking like that?") It will take some resolve on your part to be able to say, "It's *his* hair!" But as a result, even around brick-wall relatives, your teenager can affirm, "I can be me."

When I approach a child he inspires in me two sentiments:
tenderness for what he is; and respect for what he may
become.

—LOUIS PASTEUR

ONE SIDE SHAVEN WITH TWO STRIPES IN IT—HAIRDO REBELLION

Don Shaw, the former "sex and sin director" (health education
director) in our school district, said that if you let your children
make most of their own decisions (decisions that are not life-
threatening, morally threatening, or unhealthy) before they reach
puberty, they rarely take the quantum leap into serious
rebellion in the teen years, because it's hard to rebel against
one's own decision.

When my son, Joseph, was eleven years old, Don's line really
hit home. Joe came to me and announced he wanted to get one
side of his head shaven with two stripes in it. I told him I was sure
I wasn't going to like it, but since it was not life-threatening,
morally threatening, or unhealthy, and it would grow back, I
could live with it. I sat in the hair salon reading a good book as
the beautician washed Joe's hair and commented that lots of
girls would give their eyeteeth for a head of hair like his. Then
he told her what he wanted. She came over to me and asked, "Is
it all right if I shave one side of your son's hair and put two
stripes in it?" I said that I wasn't going to like it, but it was not
life-threatening, morally threatening, or unhealthy, and I knew it
would grow back. She looked at me and said, "He said the same
thing." How quickly kids learn the lines.

The beautician shaved one side and put two stripes in it.
She even got it to look good for about a day—which is a knack
beauticians have. The next day Joe could do nothing with his
lopsided head of hair. His sisters, who usually give him grief,
were in the bathroom with hair spray and mousse trying to help
him out. He survived that haircut, and the seven or eight even
more interesting haircuts that year. Then he started seventh
grade with a fairly traditional hairdo.

We also survived his sixth grade year, although family get-togethers were sometimes difficult. You should have heard some of the relatives. "Barb, you're on the road too much." It was my fault that my kid did that to his hair. I'm on lecture tours five to seven days a month, home twenty-three to twenty-five days a month, but it is my fault Joseph wanted a part of his head shaven with two stripes on the side. (If you have recently returned to work outside of the home after being at home for any length of time, be assured, if anything goes wrong with your kids now, it's your fault, because you "went to work." And if you have stayed home with your kids for any length of time and something goes wrong, it's again your fault; you smothered them. Can't seem to do it right either way.)

The next most common comment was, "If you let him do this at eleven, what's he going to do at sixteen?" I believe if you let kids make choices and mistakes when they are *cheap*, they rarely make the expensive ones later. Kids grow and learn from the cheap ones.

One aunt in particular berated Joey for his haircut. His sister Maria came to his defense and said, "Aunt, it's not life-threatening, it's not morally threatening, it's not unhealthy, and look, it's already growing back."

Sometimes It's the Choice of Words That Makes All the Difference

One of Maria's friends asked Maria to put small braids in her hair. The girl's boyfriend was so pleased with the results that he asked Maria if she would do the same with his hair. More than happy to oblige, Maria carefully braided his whole head, making sure each braid stood straight out. Looking like a scared porcupine, the boy walked into his home, the girls not far behind, anticipating a strong reaction from his mother. After taking in the whole scene, his mother exclaimed, "I really like that shirt you are wearing." She made no comment on his hair. After sleeping on the braids for two nights and getting absolutely no response from his parents on his new hairdo, he asked Maria to help him undo the braids.

How to Think, Not What to Think

Real power for parents lies in their ability to empower children, not control them and make them mind. How easy that is to say, how difficult it can be to do. We say we want our children to be responsible, resourceful, resilient, loving individuals who know how to think, not just what to think. However, we often find ourselves teaching them what to think based on what we think. From the time our children are toddlers we can hear ourselves saying to them, "Think for yourself. Don't forget your coat and mittens." "Think for yourself. Don't you have an exam you're supposed to be studying for?" "If you had put your shoes in one place, we wouldn't be looking for them now." "How many times do I have to tell you to think for yourself?" Many kids spend the first years of their adult life trying to figure out how to think for themselves, because they had learned so well what we think and rarely got the opportunity to practice how to think.

In order to believe they can solve their own problems, kids need self-esteem, integrity, and a sense of their own power. Responsibilities and decision-making skills help to create this power. An excellent way to teach the art of decision making is to let kids make decisions, guide them through the process without passing judgment, and let them grow through the results of their decisions. Mistakes and poor choices become a child's own responsibility. The hurt or discomfort arising from the choices goes away only after the child has worked out the problem constructively. By having power over the situation, the child's dignity, integrity, and self-worth are enhanced.

Since responsibility and decision making are prerequisites to self-discipline, kids need to be trusted to assume responsibilities and to be given opportunities to make critical decisions throughout their childhood. Responsibilities and decisions need to be age-appropriate and meaningful. Asking a fifteen-year-old to mow and trim the lawn is appropriate; asking a five-year-old to is not. A four-year-old can help sort laundry; a twelve-year-old could be expected to sort, wash, dry, fold, and put away the laundry, not that he would necessarily do it joyfully. A six-year-old doesn't have the skills or wisdom necessary yet to pick the school she will go to; a sixteen-year-old can look at a school catalog and select elective courses to take; an eighteen-year-old can decide to go to school or not and to know and accept the consequences for the choice he made.

Some things are not negotiable. At our home, whether you are five, fifteen, or forty, if you ride your bike, you wear your helmet. Our children know that our car doesn't start until all passengers have their seat belts fastened.

There are some decisions and responsibilities that parents need to keep for themselves. Different parents will make different choices. But first a parent needs to ask, *Am I keeping this decision or responsibility for myself because I am afraid to give it to my kids for fear of losing control, or because it is a part of being a wise and caring parent?*

Take a look at the responsibilities and decisions you keep and the ones you are willing to let your kids make. From the day we start letting them take responsibilities and make decisions, until they leave our home, it is helpful to have a plan to constantly increase the number of responsibilities and decision-making opportunities. Then, when they do leave, they will be making their own decisions and assuming full responsibility for their own behavior. It doesn't just happen—we have to make it happen.

RED PAJAMA, BLUE PAJAMA, OR A PART OF BOTH

Anna, Maria, and Joe get to make a lot of decisions. They don't get to make them all. When Joe was a toddler, I didn't say, "Do you want to go to bed or not?" That was not a decision he was going to make at three. But I did say, "Do you want to go to bed NOW with your red pajamas or NOW with your blue pajamas?" What pajamas to wear is a decision a three-year-old can make. My strong-willed, creative three-year-old showed up with red bottoms and a blue top. It was not life-threatening, morally threatening, or unhealthy, so why not? It would not have been my choice, but it was a small opportunity for him to say, "I can be me."

When he was getting dressed for preschool, I said, "Here are three outfits. Pick one." There were days when Joe would combine parts of all three outfits. Tired of the strange looks people would give me when I dropped my son off at preschool, I made a button Joe proudly wore that said in bold letters, "I dressed myself!" (I have been tempted lately to drag out that button to pin on my independent teenagers.)

As the kids got older, responsibilities and decision-making opportunities were increased. "Maria, here are your school clothes, here are your play clothes. Pick something from your school clothes." Maria still regularly shows up with the layered look—all school clothes, just definitely layered. Gymnastics day: dark green tights, pale green leotard, red knickers, white socks that go halfway between the knicker line and the ankles so the green tights stick out; high-top shoes, no laces (I have no idea if or how they stay on her feet all day), oversized shirt that is red-, green-, yellow-, and blue-striped—green of course not matching the green in the leotard and half-sleeved so that the leotard sticks out. Again I need to remind myself, it's not life-threatening.

Our eighteen-year-old has been picking out her own clothes since she was two and a half. We don't say, "Here's three outfits, pick one. Here's your school clothes, here's your play clothes." She's been through those steps. We've assumed that by now she is quite capable of picking out her own clothes. I welcome her asking me for advice, but I also trust her ability to think for herself.

Blue Sock, Pink Sock, Yellow Sock—A Thinking Girl's Choice

A parent of a six-year-old was concerned that her daughter would be unable to pick out the right clothes for school, since Mom had been laying them out every morning up till now. A few days after giving her daughter the opportunity to pick out her own clothes for school, the mom was a bit taken aback when the daughter showed up for breakfast with a blue sock on one foot and a yellow sock on the other. This would have never happened when the mother picked out the clothes. She commented on the two different-colored socks and the daughter replied, "Oh, yeah, I could only find a blue one, a pink one, and a yellow one, and you and I both know pink and blue don't go together." The girl had been thinking and had made what seemed to her to be a logical choice.

WHEN IS A CHOICE NOT REALLY A CHOICE? WHEN IT COMES WITH STRINGS ATTACHED

When kids reach the early teen years in a brick-wall family, instead of increasing responsibilities and decision-making opportunities, there is a tendency on the part of the parents to start over. ("Here are three outfits. Pick one.") By now the teenager has learned how to please the brick-wall parent. He knows that if he chooses the "wrong" outfit, the parent will yell, "You can't wear that!" Or more subtly, "You can wear that outfit if you'd like. Just don't tell anyone your last name." An even more ominous response might be, "You can wear that strange outfit to the family get-together, but remember that your grandmother has a weak heart."

The major problems arise when the teen decides he doesn't want to please his parents anymore. More than once, brick-wall parents have said to me, "Would you look at this kid. He was such a good kid, so well behaved, so well mannered, so well dressed. Now look at him!" I say, "You know what? He hasn't changed. From the time he was young, he dressed the way you told him to dress; he acted the way you told him to act; he said the things you told him to say. He's been listening to somebody else tell him what to do. He's been doing it. He hasn't changed. He is still listening to somebody else tell him what to do. The problem is, it isn't you anymore; it's his peers. The kid hasn't learned *how* to think."

No Choice, No Sense of Self, No Integrity

Responsibilities and decision-making opportunities in a jellyfish family have been nonexistent or haphazard up to the teen years and continue to be so. These adolescents will either seek out others to lead them or learn to become totally self-sufficient, refusing to rely on anyone else for support, encouragement, or advice. Those who seek out others often attach themselves to strong, charismatic leaders, who fill a hole or a need. The teenagers quickly adopt the leader's vision, even if that vision exploits their own will, spirit, and body. Lacking a strong sense of self, these teens define themselves only in relationship to whomever they have attached themselves. Those who become totally self-sufficient and fiercely independent never learn the joys and comforts of becoming interdependent. Their motto is "If it is going to get done, I'll have to do it myself."

Strong-Willed Child Plus Supportive Parent Equals Independent Thinker

For those of you raising a strong-willed child, I'd like to point out something about strong-willed children you may not fully appreciate if yours are still young. In the later teens years and early adult years these children are often much easier on their parents than are compliant kids. Compliant children are very easily led when they are young, because they thrive on approval and pleasing adults. They are just as easily led in their teen years, because they still seek the same two things: approval and to please their peers. Strong-willed children are never easily led by anybody—not by you, but also not by their peers. So celebrate your child's strength of will throughout the early years, and when the going gets tough for both of you, give that strong-willed child a hug and know that the independent thinking you are fostering will serve him well in the teen years.

Take a critical look at the responsibilities and decision-making opportunities you give your children at home, and check to see if you are increasing them as your kids get older. Keep the ones you need to keep as a wise and caring parent. The rest you can give to your children.

Teenagers in backbone families have known from the time they were young that they were listened to and cared for and were important to their parents. They could freely express their feelings, make mistakes, grow from those mistakes, and take the steps needed to become responsible, resourceful, resilient, loving individuals who could act in their own best interests, stand up for themselves, and exercise their rights while respecting the rights and legitimate needs of others. They truly begin to develop their individual selfhood. Backbone parents offer a network of support through the six critical life messages; they discipline by giving life to their kids' learning; they teach them how to think, not just what to think; they allow and encourage rebellion that is not life-threatening, morally threatening, or unhealthy. The kids say, "I can be me in this family."

If you invite your children, when they are young, to express themselves by way of small rebellions, choices, and decisions, as they grow through the third age of rebellion, they will have the backbone on which to flesh out their own identity.

Mastering others is strength
Mastering yourself is true power.
—TAO TE CHING

Chapter 5

Keeping Your Cool Without Putting Your Feelings on Ice

> Anyone can become angry—that's easy. But to be angry
> with the right person, to the right degree, at the right
> time, for the right purpose, and in the right way—that is
> not easy.
>
> —ARISTOTLE

A nine-year-old student in my special-education class had been told by his parents, teachers, and counselors that his eye-hand coordination was poor and that sometimes neither the eyes nor the hands did what his brain told them to do. One day, however, his coordination was good enough to deliver a well-placed knuckle sandwich to the jaw of another student. He looked at me and complained, "I told my hand not to do it, but it did it anyway."

He learned his lesson well and expected this defense to work as it usually did. So he was very surprised by my response: "You are angry, and *you* alone are responsible for the way you handle that anger. Nobody else. I think you need some time to cool off and figure out another way to handle it. I know you can do it. In this class if you hit, you sit, and you don't sit in our room, you get to sit in the 'opportunity room,' which is your last opportunity to stay here."

Used to having his behavior excused because of his handicap, he pleaded, "But he made me angry, it's not my fault, he *made* me hit him." He had a way to go before he would understand one of the important truths of human relationships: Other people cannot make you angry. They may tease you, provoke you, or invite you to be angry, but in the end you choose your response. And you alone are responsible for that choice and for accepting the consequences that come with it.

A twelve-year-old student threw himself on the classroom floor in a full-blown temper tantrum. As a special-needs student he had been in so many kinds of therapy that he had all the jargon down pat. He could tell me if he was coming out of his id, ego, or superego, having been in Freudian therapy; whether he was the Top Dog or the Underdog, having been in Gestalt therapy; and he would tell me if I was coming from my Parent, Adult, or Child, having been in Transactional Analysis therapy. In fact this kid probably would have scored higher than I did on the comprehensive exams for my master's degree in Emotional Disturbance. As he was throwing his arms and feet around and pounding the floor, I just stood there and stared at him in disbelief. He looked up and in all sincerity, with a tear rolling down his cheek, cried, "I can't help it, I'm emotionally disturbed!" He meant it. He didn't understand yet that it was his behavior that had gotten him into an emotional-behavioral-disorders class in the first place. If he didn't act that way, he wouldn't have the "emotional disturbance."

A young girl in the same class was always trying to take care of everybody else's feelings and apologizing for taking up space herself. Having been seriously abused, then abandoned, she felt guilty and afraid when she found herself having fun and was constantly on the alert for minute signals from adults that they were angry, upset, or ready to lash out at her.

None of these children had learned to accept and take ownership of their own feelings, nor to acknowledge that they could be responsible for how they acted on those feelings.

While I was growing up, I often blamed my own outbursts on my quick temper, inherited, I was sure, from my father, who said he got it from his father. I had been able to observe this temper in action on a regular basis and got good at copying it. Around age eighteen I realized my temper was separate from my dad's—he had his, I had mine, and I was solely responsible for the way I handled mine. The feelings weren't going to go away. What I needed to learn were more and better ways to handle them.

Even now, at forty-five, anytime I'm tired, worn out,

frustrated, and at my wits' end, I find the old behavior, the quick temper, is right at hand. But knowing it is there, I now have the skill to recognize that hatchet before I use it on my kids. I can put it away and take the time to find and use a more appropriate tool.

Those of us who grew up with destructive tools may never be able to rid ourselves totally of them, but we can make sure we don't use them on our kids. And we can rejoice that, thanks to our determination and resolve, our kids will probably not find those tools in their own toolboxes. My children give me hope. They have not "inherited" my temper. I don't believe it is an issue of genetics, but one of learning.

Children who, in anger and frustration, throw a math book across the room may not know other ways to express anger. They may have witnessed angry parents throwing plates across the kitchen. Children who beat up their peers may themselves have been beaten and berated by their parents for nothing more than making a simple mistake or for just being in the way. Children who throw themselves on the floor kicking and screaming when they don't get their own way have learned that this technique hooks the adults they are performing for. These actions are all learned.

It is possible to teach kids to replace these irresponsible actions with more appropriate, responsible expressions of their feelings. But first they need to know it's all right to feel. It is all right to be happy, concerned, joyful, sad, angry, frustrated, and hurt. Feelings are motivators for growth or warning signs that something needs changing. When we are concerned or joyful, we have energy to grow and to extend ourselves outward. When we are angry or hurt, our feelings are signaling our mind and body that something is not right and needs to be changed. Sometimes what needs changing is not the situation itself but our view of it. To be angry because I am stuck in a long line at the checkout counter after carefully choosing the line that seemed to be moving the fastest is uncomfortable, unproductive, and actually makes the wait seem longer. If, on the other hand, I decide to balance my checkbook while I wait, I have changed my own outlook on the situation, since I can't at the moment change the long line. Choosing my own way to respond to a situation is to recognize that I can't always control what is happening to me. What I can control is how I *use* what is happening to me. The same applies to emotions. Feelings are not good or bad—they are real. It is what we do with our feelings that we are responsible for. I can be angry and let that anger consume me as I strike out in rage at anyone and anything around me, or I can recognize that feeling as a warning sign that something needs changing—either my attitude toward the situation or the situation itself. The choice is mine.

Viktor Frankl, a psychiatrist and Holocaust survivor, wrote eloquently in *Man's Search for Meaning* about making choices: "We who lived in concentration camps can remember those who walked through the huts comforting others, giving away their last piece of bread. They may have been few in number, but they offer sufficient proof that everything can be taken from a person but one thing: the last of the human freedoms—to choose one's attitude in any given set of circumstances—to choose one's own way."

Feelings in the Three Types of Families

THE BRICK-WALL FAMILY

In brick-wall families, where parents demand obedience and rule by fear, kids are taught at a very young age not to express their true feelings, their true selves. Spontaneous expressions of joy, concern, and happiness are stifled, because *all* feelings are stifled by the parents. Anger, hostility, opposition, and sadness are all punished. Eventually the child becomes so wary of her parents that *no* feelings are spontaneously expressed; she must first "check in" with her parents to see if the feeling is okay.

When young kids in a brick-wall family explore their environment, they are slapped or yelled at for touching something and told to quiet down and be still. When they walk through a mud puddle just for fun, they are told to get inside, clean up, and don't ever do that again. As they try to comfort crying siblings, they are warned to leave them alone. Stopping to catch snowflakes, they are told to hurry up and get inside so that they don't catch a cold. If they are often discounted in these ways, kids begin to believe that they have no worth and to feel guilty and anxious if they are happy. They are constantly alert to subtle signals from their parents of impending rage. Since they rarely see their parents laughing and enjoying life, the kids rarely laugh and enjoy life themselves. The implicit message is life is to be endured, not enjoyed.

The feelings of anger, fear, sadness, or hurt are not just stifled; they are directly punished or denied. ("Don't stomp your feet, or I'll spank you." "Don't talk to me like that, or I'll wash your mouth out with soap." "At your age you ought to be able to sleep with the lights off." "You're a scaredy-cat." "Don't cry, it was only a gerbil." "Big boys don't cry." "I'm going to keep paddling you until you stop crying and tell me you are sorry." "Get up, you didn't fall that hard.")

Forbidden to express these emotions themselves, kids get stuck in their anger, fear, sadness, and hurt. Sometimes they even refuse to acknowledge that they are angry or hurt and have no way of getting rid of the energy produced by those feelings. ("That's just the way my dad is. I've learned to live with his strappings. He's only doing it for my own good." "I never cry when she slaps me. I'll never let her see me cry." "It doesn't hurt much.") The energy builds up inside, like steam pressure in a boiler. Eventually one of three things results:

1. Passive-destructive acts against the self

Passive-destructive acts against the self signal poor self-esteem or even self-hatred. Examples are derogatory statements directed at oneself, body mutilation, sexual addiction, drug addiction, alcoholism, psychosomatic illness, melancholy, eating disorders, depression, and the ultimate self-destructive act, suicide. A passive-destructive person often avoids dealing openly with feelings or blames others for "causing" them. ("It's okay, I'm not sad." "He made me do it." "Nobody cares about me anyway.") Instead of solving the problem, passive-destructive acts destroy the person who has the problem.

2. Aggressive acts against others

Aggressive acts against others are actions deliberately intended to harm others. Examples are physical fights, arguments, blaming others, extortion, kicking the cat, child abuse, spousal abuse, and murder. Aggressive people try to control others with brute force, verbal abuse, or a combination of both. ("You give me your lunch money, or I'll stomp you to the ground." "Hey, stupid, can't you even tie your shoelaces yet?" "You took like a tramp! Get in here and see how it feels to have that garbage scrubbed off your face.") Aggressive acts against others don't solve the original problems. Instead they create new ones.

3. Passive-aggressive acts (a combination of the other two)

Passive-aggressive acts combines the first two in a creative way that signals that the person is responsible neither for himself nor to others. Constance Dembrowsky, a noted authority on responsibility-oriented education, describes, in *Personal and Social Responsibility*, passive-aggressive people as those who

> set others up to fail in sneaky, non-direct ways. They don't deal with people or issues directly, but use devious ways to get back at them.... They use sarcastic remarks or put-downs and say they were just kidding. They pretend to forget their anger, but do their best to get even by: undermining things; forgetting things; pretending to misunderstand and doing it wrong; being late but always having a good "excuse"; and by taking someone's words literally and doing EXACTLY as they were told, knowing that was not the intention of the person. They actually harbor the anger and use the negative energy to figure out ways they can get back at the person they are angry with in indirect ways that look like they didn't do it on purpose.

The passive-aggressive individual destroys herself physically, mentally, and emotionally; harms others; and creates more problems.

god save the children
trapped in the game
living in fear
hiding the pain
battered by devils
screaming in vain
feeling the wrath
then doing the same
—STEVE LYNCH, IN *THE CARLETON VOICE*

THE JELLYFISH FAMILY

In jellyfish families kids are not taught how to identify or responsibly express their feelings. Often the adults express their own feelings and respond to their child's feelings in extreme ways. The parent will either smother the child and try to own the feelings for her, not encouraging her to work through her own feelings and protecting her from the consequences of the expression of her feelings. Or the parent will totally disregard the child's feelings through abandonment or neglect. ("Perk up, it's not that bad. Let's go get an ice cream and forget about it." "Oh, I'll call your friend and tell him you didn't mean to hurt him. We'll invite him over to play." "Don't be sad about your gerbil. I already have a new one for you." "I know you didn't mean to hit her. Besides, she shouldn't have been bugging you in the first place." "Don't bother me now. Can't you see I have enough problems of my own?")

Since boundaries are few or nonexistent in the jellyfish family, the parent's feelings and the child's feelings often get intertwined, and the child gets confused about whose feelings are whose. A child wins the district spelling bee. Mom is ecstatic and praises her son profusely: "I'm so proud of you. You've made me so happy." His feelings are never explored or even acknowledged; the emphasis is all on the way Mom feels. The result is that the child feels an obligation to keep Mom happy by winning more and more events, even if he doesn't want to enter them. The child thinks, "Mom is so happy, and I feel guilty for not wanting to do things that make her happy, so I'll try to be happy about being in the spelling bee even if I do get sick to my stomach." He never feels free to tell Mom, "I get scared even thinking about another contest." The son learns to fake it, stays confused about what he is really feeling, and does what he needs to do to please his parent at his own expense. He is overly aware of others' feelings and needs at the expense of his own self-awareness. He learns that his feelings are not as important as other people's; he learns to take care of others at the expense of his own mental and physical well-being.

If the jellyfish parent constantly rescues the child from feelings and situations, the child learns to be dependent on others to define her own feelings. She also becomes helpless at solving her own problems and is quick to lay blame on others. "Don't cry about the goldfish, Susan, I know you meant to feed him," Dad says. "We all forget sometimes. Besides, I'll bet it was sick when your friend gave it to you. Let's go out and get a real pet." Eventually the child begins to feel angry and resentful at not being truly listened to; she begins to doubt her own feelings and either leaves it up to others to pick up the pieces after her or attacks those who suggest that she is capable of handling her own problems.

If the parent abandons or neglects the child, the child learns to put aside or hide feelings of fear, hurt, sorrow, and anger because they get in the way of taking care of the parent's feelings and thus being able to stay connected. He learns not to trust others and to manipulate them to get what he needs. Joy, concern, and happiness are smothered. The child eventually becomes either too self-sufficient, allowing no intimacy in his life, or a needy adult, constantly seeking others to make him feel safe, loved, and secure. He could become a prime candidate for a cult, gang, prostitution ring, or a chronically unhappy and disappointing marriage. He goes through the motions of living but neglects his mind and body, or becomes an angry bully who physically and verbally assaults people. Or at worst he becomes a hollow shell of a human being without remorse and with terrible vengeance, who strikes out at anyone and anything in his way.

THE BACKBONE FAMILY

In the backbone family, feelings are dealt with in a radically different way. Parents in a backbone family regularly do five things:

1. **They acknowledge their own feelings and label them.** "I'm angry. I'm hurt. I'm upset. I'm happy. I'm sad. I'm frustrated. I'm concerned." They express a full range of emotions. Their children see them laughing, crying, joyful, sad, angry, hurt,

frustrated. The kids learn it is all right to feel and to express their feelings.

2. They admit that they are angry, or hurt, or afraid, then do something responsible and purposeful to address these feelings. They not only verbalize their feelings, they also let their whole body speak those feelings in an assertive way. They don't deny that they are sad when their eyes are filling with tears. They don't deny that they are angry, then stomp out of the room. Kids learn that there are constructive ways to work through a feeling. They don't need to deny or make excuses for their own feelings.

3. They make assertive statements about themselves. ("I can do this!" "I'll handle it!" "I can change!" "I blew it this time, and I'll fix it!" "I can accept it.") These statements create a sense of power and control over one's own life. Kids learn that they, too, can have this same power. Passivity is not there to be copied.

4. They acknowledge their children's feelings as real and legitimate, without passing judgment on those feelings. ("You look like you are having fun catching snowflakes. It's too cold for me out here; I'm going inside. Let me know how many you catch." "You seem to be really sad about your dog. Would you like to sit here and be held, or would you rather be alone for a while?") Kids learn that their own feelings are important, that they can be trusted to handle those feelings, and that it is okay to count on others for support.

5. They teach their children to handle their own feelings assertively. When kids express their feelings irresponsibly, backbone parents accept the feelings as real, label the feelings, and help their children find alternative expressions that are both responsible and assertive. An alternative might be going out for a long run or a short walk, making a firm statement of anger, or assertively confronting the person with whom they are angry.

Sometimes helping kids arrive at alternative actions means starting at the beginning with simply identifying a feeling and affirming a child's right to that feeling. ("You seem really angry." "It's okay to cry when you feel sad." "I know it's frustrating to have to leave the park when you are having so much fun.") As easy as it seems to simply identify a feeling and affirm a child's right to that feeling, parents can be sorely tested when their child is in the middle of a full-blown temper tantrum.

THE TEMPER TANTRUM

Temper tantrums happen—they are not planned. Parents can anticipate them intelligently, or they can fear them and then ignore them when they happen. Neither approach will prevent the tantrum, and the second approach will often make it worse. But understanding the causes of tantrums will help parents anticipate when one is about to happen.

Tantrums usually occur when kids are tired, hungry, frustrated, or all three. If parents remain calm, they can help their children by eliminating the cause or by redirecting the energy in a more responsible and productive way.

Often when they are on the verge of a major breakthrough in their physical, mental, or psychological development, kids will become very agitated, frustrated, sullen, or angry. Just before he learns to walk, or she takes off on the two-wheeler, or he learns to combine letters to make words, or she begins to menstruate, temper tantrums seem to be the norm of the day, with calm and reason but a passing memory.

Tantrums are not limited to the time just before major break-throughs. Kids also tend to pitch their fits at the three ages of rebellion: two, five, and puberty. At each of these ages children are trying to define themselves as distinct individuals, separate from those around them. Also at these ages children's verbal skills often do not match their emotional states. You may have a very verbal five-year-old who throws temper tantrums, but being very verbal and having the verbal skills to match an emotional state are not the same. She may talk a lot and use words impressive for her age, but connecting the right words with things in the external world is much easier than connecting the right words with a feeling. For kids, being able to verbalize that they are tired, hungry, or frustrated is a skill to be learned over and over again. If a child learns that his feelings are accepted as real and legitimate and he is helped to express them in words and to act on them responsibly when he is in the first age of rebellion, he will find it easier to adapt those skills to the challenges of the next two ages of rebellion. He will have in his own toolkit the appropriate ways to handle his exhaustion, hunger, and frustration. He will know that he has the support and encouragement of the adults around him during the next two ages—especially the third age when he will be dealing with exhaustion, hunger, frustration, and hormones!

These ideas look good on paper, but not so simple when you are in the middle of the aisle at the grocery store, or in front of the relatives who swear their children never behaved that way, or on a city bus with twenty people watching to see what you are going to do. In these situations brick-wall and jellyfish parents have fairly predictable, and predictably nonproductive, responses.

The brick-wall parent grabs the kid and starts yelling. ("Stop it now, or I'll give you something real to cry about." "You get off that floor right now, or you will spend the rest of the afternoon in bed.")

As a result of these threats the kid increases the pitch of her temper tantrum until she physically loses control and collapses on the floor. She eventually falls asleep from the exhaustion that has been magnified by the temper tantrum. Or worse, fearful of a beating, she immediately stops crying, repressing her own feelings of hunger, frustration, or exhaustion. She is learning that her feelings don't count.

A jellyfish parent will at first try to ignore the tantrum and pretend it's not happening (which is pretty hard to do), or brush it off as something that has to be tolerated: "She always does this when she doesn't get her way. It will stop soon." When it doesn't (and it usually doesn't), the parent will try to bribe the child to stop: "If you stop crying, I'll give you this candy," or "Be a big girl for Mommy and stop crying, and I'll let you ride in the front seat of the car." Or the parent gives in and lets the child have whatever it was she wanted: "Okay, you win, you can have the truck. Just stop crying, I can't stand it."

If that doesn't work, a jellyfish parent, himself raised in a brick-wall family, will pull out the one tool he knows will work because it "worked" on him: brute force with a healthy dose of loud voice. He grabs the child and screams at her, "Stop that right now, or I'll give you a good reason to cry." The kid is not only frightened and learns to be hypervigilant out of self-defense but she also learns that her feelings are not important to, or even acknowledged by, her parent. She learns that she can get what she *wants* if she howls long enough but that she is powerless and helpless to get what she really *needs*.

In contrast the backbone parent tries to be in tune with the child's needs. Recognizing the roots of a temper tantrum, she tries to avoid situations where the child gets overly tired, extremely hungry, or too frustrated. She recognizes that the child is in need of a nap, not a trip to the grocery store right now; or that he needs to eat a snack while walking down the grocery store aisle and that not being able to have the cereal he saw on TV can be pretty frustrating.

But the reality is that sometimes, even with the best of plans, temper tantrums can't be avoided. You are already in the cereal aisle, halfway through your shopping, and your child throws himself on the floor, wailing about not getting that prized cereal. Suddenly ten adults are in the same aisle staring at you and your out-of-control kid. You'd like to pretend he isn't related and you never saw him before.

Or you are at a family reunion, and your two-year-old wants a piece of the cake *now*, not later. Everyone tells you what to do with your "spoiled kid." Your own mom has just launched into the beginning of what promises to be a long lecture about "I told you so." Uncle George thinks your son needs a good swat, and his wife is yelling at him for being such a brute. Aunt Ann is trying to sneak a piece of cake to your child. And you just want to sneak away.

Or you are stuck in a bus in a rainstorm and traffic with a tired, hungry, and cranky two-year-old and twenty tired, hungry, and cranky adults, including yourself. Everybody is in a hurry, and the bus is getting nowhere fast. You've run out of crackers and ideas. There aren't too many ways to avoid the oncoming temper tantrum—in fact there are none. And if the bus takes much longer to get to your stop, you may throw a temper tantrum yourself.

But in all these situations, as a backbone parent you know the last thing an out-of-control kid needs is an out-of-control parent. Give yourself a moment to tell yourself you can handle this. If it is possible to remove yourself and your child from the scene, all the better. If that is not possible, do the next best thing: pretend that you have removed yourself from the scene and that those people staring at you are not really there.

If in the grocery store she has thrown herself on the floor, get down there with her and start rubbing the top of her head and across her back, calmly affirming her, labeling her feelings, and letting her know you are there to help her handle them. "I know you are tired [or hungry or frustrated or all three] and I am going to be here for you. It's okay, you're going to be all right." You can expect some disapproving looks and aggressive comments for this one! Once your child has calmed down, you can give her a hug and try to figure out a way to relieve her hunger, or get through the store faster so that she can get the sleep she needs, or redirect her attention away from the cereal by giving her an errand to run in the next aisle.

Tough as it is, it is easier to be patient with a two-year-old who is throwing a temper tantrum than with a teenager doing the same thing. Yet he needs the same help labeling his feelings and figuring out constructive ways to handle them.

You are sitting at the dinner table for a family meal, and your seven-year-old casually comments about the zit on your fourteen-year-old's face. That's it! Your teenager screams at his sister, tells you that you never do anything about his sister's rude comments, and storms up to his bedroom, slamming the door behind him.

The brick-wall parent jumps up from the table and charges to the son's room, all the while screaming, "You ruin all our dinners. I am sick and tired of you picking on your little sister, and you should be ashamed of yourself, acting like a two-year-old." The parent then throws in a minilecture for good measure: "If you hadn't eaten the french fries and the chocolates, you wouldn't have those zits."

The teenager's feelings are denied, and he has no appropriate outlet for the energy produced by those feelings. He will get passive: *I am ugly. I'm hurt. Nobody cares about me. I am acting like a two-year-old and I don't know what to do.* Or he will become aggressive, finding opportunities to tease and torment his younger sister, creating a cycle of chaos and abuse. Or he will become passive aggressive, setting his sister up in a sneaky way, making sarcastic remarks, then telling her he was just kidding, can't she take a joke? He doesn't feel good about what he is doing but doesn't know how to break the cycle and ends up creating more problems for himself and his sister.

The jellyfish parent tells the teenager that he shouldn't be so sensitive—in essence that his feelings don't count. Or the parent berates the seven-year-old for picking on her brother, and rushes up to "console" (read "rescue") the teenager. ("Oh, hon, your zit's not that bad. I can't even see it. When I was your age, I had at least thirty. You are such a handsome boy. Look at your shoulders and your gorgeous hair. Stop crying and come have some dessert with us. Make your mom happy by smiling for me.") The teenager learns not only that his true feelings don't count but that he is responsible for keeping his mom happy, no matter what he is feeling inside.

As a backbone parent you can respect your son's need to leave the dinner table and calm down. Later give him a hug and tell him you understand how it feels to have a zit in the middle of the face; it's no fun. And having a seven-year-old comment on it, even pleasantly, is like adding salt to a wound. After acknowledging the kid's feelings as real and legitimate, you can talk about how he might express his feelings without stomping up the stairs and slamming his door. Yes, it was better than knocking his sister off her chair as he left the table, and yes, it's okay to get away, but if he wants to handle his feelings maturely, the stomping and slamming have got to go. As he looks at the anger, he can begin to see that it was masking other feelings, such as embarrassment and frustration.

It takes time to teach kids to handle their feelings assertively, but in doing so you teach them that their own feelings are important, that they can be trusted to handle those feelings, and that they can count on you for support and guidance when they have handled them poorly.

ASSERTIVE CONFRONTATION

Confrontation is sometimes necessary, but all too often it means endless arguments that waste a great deal of energy, lead only to further argument, and solve nothing. Kids need to learn better ways. In order to confront effectively, they must first understand their anger:

- Where did it come from? (*From inside myself.*)
- Is it masking another feeling? (*I am hurt, or frustrated, or disappointed or afraid.*)
- Why be angry anyway? (*Because I care. If I didn't care, I wouldn't be angry. I can't be angry about something I don't care about, with someone I don't care about.*)

Once the anger is understood, kids are prepared to confront the person they are angry with.

If you are going to teach your children how to confront assertively, the best way to begin is to demonstrate it for them. Think about how you handle conflicts. Your teenager leaves her smelly running clothes and shoes right where she took them off—outside the shower. Do you choose a passive response, pick up the clothes, and tell yourself that you are lucky she is doing cross-country running instead of just running around the shopping mall? Or is your style aggressive, throwing the clothes out onto the front porch? Or passive aggressive, picking up each garment and pasting an angry stamp in your mental notebook? The issue is not big enough to have a full-blown fight over, so you keep picking up the clothes, day after day, until finally your notebook has room for only one more stamp. The teenager walks in and throws a coat over the chair, and you cash in your stamps: "What do you think I am, hired help? You are such a slob! I'm never picking up a piece of your clothes again. You can live in a pigpen for all I care." Your teenager looks at you in astonishment, never expecting such an outburst, blames it on PMS, and vows to stay out of your life until you cool off.

None of these responses is an acknowledgment of your feelings, nor a responsible and purposeful way of addressing those feelings. The problem has not been solved and is likely to keep coming up. The feelings will either fester inside you or spill out all over someone else. Your children will then try to solve their problems the way you taught them, passively, aggressively, or passive aggressively.

As a backbone parent you can serve as a model for your children and show them a way of confronting someone else that demonstrates that you accept your own feelings and have a responsible way of addressing them. Using the following seven steps for a fair fight as a backbone, you can begin to construct a productive, assertive confrontation:

1. **When you are upset or angry, say so in an upset or angry tone of voice.** Let your whole body speak the message in a straightforward, assertive manner—not aggressively or passively. Say what you are feeling in a firm voice. Your tone can convey anger without a loud scream or a shaky whisper.

2. **Tell the other person about your feelings.** "I am angry!" It is critical that your body and mouth are saying the same thing. To grab the coat and throw it on the floor and say that you are not upset about anything is passive aggressive. To say in a soft whisper that you are angry is to not involve your body in delivering the message. In fact, if you quietly say you are angry, anger is probably masking another feeling, such as disappointment or sadness. You then have to ask if your body is speaking your true feeling.

3. **State your belief out loud but avoid killer statements.** "I believe each one of us needs to pick up our own dirty clothes and put them in the laundry basket." Avoid comments such as "You never pick up your clothes." "You are such a slob." These killer statements only attack the other person. Stick to your belief. This step is often left out of confrontations, yet it is critical that the person whom you are confronting know what your opinion is.

4. **Close the time gap between the hurt and the expression of that hurt. Give direct feedback.** ("This week I have picked up your underwear and running clothes every day. You drop them outside the shower and leave them there.") Tell her what she has done. Don't tell her she's been this way since she was two, or that you never had to pick up after her older sisters. These not only put her down, they are likely to arouse resentment and anger. Don't tell her she also forgot to put out the trash four weeks ago and ruined one of your blouses two months ago. To tell a teenager you are still angry about several other things she did a while ago is both unproductive (she can't remember the incident) and an indication that you need to work

on dealing effectively with your anger: You are saving "red angry stamps" and cashing them all in at once.

5. **State what you want from the other person.** ("I want you to pick up your running clothes and throw them in the laundry bag after you shower and to put your running shoes back in the closet.") Often it is enough to tell the other party what you want without adding an ultimatum. Sometimes just having the problem brought to her attention is enough. But if you do give an ultimatum, make sure you say what you mean, mean what you say, and do what you said you were going to do. ("If you don't pick them up after your shower, I will put them in a plastic bag in the bathroom, and you can wash them yourself.") If you said it, mean it and follow through. Don't pick up the clothes and wash them the next day because you know your daughter was in a hurry to get to school. Don't make an idle threat or one you are not willing to carry out.

6. **Be open to the other person's perspective on the situation.** Give your teenager an opportunity to talk, and be willing to listen. Perhaps the two of you had different expectations, or she never gave it any thought, or maybe she does expect you to pick up after her. Often in assertive confrontation the problem is solved at this stage. The person being confronted agrees to do what she is asked because it makes sense and is fair.

7. **Negotiate an agreement you can both accept.** If there is a difference in opinion, or a disagreement about your proposed solution, you will need to negotiate a solution you can both accept. Maybe she will shower in the basement and let her clothes collect in the corner until she can wash them herself on Saturday. Maybe you both agree she will purchase a small garbage can with a tight lid to place in the bathroom so that she can throw her running clothes in it as she is undressing. Decide on a time that you will get together to discuss how the proposed plan is working.

If assertive confrontation feels awkward to you, choose an issue that is upsetting you, practice the steps in front of a mirror or with a trusted friend, then confront the right person for the issue at hand. You can begin to make assertive confrontation your tool of choice by recognizing your own feelings of hurt, sadness, frustration, or anger and by taking time to think before you respond rather than react and regret later.

Once you are comfortable with the tool, help your children work through the seven steps. Since they don't have old habits to replace with the new, they may learn more quickly than you. If so, you will get an opportunity to learn from them.

Even when you are using the seven steps for a fair fight, a confrontation can be frightening. Both children and adults need to recognize that to *keep* it a fair fight, it is always acceptable to

1. *Call time out* ("We are both too angry to talk right now. Let's talk about this later." "I am too upset to work through this right now. I need to take a break.") If either party is too angry or too upset to speak calmly and responsibly, it is important to call time out and come back to the confrontation at a later time.

2. *Refuse to take abuse* ("It hurts when you call me a slob." "Please don't attack my family that way." "You can be angry at me, but you can't hit me.") If one party becomes verbally, physically, or emotionally abusive, the other party has the right to refuse to take the abuse.

3. *Insist on fair treatment* ("I won't borrow your clothes without asking you first, and I want you to ask me first if you can borrow mine." "I will knock on your door and ask permission to come in; I want you to do the same for me." "It is not fair to throw my running clothes in the trash just because I didn't pick them up. We've got to come up with a better solution.") Fair treatment is not always equal or identical treatment, but it is *honest, adequate, and just.*

We need to help our children learn to recognize when it is necessary to call time out; to know they have the right not to be verbally or physically abused by anyone and that they have the right to be treated with respect, dignity, and fairness. They also have the responsibility not to let their feelings take over a situation; to see that they do not physically, verbally, or emotionally abuse another person; and to treat other people with the same respect and dignity they themselves ask for. Fighting fair enables parents and kids to use their feelings as a positive energy source to establish and maintain productive relationships with one another and with other people outside the family.

Recently my daughter Maria told me she was angry with a friend who told a boy that Maria was going to invite him to a party. We went through the seven steps very quickly, and she decided that the first five would be all she needed to use with her friend. Here are the steps she took to confront her friend:

1 and 2. "I am hurt" (No problem showing it! Notice that the feeling went from anger to hurt. Anger was really masking her hurt.)

3. "I think I ought to be able to ask any boy I want to ask to a party without you telling him first."

4. "I told you I was going to ask the new boy to the party. I trusted you not to tell anyone, especially him. But you told him in second-hour class that I was going to ask him."

5. "I need to know I can tell you this kind of stuff and you won't tell anyone else."

The confrontation was simple and quick, and both kids won. Maria expressed her feelings, and her friend apologized and said she didn't realize she had hurt Maria. How quickly kids can learn!

We can learn to keep our cool in tense situations without putting our feelings on ice. Once we realize that our feelings are real and legitimate and that we have the freedom to choose what we will do with them, the freedom, as Frankl says, "to choose one's own way," we will be able to acknowledge our children's feelings as real and legitimate and will begin to model appropriate ways of expressing them. If we honor our feelings and theirs, assertive confrontation will become an increasingly natural way of resolving conflict.

The Sufis advise us to speak only after our words have managed to pass through three gates. At the first gate we ask ourselves, "Are these words true?' If so, we let them pass on; if not, back they go.
At the second gate we ask, "Are they necessary?"
At the last gate we ask, "Are they kind?"

—EKNATH EASWARAN, *MEDITATION*

Chapter 6

Realities, Mistakes, and Problems

Grant me the serenity to accept the things I cannot
change, the courage to change the things I can, and
wisdom to know the difference.
—REINHOLD NIEBUHR

How our children learn to deal with life has a lot to do with
how we as parents view life and handle our own mistakes and
problems. Our attitude, as well as our action, is important. If we
are optimistic, we seek solutions to our problems; if we are pes-
simistic, we seek someone to blame.

When a brick-wall parent makes a mistake, it must be
someone else's fault. ("If you hadn't left your bike in the
driveway, I wouldn't have run it over." "You should have called
me sooner, and I wouldn't have been so late." "If you two hadn't
been arguing all day, I wouldn't have lost my temper tonight.")

A jellyfish parent either tries to make the mistake seem in-
consequential or sees it as proof that external forces control what
happens. ("It's okay. That bike was old, and we needed to get
you a new one anyway." "I'm always late. It runs in the family."
"I can't control my temper. It just gets the best of me every
time.")

A backbone parent admits that she made a mistake, takes
full responsibility for making the mistake, avoids making excuses,
figures out how to fix the problem created by making the mistake,

recognizes if and how another person was affected, and figures out what to do the next time so it won't happen again. ("I ran over your bike as I backed out of the driveway today. I should have looked before I put the car in reverse. I will see if I can fix it myself; if not, I'll take it to the repair shop. I am sorry you won't have a bike to ride for a couple of days. Next time I'll walk around the car before I get in to make sure there is nothing in the way.")

By taking ownership of the problem, you are showing your children a way to accept responsibility for their own mistakes. You might argue that your child should not have left his bike in the driveway, and you would probably be right. But if you take ownership of your own mistake (not looking before you backed out) you have set the stage for your child to be able to say that it was his mistake to leave his bike in the driveway. You have also shown him that when he is old enough to drive, it is a good habit to walk around a car before he backs it out.

Your son can decide on a place away from the driveway to park the repaired bike. If the bike is left in the driveway again, you won't be backing over it, because you will see it when you walk around the car. And your son won't be riding his bike for a week, because you will remove it from the driveway and lock it up. Chances of him leaving the bike on the driveway again will be greatly reduced.

Sometimes you are faced with problems you had nothing to do with creating. They, too, can be opportunities to seek blame, to use an excuse to escape reality, or to accept reality and solve the problems that come with it.

Several years ago I was stuck for eight hours in an airport when a snowstorm delayed my flight. You should have seen the way some of the passengers carried on. "You can't do this to me." "I'll never fly this airline again." "I want my money back."

Some people ranted and raved for eight hours; some hit the bar for eight hours; and some read for eight hours. All three groups got on the plane eight hours later. Some were still so angry that they were ready to throttle the pilot, which would have only made us later; some, after eight hours in the bar, weren't even sure and didn't care if they were on a plane; and some had finished reading their book. When is the last time anyone gave you eight hours of uninterrupted time to read for enjoyment?

It's your point of view that matters. You often can't control what happens to you, but what you *can* do is use what is happening to you. A big part of using what is happening to you is distinguishing between what can be changed and what has to be accepted. The fact that the plane was eight hours late was a reality, something to be accepted. What to do with the eight hours was mine to choose and use. Some people rant and rave their way through life, some drink their way through life, and some read a good book.

I was once working with a sixteen-year-old who was five months' pregnant. I asked her what her problems were; she looked at me as if I were crazy, patted her protruding womb, and said, "I'm pregnant!"

I said, "That's not the problem. At five months that baby is very real. I could show you five women who would give almost anything to be in your place—five months' pregnant with a healthy baby. Being pregnant is the reality. What are the problems that come with it?"

She began listing them: "My parents are throwing me out. My boyfriend won't marry me, and I want to keep this baby."

"Kid, you have a problem. In fact, you have three big problems, and anytime you put two or more problems together, you have a predicament. And the best way I know to solve a predicament is to break it into solvable problems. Every one of those big problems is solvable. You can do it, and there are people here who can help you."

One of my fifteen-year-old students came in one day and announced that he was leaving school. I asked what the problem was, and he said, "I'm quitting."

"That's not the problem," I said. "In fact I can show you three of your teachers who will help you unpack your locker and get you out the door! What is the problem?"

"I'm flunking five subjects."

"That's a problem." ("I *flunked* five subjects" is a reality, and summer school becomes the problem. "I'm *flunking* five subjects" is still solvable.)

When working with parents of children with special needs, I have been amazed at the time, energy, and money some parents have spent trying to solve the *reality* of their child's handicap. They and their children would have been a lot better off accepting the reality of the handicap and putting the time, energy, and money into solving the problems that came with the reality.

If we can accept realities and solve the problems that come with them, we will save ourselves a lot of grief and we will teach our children how to view life with optimism and resolve.

MISTAKES ARE FOR LEARNING

When your son comes in with an A-plus on his spelling, how you respond will determine whether he thinks he can tell you the following week that he missed ten out of a possible eleven. If you get all excited about your child's performance, connecting his performance with his dignity and worth as a person, you are encouraging him to view mistakes as a negative reflection of himself; something to be denied or blamed on someone else.

"I am proud of you; you take after Mom's side of the family. We are going to put this up on the refrigerator for your dad's side to see." You do that and I promise, you will go to Parents' Night at school, lift the lid of your child's desk, and find every paper that's not an A-plus. He can't bring them home because he has learned that in your home mistakes are bad.

Instead, whether the paper is an A-plus or a D-minus, simply ask your child to tell you about it. He might express his pleasure with the effort that went into getting the A-plus, or tell you how discouraged he feels, having studied hard and missed ten, or he might explain that he now realizes that he hadn't taken the exam seriously and that he plans next week to improve his spelling. He has no need to make excuses for his mistakes. ("The work sheet wasn't dark enough." "She didn't give enough time to finish." "The girl behind me kept talking." "I take after my father.") Instead mistakes are used as learning opportunities.

WHOSE PROBLEM

Before starting to solve a problem, it is critical to know who owns it. If you are going to solve a problem, first make sure it is yours to solve. Most of the time it does neither of you any good if you solve someone else's problem. However, sometimes logic and emotion send two different signals to your head. You know you shouldn't rescue your child from the mess he created himself, but it would be so much simpler and more efficient to get him out of a mess just this one time; and besides, he'll love you more (or dislike you less) if you take care of the problem for him. These two signals are warnings that you need to pause and question the messages you are giving your child by rushing in and solving the problem for him. Remember, parenting is neither an efficient profession nor a popularity contest.

The opposite of rescuing—washing your hands of any involvement in your kid's problems, even when she is in way over her head and really needs your help and support—also confuses and complicates the issue of who owns a problem. It sends a message to your child that you will not be there when she really needs you.

If you find yourself either rescuing or avoiding your kid's problems it may be time to consider some of the old parenting tools you are still carrying around. What were your parents' responses to your problems as a child? Did they rescue you? Did they wash their hands of your problems? Did they sometimes do one and sometimes the other so that you never knew what to expect? Are you unconsciously repeating patterns you learned as a child?

BROKEN GLASS—A REALITY TO BE ACCEPTED, A COUPLE OF PROBLEMS TO BE SOLVED

The three kinds of families handle reality, mistakes, and problems differently.

A three-year-old drops a glass after you have repeatedly admonished him to be careful with the glass he insisted on using instead of his plastic one. Crash! The glass is now in a hundred pieces all over the floor.

The brick-wall parent: "You klutzy kid. I swear, you are going to use plastic ones for the next thirty years. Get out of the kitchen right now!" The message is not "You have a problem," it is "You are a problem."

The jellyfish parent: "Move out of the way, sweetie. Be careful, you might get cut. Mommy made a mistake. I gave you a slippery glass. It is all Mommy's fault. Here, let me get you a new glass, and let's add chocolate to the milk for a treat. I'll pick up the mess." The message is "I'll take care of you. You can't take care of yourself. When you make a mistake, it's somebody else's fault."

The backbone parent: "You have a problem. I know you can handle it. Run get a paper bag." Three-year-olds can't pick up glass, but they can hold a bag while you put the broken glass into it. When the glass is picked up, the toddler can help mop up the spilled milk. Then you hand him two plastic glasses and say, "Which of these two plastic glasses would you like to use today?" You are giving your child the message "You have a problem; I know you can handle it. I'm not here to rescue or punish; I'm here to help, encourage, and support."

The reality is the glass is broken. That's not something to be solved; it just has to be accepted. No amount of ranting and raving, weeping or wailing, is going to put that glass together. The problems are cleaning up the mess and finding an appropriate glass to use; these are solvable. Your toddler has no reason to lie ("The cat did it"), make excuses ("You gave me a slippery glass"), or try to hide the evidence behind the trash can. Your response to his mistake helps him understand that realities are accepted, problems are to be solved.

We can empower kids by giving them the message "You have a problem; I know you can solve it." We can destroy their sense of dignity and self-worth by giving them the message "You have a problem, but I don't think you can solve it." Or an even worse message: "You don't have a problem: you *are* the problem." It's easy to give these negative messages without even realizing it especially if we were raised with those messages from our own parents. It takes conscious effort and constant awareness to give the positive message.

DECORATED-CAKE DILEMMA

My oldest daughter dropped my mother-in-law's birthday cake shortly before it was time to go to Grandma's. I had spent two hours decorating the cake, put it on a white cake pedestal with a white paper doily. Wanting to show her friend the cake, Anna grabbed the platter and quickly moved it from one counter to the other. Cake and platter did not move at the same speed or in the same direction. The once carefully decorated cake was now upside down on the kitchen floor, icing smashed beyond repair.

After all the time I had invested in decorating that cake, I had to step back a moment, take a deep breath, and realize that getting hysterical would do no good. Screaming would only hurt my lungs and Anna's ears; it would not put the cake back on the platter.

I looked at Anna and said, "Anna, you have a *big* problem."

Anna responded, "Mom, I tried to catch the cake!"

And I said, "You tried to catch it, your friend tried to catch it; it didn't work. The *reality* is the icing is smashed. The *problem* is that we need to take a cake to Grandma's. I know you can handle it."

She looked at the cake, then she looked at me and said, "I think I can salvage this cake."

And I think we can help our kids. Anna held the platter, I reached under two inches of smashed icing, and together we plopped the cake back over. Crumbs from the breakfast toast that had not yet been swept from the kitchen floor were now embedded in the smashed icing. Anna knew without being told that all of the crumb-covered icing had to be scraped off and fresh icing put on.

I went into the other room, knowing Anna could handle the problem. And she did, all the while having fun! You're not supposed to have fun if you're being punished, but it is all right to have fun if you're being disciplined. By having ownership of the problem and the solution, Anna was able to experience the four steps of discipline:

1. **Show her what she did wrong.** She knew she had moved the cake carelessly, so no need to point it out.

2. **Give her ownership of the problem.** I could have said, "Get out of the kitchen right now!" Instead I told her I believed she could handle it.

3. **Give her ways of solving the problem.** "We're not taking this cake to Grandma's, and you tell her why we don't have a cake for her" says the problem is not

solvable and asks the child to feel miserable and guilty. She figured out a way of solving the problem, so I didn't need to give her options.

4. **Leave her dignity intact.** "You stupid klutz, you can't do anything right, you're just like your brother" diminishes her self-esteem and gives her the message that she is the problem, not that she has a problem that is solvable. "Anna, you can handle it" affirms her ability to solve problems.

I want my children to understand that when they have a problem, what they need is a good plan, not a good excuse. Blaming a kid is virtually asking for an excuse, not a solution. If kids early on learn to find a solution to the problem of the smashed cake, then when they get older, we won't be as likely to hear things such as "It's not my fault I got drunk." "She made me do it." "You didn't give me enough time." "You forgot to remind me." "He hit me back first."

To Bring or Not to Bring The Gym Uniform

You get the fourth phone call in a week from your kid at school: "I forgot my gym uniform again." Cheers for the parent who says, "I see it right here on the counter. I can't bring it today. I know you can figure out a way to get through P.E. without your uniform." How often, though, do you take that uniform to the school and then minilecture your child when you get there: "If you'd have put your uniform in your backpack like I told you to, you would have it for gym. What do I have to do, tie this around your neck? This is the last time I'm bringing this uniform. Do you know how much time it took out of my day to get this to you? Your brother never forgot his uniform!" But you bring it nevertheless. It is not life-threatening to forget a gym uniform in most schools; uncomfortable, yes, but not life-threatening.

I can hear you saying, "Wait a minute, you mean I can't ever bring a gym uniform or a band instrument or a term paper my kid left on the kitchen counter?"

Brick-wall parents say, "Never, never, never. Let 'em feel the pain. It will teach them responsibility."

Jellyfish parents say, "All the time. In fact I'll get it there even before he misses it."

Backbone parents say, "Yeah, once in a while you do; once in a while you can bring a gym uniform, a band instrument, or a term paper your child left on the kitchen counter." But listen to your gut—your intuition. If you are bringing a gym uniform for the fourth time, your gut ought to be letting you know that you are probably rescuing your child. On the other hand, it might tell you the opposite. It sometimes can and should override both logic and emotion. I have taken things to school for my kids. One day my oldest called and asked if I would bring her backpack. I was very busy and asked what was in it that she couldn't live without that day. She started to cry and said, "My valentines." It was second-grade Valentine's Day. I took the backpack with her valentines in it to her. The logical thing to do was to tell her she could bring them for her friends the next day. But the distress and embarrassment she would suffer by not having her valentines would far outweigh any good I would do her by refusing to bring them.

Have you ever locked yourself out of your car and watched yourself do it? I have. I was on my way to a workshop, called my husband, and said, "The car is running, the keys are in it, and I'm not. I need your help." Don said he would be right there with another key; that's what I needed to hear. I didn't need "That's a bummer. I know you can handle it." I needed "Barb, I'll be right there." But when we purchased our next car, Don's first question was "Can you lock yourself out of it?"

INTUITION IN PROBLEM SOLVING

Intuition is a misunderstood and neglected aspect of our personal life. It is often confused with emotion or subtly invalidated by the term *women's intuition*. But intuition is very different from emotion, and every woman, man and child has it. Being able to acknowledge, trust, and act on intuition is essential to a harmonious, healthy life and is particularly useful when you are faced with complex difficulties and problems. It can, if listened to, often point the way out of an impasse that thinking and emotion have only confused.

Intuition is really your inner self speaking and reaching out. Clarissa Pinkola Estés, in her books *Women Who Run with the Wolves*, speaks of intuition as "a divining instrument and ... a crystal through which one can see with uncanny interior vision. ... This great power, intuition, is composed of lightning-fast inner seeing, inner hearing, inner sensing, and inner knowing."

Intuition often provides options that aren't immediately obvious to logic or emotion. When you are in touch with the instinctual, intuitive self, you have more choices. If your logic and your emotions are not connected to and fed by your intuition, they can easily go astray. But if they are connected, you can, in a crisis (large or small), *respond* rather than *react*. When your intuition, logic, and emotions are all connected, they work simultaneously to find the best solution to the problem.

Expressions we use such as "listen to your gut" and "my gut said it was not such a good idea" and "I have a feeling that ... " are really expressions of intuition, that "lightning-fast inner seeing, inner hearing, inner sensing, and inner knowing." Trust it.

INTUITION IN ACTION

It is usually best to allow kids to experience the consequences of their mistakes and poor choices, which then become their own responsibility. Kids learn that they have positive power in their own lives. The hurt and discomfort arising from the choices go away after they have worked through the problem themselves constructively. Backbone parents, though, recognize that there are times to bend, times to override this principle. The logical mind says, *No, don't help the kid, don't rescue her*. But the intuitive self says, *Yes, in this case, help her, for her sake*. Knowing when to ignore logic, principles, or rules is one of the great gifts of well-developed intuition.

Your seventeen-year-old has just broken up with his girlfriend, dented the fender of the family car, got cut from the varsity basketball team, is in pain from his new braces, and woke up this morning with a face full of zits. This is not one of his best days. In fact his world seems to be crashing in on him. He calls you from school in a panic. The assignment for photography class is sitting on the counter and is due by third hour. Could you please bring it to him? My gut would say yes. And when I got to school, I'd give him a hug and tell him to hang in there; he's going to make it through; I know he can do it.

Your toddler has just been moved out of her nursery into a "big-girl bedroom" to make room for her baby brother. Yesterday she fell off the steps, skinned her knees, and was reprimanded by Grandma for trying to take the blanket from the baby. She's tired, cranky, and wants you to dress her today. She knows how to dress herself. Logic says, Don't give in. She needs to dress herself. Intuition says, "I'll put on either your shirt or your pants, you can do the other, and together we'll get those shoes on. Let's make a game of it."

Six Steps to Problem Solving

A problem well stated is a problem half-solved.
—CHARLES F. KETTERING

1. Identify and define the problem.
2. List viable options for solving the problem.
3. Evaluate the options— explore the pluses and minuses for each option.
4. Choose one option.
5. Make a plan and DO IT.
6. Evaluate the problem and your solution: What brought it about? Could a similar problem be prevented in the future? How was the present problem solved?

Dropping a glass, forgetting a gym uniform, or leaving a term paper on the kitchen counter are relatively simple problems to solve. Sometimes, though, kids and parents are faced with more difficult or complicated problems, ones that have no easy solutions. If the problem belongs to one family member, the Six

Steps to Problem Solving can provide the necessary backbone structure on which to build a solution. When the problem is a shared family concern, a family meeting can be an effective tool for confronting and solving the problem. Some problems can be solved using one or the other or a combination of both.

1. Identify and define the problem.

Jeni has lost her best friend's baseball mitt. Her friend wants it back right now. But Jeni remembers putting it in the large bag she thought was the toy bag; instead it was the bag full of toys to be given to a local charity. The bag and mitt are long gone.

2. List viable options.

Jeni is able to come up with two options on her own: (a) Stay away from her friend; or (b) pretend she never had the mitt. You may scoff at some of the options your child gives you, but have you ever seen adults avoid someone to whom they owe money or pretend they never borrowed a book you lent them?

Kids are people too. Jeni has come up with two options that some adults would come up with. That doesn't mean they are good options. At this point let her continue to list options without judgment being placed on any of them. In the end she needs to choose the option that makes the most sense to her. Remember, you are helping her learn how to think— not what to think. Other possible options might be buying a new mitt to replace the lost one; or Jeni's giving her own mitt to her friend.

3. Evaluate the options.

It is important that Jeni be the one to evaluate the options, with you there for guidance, support, and encouragement. "The first one won't work: We walk to school together every day, and I don't want to avoid her, she'd be hurt. The second one won't work either: She never forgets anything, and I don't want to lie to her. The third won't work: I don't have enough money to buy a new mitt. And the fourth won't work: If I give her mine, I won't have a mitt." None of the options looks good, but if they looked good, there wouldn't be a problem to solve in the first place. It's a matter of choosing which ones could possibly work. Using the following four questions, Jeni was able to eliminate the first two herself.

Is it unkind?
Is it hurtful?
Is it unfair?
Is it dishonest?

Solution A would be unkind; solution B would be dishonest. The last two have the most potential. If she had not seen anything wrong with the first two options, it would be time to offer her guidance.

4. Choose one option.

Jeni decides that the easiest for her would be to give her friend her own mitt. Earning the necessary money would take too long, and besides, Jeni can use her brother's old mitt. In choosing an option, it is important that the solution to the problem does not create a problem for someone else. If Jeni decided to give her friend her own mitt and use her brother's mitt but her brother needed his mitt, a problem has been created for her brother, so it's not a good solution. Jeni would have to look at another option.

5. Make a plan and DO IT!

Probably the most difficult step is for a kid to make a plan and actually follow through with it. Taking full ownership for the mistake she has made, Jeni goes to her friend and, without making excuses, explains what she has done and offers her own mitt to replace the original mitt. A new problem arises. Her friend tells her she does not want the used mitt; she wants her own mitt. Kids need to learn that if the first option doesn't work, they need to go back to the other options to see if another might work, or if not, to explore new options. Jeni explains that she can't get the original mitt back, but will lend her friend her own mitt until she can earn enough money to buy a new one. She then mows lawns in the neighborhood to get the money and replaces the mitt with a new one.

6. Evaluate the problem and your solution.

This is probably the most neglected step in problem solving, but it is critical to the learning process.

- What brought the problem about? Putting the mitt in what appeared to be the toy bag was a mistake, but the chances of it happening again are remote. However, if Jeni often misplaced borrowed items, she would need to look at her behavior, and the following questions would be answered differently.

- Could a similar problem be prevented in the future? Jeni will look very carefully before she places a friend's mitt in any bag. She might also find one place to put anything borrowed. (We have a bench by the front door to hold items borrowed from friends or inadvertently left at our home.)

- How was the present problem solved? Jeni tried one option, but it didn't work. The second option did. She can feel good about her ability to take ownership of her mistake and her ability to solve the problems that came with that mistake. Her sense of self-esteem and her personal integrity are greatly enhanced.

A brick-wall parent would probably berate Jeni for being so irresponsible and then dictate how the problem is to be solved. "You irresponsible kid, don't you ever borrow from your friends again. You will lose your allowance for the next six weeks so that we can buy a new mitt for your friend!"

A jellyfish parent would probably minilecture, then solve the problem for Jeni. "If you had looked at the bag more closely, you wouldn't have put the mitt into it. Don't tell your friend; instead we'll replace her mitt with one just like it."

It is so much easier as a parent to make the decisions and tell a child what to do, but so much more rewarding to teach her to make her own decisions. Through the problem-solving process Jeni can learn to be an assertive and responsible individual who can act in her own best interests, stand up for herself, and exercise her own rights while respecting the rights and legitimate needs of others. She can be trusted to take ownership of the problems she creates and the solution to those problems.

Family Meetings

No problem can stand the assault of sustained thinking.
—VOLTAIRE

Many problems can be solved with the previous six steps alone, but sometimes the problem is more complex or affects several people, so something more is needed. If the people affected are family members, as they often are, the family meeting can be a valuable tool in problem solving.

A family meeting can be a forum for kids to learn to examine situations, propose solutions, and evaluate the results with guidance, support, and demonstrations from parents and older siblings. It is an opportunity to reinforce the notion that the goal for our children is not dependence or independence but rather a sense of interdependence. We are all connected; what we do or do not do influences and affects those around us. Once children are old enough to offer ideas for solving a problem, they can be included in the problem-solving process. Younger children can learn a lot about the process just by observing older family members go through the steps in a family meeting. There are three basic requirements for such a meeting:

1. **The problem must be important and relevant to all concerned.** Sue's forgetting her gym uniform isn't important or even relevant to her sister, but Sue's wet clothes hung all over the bathroom are both important and relevant to her sister—and brother, and mom, and dad.

2. **The parent needs to provide nonjudgmental leadership.** It's not really a "family meeting" if everyone offers ideas, opinions, and solutions, and Dad tells everyone else how it will be solved. "You will have to hang your wet clothes somewhere else, and you will clean up all your makeup from the counter, unplug the curling iron, hang up your towels, put the soap in the soap-dash, and clean off the mirrors before you go to school. Do you understand?" All participants need to feel that their opinions, feelings, and ideas count.

3. **The environment needs to be conducive to sharing.** A dinner table where everyone is seated and able to see one another is far more conducive to a family meeting than the five of you seated in the car hurrying to get to school and work and screaming at one another about the wet clothes, curling iron, soap, and dirty mirror.

In a family meeting, problems are stated simply and clearly, then clarified. ("I get upset when I try to fight my way through all the wet clothes to get to the bathroom sink in the morning." "I'm afraid the house will burn down if the curling iron is not unplugged." "The mirror looks like someone airbrushed confetti on it. I can't tell if it's spots on the mirror or a bad case of acne on my thirty-year-old face." "But there isn't time in the morning for me to clean the bathroom before someone is pounding to get in after me." The problems are wet clothes, plugged-in curling iron, splattered mirror, and too little time in the morning in a bathroom shared by five people.

All family members look at various options and discuss the feasibility of their choices. Adding a second bathroom may be feasible or might be just wishful thinking. Hanging wet clothes outside might work in Arizona but is not practical in Anchorage. Putting a paper-towel rack in the bathroom would not make the home eligible for *House Beautiful* but might make it easier for everyone to wipe up after they have speckled the mirror with toothpaste, hair spray, makeup, and shaving cream.

Solutions are proposed, and a plan of action is agreed upon and carried out. Sue will shower in the evening, Jan in the morning; everyone will clean up their own mess before leaving the bathroom; the family will invest in a curling iron with an automatic shutoff; Joe will design and make a rack that can be used to hang wet clothes in the laundry room.

The results are then evaluated. One month later everyone agrees that the schedule change for showers is working, the mirror still needs a bit more elbow grease and less hair spray, the rack looks great but would be more convenient if moved from the laundry room to the bathroom; and the kids swear that when they buy their own homes, they definitely will make sure they come equipped with two bathrooms.

Having presented their own ideas, listened to one another's

reasoning, and worked cooperatively to arrive at a solution, all family members begin to see that there is no definite right or wrong, no one correct way to solve most problems. Group choices involve give-and-take, openness, and cooperation on the part of all concerned. Everyone feels that they are listened to, cared for, and important. The skills learned in family meetings will help kids deal effectively with problems they may have in other social settings.

If we parents accept that problems are an essential part of life's challenges, rather than reacting to every problem as if something has gone wrong with a universe that's supposed to be perfect, we can demonstrate serenity and confidence in problem solving for our kids. We can teach them that no problem is so great that it can't be solved. By telling them that we know they have a problem and we know they can solve it, we can pass on a realistic attitude as well as empower our children with self-confidence and a sense of their own worth.

Wisdom is knowing what to do next, skill is knowing how to do it, and virtue is doing it.
                                                   —DAVID STARR JORDAN

Chapter 7

Getting Your Kid Out of Jail and Other Mega-Problems

We can love completely without complete understanding.
—A RIVER RUNS THROUGH IT (SCREENPLAY)

Simply because our teenagers have free will and are subject to one of the strongest forces in the universe—peer pressure—any of us parents may have to deal with mega-problems our teens have created for themselves. Although more difficult to handle than clothes left on the floor, mega-problems are still solvable. It's hard to tell the parent of a sixteen-year-old who has mainlined smack that there is no problem so great, it can't be solved. It's just as hard to tell a parent of a fifteen-year-old who has attempted suicide that there is no problem so great that it can't be solved. The same with a parent whose son has just landed in the jail. The last things these three kids need is for someone to try to rescue them (it can't be done) or to punish them.

As their whole world is crashing in on them, what they do need is someone to stand behind them and tell them, "I believe in you. I trust you. I know you can handle this. You are listened to, cared for, and very important to me. We aren't concerned what the rest of the community is saying. We love you and we're here—not to rescue, blame, or punish but to support and discipline." It's vital to remember the last, discipline, because without it, help can easily turn into rescuing. Take the case of getting your kid out of jail.

GETTING YOUR KID OUT OF JAIL

Your kid phones to let you know why he is not coming home before curfew—he's making a pit stop at the jail. The parents in the three families are going to handle the situation very differently.

Brick-wall parents are inclined to punish. They themselves grew up in a family where retribution and punishment were the normal fare. ("You're in jail. Tough cookie. Sit there all night. See you in the morning. Good-bye.") What is implicit in those comments is "If you are well behaved, we'll love you; if not, we won't. Our love for you is highly conditional."

Our love for our children needs to be unconditional. Our likes and dislikes can be and usually are highly conditional. We don't have to like the funny-looking hair, the earring in the nose, and the silly-looking shoes. But our love needs to go beyond all that. Besides getting all the wrong messages, by spending even one night in jail to learn a lesson our teenager could be in a situation that is life-threatening, morally threatening, and unhealthy. It's not time to punish; it's time to help.

But it's not time to rescue, which is what jellyfish-A parents will try to do. They hurry down to the police station as fast as they can, minilecturing their spouse all the way. ("I told you this would happen if you let him go out with those kids. I knew it. You gave him the keys to the car too early. He's too young. He takes right after your side of the family. It's all your fault.") They then minilecture the kid. ("I knew it. How could you do this? You shouldn't have gone out with those kids. I told you they'd get you into trouble. You never listen to me.")

Nevertheless his parents bail him out. And they show up in court for him—if they even let it get to court. If these parents have enough clout in their community, their kids will never see the inside of a courtroom.

The chances of the kid staying out of trouble are directly proportional to the energy the *kid* expends, not to what you expend. It does no good to rescue your kids: you'll be bailing them out in your old age from your rocking chair because they never had to grow up and accept the consequences for their own mistakes.

Jellyfish-B parents, if they can even be found, are quick to turn over their responsibilities to the juvenile authorities. ("You keep him; I can't handle him anymore.")

As a backbone parent you get to the police station as fast as you can, put your arm around your teenager, and tell him, "I love you. You're in trouble. I know you can handle it. I'm here to support you." You can help him find a lawyer if he needs one, but let him do the talking—and the paying. He may spend many a Saturday as a 'gofer' at the law firm to pay off his legal debt.

You show up in court standing *behind* your teenager with your mouth shut. It's hard not to intervene. Just remember you are there to support, not rescue.

Let's say the reason your teenager was arrested is that he vandalized an elderly couple's house and front yard as a prank with several friends. Don't pay for the damage. Let your kid work out a plan to make good for the vandalism. Maybe he has to mow the lawn weekly, plant flowers, and help paint the house that he vandalized.

He's not been rescued; he's not been punished; he has been disciplined: shown what he did wrong, given ownership of the problem, given ways to solve the problem, and his dignity has been left intact, perhaps even enhanced.

Sounds easy, and it is when the legal problem is a minor offense or misdemeanor, such as vandalism, shoplifting, petty mischief, or minor scuffles. It gets more difficult when there are repeat offenses, or the crime is serious, such as armed robbery or assault. When your teen is in serious trouble with the law, along with the necessary legal counsel, it is important to get professional advice and support for both you and your teen. Counselors trained in dealing with troubled teens and their families can help you get at the core of the problem as well as address the immediate offense. They can also be there to give you and your teen a hug, a shoulder to cry on, and options for solving the mega-problem, while brick-wall members of the community push to "throw the book" at him and jellyfishes try to find excuses for his behavior.

In the U.S. if your teen has been arrested for a status offense, both you and he may feel that he has been unjustly arrested. Status offenses include runaway, truancy, beyond parental control, minor in possession of alcohol, and curfew violations. In the

U.S. "Status Offender" is defined as any juvenile who has been charged with or convicted of an act that would not be a crime if committed by an adult. The urge to rescue, punish, or give up can be strong, but stronger still is the need to solve the problem that brought about the arrest.

In the U.S. in keeping with the doctrine of *parens patriae*, that is, the concept that the state plays the role of parent rather than adversary to the juvenile, most police working with young offenders are committed to delinquency-prevention methods that can help the juvenile to become a productive, responsible member of society. They will work with you if you are willing to work with them in helping your teen solve the problem he has created.

Today, see if you can stretch your heart and expand your love so that it touches not only those to whom you can give it easily, but also to those who need it so much.

—DAPHNE ROSE KINGMA

Don't Tell Alice When She's Ten Feet Tall—What to Do When You Suspect Your Teenager Is Using Drugs

It does no good to try to reason with your teenager if she appears to be under the influence of a drug. If she is in a drunken stupor or an LSD high, you'll know it. And you'll know something has to be done, even if you're not sure what it is that has to be done. But often the symptoms of drug use are not so obvious, are gradual, or are the same as symptoms for depression and other emotional problems or physical problems.

It's raining hard, you pull into the gas station, and your teenager leaps out of the car to fill the gas tank, and you're thinking, "How thoughtful of him to do that for me." Then you notice he is leaning over with his face inches from the gas nozzle. He must be checking to see if the tank is almost full. *Sure!*

Your daughter grabs the almost-empty whipped-cream can and holds it to her mouth to get the last of the whipped cream.

You tell her to take that nozzle out of her mouth. She says, "Don't worry, Mom, the cream's all gone, I'm just emptying the air." *Wrong.*

You find three empty eyedrop containers in the bathroom. Your son must be having trouble with his allergies. *Think again.*

A strong, sweet odor of incense fills your son's bedroom and you wonder why he didn't just open the window if his dirty laundry was stinking up his room. *Bad assumption.*

Your daughter calls to tell you she has decided to stay at a friend's house tonight. She's too tired to drive home. She sounds tired; her words are not coming out clearly. You're glad she used such good judgment. *Don't be so sure.*

Your cough medicine is gone. The guests didn't drink that much wine, did they? You thought you had two twenty-dollar bills in your purse. Your husband probably took it and forgot to tell you. *Not likely.*

Your teenager won't eat anything you put in front of him; he's belligerent; and those new kids he's hanging around with certainly act strange. They keep talking about "getting wasted," "the good stuff," "toke it, smoke it, stroke it." Must be those crazy teen years everyone is talking about. *Not hardly.*

What you have just missed are some of the telltale signs of drug use. These are not proof, just signs. But if your teen has a drug problem, she also has a better chance at solving it if you are an aware and involved parent. Partnership for a Drug-Free America gives the following signs a parent can look for:

The Telltale Signs

Chronic eye redness, sore throat, or dry cough
Chronic lying, especially about whereabouts
Wholesale changes in friends
Stealing
Deteriorating relationships with family members
Wild mood swings, hostility, or abusive behavior
Chronic fatigue, withdrawal, carelessness about personal
  grooming
Major changes in eating or sleeping patterns
Loss of interest in favorite activities, hobbies, sports

School problems—slipping grades, absenteeism
Partnership for a Drug-Free America

Other Warning Signs

Drug slogans on clothes
Language laced with drug terminology
Having lots of money or no money and no reasonable
   accounting for either
Hysterical crying or hysterical laughter
Paranoid behavior
Incense burning

Direct Evidence of Drug Use

Drug paraphernalia
Marijuana plants, seeds, or leaves
Actual drugs or evidence of drugs
Drug odors
Needle tracks, skin boils and sores
Sniffing gasoline, glue, solvents, or aerosol

BRICK-WALL DRUG SURVEILLANCE

A brick-wall parent will constantly be on the lookout for any signs of drug use, but will carry the surveillance to an extreme. Any use of eyedrops is suspect; chewing spearmint gum must be an attempt to cover up alcohol. The game of twenty questions follows every outing. He doesn't trust the teen to make good decisions about her own body and doesn't give her good information about the dangers of drug use. Absolutes are handed down. ("Don't you ever use alcohol." "No kid of mine is going to do drugs and live to tell about it." "If you are caught smoking, you might as well pack your bags.")

The teenager, lacking a strong sense of self, having few problem-solving skills, easily led, and wanting to assert herself apart from her parents, is at high risk for drug abuse.

Interestingly when brick-wall parents are confronted with

proof of their teen's drug use, they often protest, "I'm tired of people accusing my kid." Or they go into denial: "No, my daughter does not have a drug problem." Or they try to "beat some sense" into her. Or blame her for all of the problems in the family. ("If it weren't for you, your mom and I wouldn't fight so much.") Or have her immediately committed to a drug program, refusing to get involved themselves, because it is her problem—she is a bad kid.

JELLYFISH DENIAL AND DEFENSE

The two types of jellyfish parents handle the suspicion of drug use very differently. When faced with the signs, a jellyfish-A parent often goes into denial. ("My kid use drugs? Never. He'd tell me. His eyes are glassy? He drives a Jeep!") Or he blames the other parent, taking the attention off the teen. ("Look what you have done to your kid.") Or looks for another reason for the strange behaviors. ("She has a learning disability. He's just upset about our divorce.")

Jellyfish B denies that drugs are a problem. ("Having 'one too many' once in a while won't harm him. Didn't harm me.") Or defends the teen's use of drugs. ("Everybody's doing it. As long as he doesn't use the hard stuff, I don't mind.") Or provides the drugs. ("Share a joint with me." "Tell your friends I'll buy the keg for your next party.") And the cycle continues.

In both kinds of jellyfish families there is a lack of any meaningful structure. With no limits set for him as a child, when he is offered drugs in the teen years, he has no basis for judging if it would be good or bad, healthy or unhealthy. He may use drugs to fill an emotional hole, to please his peers, or to be accepted into a group.

BACKBONE AWARE, INVOLVED, AND THERE

When confronted with the signs of possible drug use by your teen, you first accept the possibility that it is true, recognize that it is her problem to work through, and then commit to being there for her over the long haul. The Premier National Law Enforcement Publishing Company, in their booklet *Children and Drugs—The Next Generation*, lists ten steps a parent can take:

1. Don't panic or react out of anger or fear.

2. Make yourself as knowledgeable about drugs as you can: check with your local library, local drug-related assistance programs, school authorities, etc. Remember also that your children may know a great deal.

3. Determine who has the best rapport with your child (it may not be you) and ask his or her assistance. Keep the lines of communication open.

4. Commence a "low key" dialogue to determine why and how the child reached a decision to use drugs or what brought him to use drugs. Remember the involvement may be brief and experimental; don't back him into a corner by prejudging, threatening, or moralizing.

5. Drug use, or heavy involvement in drugs, may well be symptomatic of other problems perhaps more urgent. Don't ignore them or think them irrelevant.

6. Involve others along the way if this seems appropriate, preferably with the voluntary approval of the child. Be careful in your selection, use persons or services who specialize in treatment of drug or alcohol abuse.

7. Be honest and factual: accept that the child may bring up inconsistencies or hypocrisies on your part. Don't lose your cool over this.

8. Drugs may be an issue over which your whole relationship with the child may be examined and talked over. It may be a valuable opportunity in many areas.

9. If, in spite of all your efforts, you still consider the problem so serious that more action must be taken, **professional or other help should be sought.**

10. Remember, if your child is using drugs, some of his friends will be too. Thus there is room for you, along with other parents, to try to offer the whole group something better than drugs.

A backbone family cannot prevent a teen from experimenting with drugs, but it can give her the tools that can buffer her from the lure of the drug culture. Backbone parents begin creating that buffer before their child is born. Treating their own bodies with dignity and regard, they in turn treat their infant's body with dignity and regard. They provide her with a loving concern, emotional presence, food, warmth and a loving touch. They don't physically abuse, sexually abuse, neglect, or abandon her. As she grows, she is taught to treat her own body with dignity and regard. She learns to listen to her own body. When she is full, she is not forced to eat more. She is encouraged—not bribed or threatened—to control her own body functions, including bowel movements. She is given lots of opportunities to make choices, and to be responsible for those choices. She solves problems and fixes mistakes. She learns to honor her feelings and express them responsibly. She knows she can ask for help.

An ounce of prevention is worth a pound of cure.
—BENJAMIN FRANKLIN

A Cry for Help—Attempted Suicide

Visiting a young girl hospitalized for attempting suicide, I asked her why she had slashed one wrist and then called 911. She sat up straight and said, "I wouldn't slash the other one: that's my pitching arm." Her attempt at suicide was an obvious cry for help. She didn't want to die, she was just overwhelmed with life in general, and her family life in particular, and didn't know what else she could do. She had a brick-wall father, who ruled with an iron fist, and a jellyfish mother, who was physically and emotionally exhausted trying to avoid a beating, run a home, hold down a job, and raise three kids. After picking up the pieces of broken dishes, comforting her mom, and getting herself and her younger brother and sister off to school, she fell asleep in her first-hour class. Berated by her English teacher and laughed at by the boy in the seat next to her, she had had about all she could take. The final straw came when she saw her low test score posted on the classroom door. She had studied so hard for that exam. She slashed her wrist at noon.

Many attempted suicides are not failed attempts but desperate cries for help. Both the brick-wall family and the jellyfish family can set the stage for these desperate cries.

The brick-wall parent has told the child for years to stifle his feelings of hurt, anger, and frustration. ("Stand up and take it like a man." "Boys don't cry." "Don't walk away from me. You will listen to me." "Do what I tell you to do, and no arguments, please.") Solutions for problems are dictated by the parent to the child, with no opportunity for discussion or dialogue. ("You will bring your test scores up by studying every night for two hours." "You will replace Mr. Smith's planter, and tell him you are sorry." "Share that toy with your sister, right now.") Love is held out as a reward for behavior the parent approves of, and withheld for behaviors the parent doesn't like. ("If you are well behaved, I'll love you. If you are not, I won't." "Get away from me. You are a bad boy." "Let Mommy give her big girl a big kiss for winning the spelling bee.") Perfection is good. Mistakes are bad. (For example, an honor student gets a B and thinks his whole world should come to an end. A young girl starves herself to become like the model waifs that are the "ideal" weight.)

The jellyfish parent has been inconsistent in his own expression of feelings, one moment flying off the handle for a minor infraction, the next laughing at something his child got punished for yesterday. The child's feelings are ignored. ("Go to your bedroom right now and stay in there until morning. That should teach you to talk to me like that." "Did you hear how he told his teacher off? What guts he has." "He's not sad. He has nothing to be sad about.") Problems are not solved. They are ignored or glossed over. ("Don't worry about Mr. Smith. He'll get over his anger. It was only an old planter, and I know you didn't hit it on purpose." "Three Ds and four Fs. That's not as bad as it looks. You should have seen my report card when I was your age.") Love is also highly conditional. However, in a jellyfish family the conditions for it are inconsistent. One day a hug is given, "just because I wanted to give you a hug." The next day a hug is withheld because the child "upset Dad."

Reaching adolescence with a sense of learned helplessness, coupled with hurt and anger, a teen from either family can become depressed and self-destructive when faced with the normal frustrations of the age. Wanting help, but not knowing how to ask for it, he physically hurts himself to get someone to notice his real pain. If the anger is greater than the hurt, the teen might attempt suicide to punish his parents. "See what you did to me? I'm going to make you suffer now."

If the hurt, the anger, and the depression become chronic, a teen may see no way out of the pain except death. Then the attempt is not a cry for help; it is really a botched suicide. Suicide is the third leading cause of teen deaths, with accidents and acts of violence being first and second. Some accidents are actually veiled suicide attempts. Taking drugs can be a slow form of suicide.

A backbone family is rarely confronted with attempted suicides. The environment the child grows up in where his feelings are accepted, his ideas count, his basic needs met, and his mistakes seen as learning opportunities provides the structure to flesh out a sense of his true self and the tools necessary to help him solve the myriad problems he will face. Nevertheless no cry for help is ignored, laughed at, or dismissed as foolish.

Signs of Suicidal Tendencies

1. Previous attempts at suicide. These may be drug-related.
2. Deteriorating relationships with family members.
3. Chronic fatigue, withdrawal, carelessness about personal grooming.
4. Major changes in eating or sleeping patterns.
5. School problems—slipping grades, absenteeism.
6. An obsession with perfection.
7. Loss of interest in favorite activities, hobbies, and sports.
8. Giving prized personal possessions away.
9. Writing about death.
10. Chronic depression.

The ten steps parents can take to help their teen with a drug problem are the same ten they can use to help their teen who is showing suicidal tendencies. The key is to be there to give him your love, support, and help.

All of our kids will make mistakes; that's part of growing up. Growing up can be painful, and it's hard for us to see our children in pain. But let the mistakes and poor choices become your kids' own responsibility. That doesn't mean you stand back and let them destroy their lives. If it is life-threatening, morally threatening, or unhealthy, you do step in with loving support and guidance—and sometimes a straightjacket. Just as you might restrain an angry toddler who was hellbent on hurting himself or his younger brother, you might have to get professional help to restrain a drug-crazed son or to intravenously feed an anorexic daughter. The intervention and control is only temporary and will need to give way to the teens' eventually taking ownership of their own problems and the solutions to those problems. The hurt or discomfort arising from their choices goes away only after they have worked out their problems constructively. By having positive power over even such painful situations as mega-problems, their dignity, integrity, and self-worth are enhanced.

Every time you meet a situation, though you think at the time it is an impossibility and you go through the tortures of the damned, once you have met it and lived through it, you find that forever after you are freer than you were before.
—ELEANOR ROOSEVELT

Chapter 8

Settling Sibling Rivalry Without Calling in the Cavalry

If we know how to look at violence, not only outwardly in society ... but also in ourselves, then perhaps we shall be able to go beyond it.

—J. KRISHNAMURTI

Kids fight. The next time your kids are going at it, take a big breath and tell yourself, "They're normal." Conflict is inevitable, as much a part of life as sleeping and eating and paying taxes. So is the pain that goes along with it. But you can resolve conflict and make it less painful if you deal with it directly and creatively. As hard as it is to believe when you're in the midst of a home-grown version of the Civil War, conflict can even become an opportunity for growth.

Kids fight, and virtually every parent in the world wishes they didn't. Since conflict isn't anybody's idea of a good time (at least not anybody you'd want as a neighbor), wanting to avoid it seems to make sense, but avoidance can be unhealthy in the long run. Kids who don't fight, those who avoid conflict or always give in, grow up to be passive adults, or adults seething with suppressed anger and rage. Passive adults are likely to take all kinds of abuse lying down, whether it's exploitation by the government or dishonesty from the local car mechanic. And they make really lousy spouses. If you are currently living with one who refuses to confront, who walks away from conflict, or hopes it will go away by itself, you'll know what I'm talking about. Adults seething with suppressed anger and rage direct the hostility outward in acts of violence against others or inward against themselves.

Knowing how to handle conflict is more than a matter of creating peace in the home; it is a matter of creating a peaceful attitude in ourselves and our children so that we can create that peaceful atmosphere in our home. And unfortunately this knowledge does not come naturally. Kids don't come out of the womb knowing how to deal with conflict. It is a skill that needs to be learned. And it *will* be learned, one way or the other. Without conscious, wise, parental care the "skills" they are likely to learn are violence and aggression or passivity and evasion. Kids need to be taught how to enter into conflict and deal with it nonviolently, constructively, creatively, and responsibly.

As parents we don't have to purposely create conflict to teach our children how to handle it nonviolently. Conflict happens. It's how we view conflict that will make a difference in how we approach it. Both brick-wall and jellyfish parents tend to view conflict as a contest, something that somebody has to win and someone else will inevitably have to lose. In a contest, especially one involving intense feelings, emotional or physical aggression becomes the tool of choice. And if we think that an unpleasant situation is a contest that needs to be won and that we may therefore lose, we are more likely to pretend it doesn't exist or try to run from it. But it doesn't go away. If not resolved on the outside, the conflict/contest will come inside and grow of its own accord, with our bodies and minds keeping score. And the score will always be against us.

Viewing conflict as a contest, a victim-victor activity, a brick-wall parent uses threats of punishment ("You will get over here right now, or get a spanking." "Don't you dare!" "Just wait until your father gets home." "I'm in charge here, and you will do as I say, or else.")

The jellyfish parent tends to avoid conflict, moralize, or play peacemaker. ("Just leave him alone when he's like that." "Don't fight, kids, you need to love one another." "One of you come and sit next to me if you can't get along with each other in the backseat.")

A backbone parent views conflict not as a contest but as a crisis. "Of course," you say, "what's new about that? Every time my kids fight or I have a fight with my spouse, it sure seems like a crisis to me!" You're right, but the difference is that we are used to thinking of a crisis as something negative to be avoided. Crisis is a neutral term meaning "a sudden change or turning point in a situation." The Chinese were keenly aware of the connection between *crisis*, *danger*, and *opportunity*. *Wei-ji*, the Chinese term for "crisis," is made up of the characters for "danger" and "opportunity." A backbone parent doesn't attack or flee from conflict but embraces it, seeing it as a challenge and an opportunity to grow. ("I need to talk with you about this." "We can work this out." "It's okay to be angry; it is not okay to hit your brother.") *Embrace* is not exactly the word that comes to mind when we find ourselves in conflict with our children, but it sure beats the alternatives of fight or flight.

Your sixteen-year-old daughter just walked in wearing an outfit you told her she couldn't wear—it's yours. She didn't unload the dishwasher as she said she would—in fact she put dirty dishes in with the clean ones. And she's hanging around with a kid you don't like.

The brick-wall parent tends to lock herself physically and mentally into a fighting stance. The space called home becomes a battleground of wills, and someone is going to win at the other's expense. Arguing, yelling, threats, and brute force are the weapons.

The jellyfish parent attempts to fix it or avoid the conflict totally, wishing it would go away; or simply sends the teenager away to "finishing school" (in other words, "We're finished with you"). Denial, rescuing, pleading, and abandonment are poor substitutes for conflict resolution.

A backbone parent views the conflict as a challenge and embraces it as an opportunity to grow and change, using assertive confrontation and other nonviolent tools. By embracing the conflict, the parent and daughter can begin to see not a battle but a dance. Conflict then becomes a cooperative challenge, a process, a movement back and forth between two or more people. If it is a battle, we move forward and attack and defend and fall back; we claim, win, and lose territory, emotional "space." If it is a dance, we share the space, move through it together, move with and around each other, sometimes leading, sometimes following. Sometimes we guide and speak; at other times we watch and listen. We accept the feelings and are open to the ideas and wishes of all involved, including our own. Rather than joining in a battle, we can "dance" a solution to conflict. Who wouldn't rather dance than fight?

TEACHING CONFLICT RESOLUTION

Example is a powerful way of teaching our kids to handle conflict. Kids tend to handle it the way they see us handle it. We often give examples without a lot (or any) thought of what we are doing. We will tend to respond to conflict the way *we* were taught to respond to it—with techniques learned from our parents, schoolteachers, peers, and the media. If we were taught to see conflict as a contest, we will probably fight physically or verbally with our "opponents" until one of us has won and one has been soundly defeated. If we saw our parents run from conflict, we will probably show our children how to run as well. If we were lucky enough to see significant people in our lives handle conflict assertively, without aggression or passivity, we can model for our children the same behavior.

If you throw a dish across the room in anger, don't be shocked if your child throws a math book across the classroom. If you hit your spouse or your child, you can probably count on your child regularly slugging a younger brother, a neighbor, or even the cat or dog. If screaming is the only way you feel you will be heard, don't be surprised if you hear the same volume and tone of voice coming out of the mouth of your five-year-old. If you make light of every conflict, don't be surprised if your child stops telling you what's bothering or hurting him. ("Cheer up, son, it can't be that bad. What's wrong, now?" "Nothing, Mom, just forget it.") But if, when you are in a disagreement with your spouse or a friend, you use the "fair fight" rules and your kid hears you say, "When you do that, I feel hurt," or "What do you need from me to feel better about this situation?" you'll notice her using similar techniques in her own conflicts. And if, when you get angry with your kid, you tell him that you are going to your room (or the kitchen, or the bathroom) to cool off before continuing the conversation, you may discover him doing the same thing next time he's angry.

Not that any parent doesn't "lose it" sometimes. Tired, worn out, frustrated, under pressure, you see your favorite shirt walk through the door on the back of your at-the-moment-least-favorite teenager. Words you swore you would never say spew from your lips: "I'll break your arm, I'll wring your neck. You are never, ever going to borrow another piece of my clothing. You are grounded for six months!" The adrenaline has risen and shut off the thinking portion of your brain. It's time to walk away; no, run away—cool off—then come back and start all over. The example you just modeled for your teenager is one you would rather she not emulate. But you can say at this point, "I lost it! I am not going to break your arm, or wring your neck, and you are not grounded for six months. Give me five minutes to come up with something that makes sense, and by the way, I am open to suggestions." You are ready to embrace the conflict and dance a solution with your daughter. Most of us are going to "lose it" sometime. Kids need to learn that if they lose it, they can come back and try again.

Guidance and *instruction* often go hand in hand. As we provide the backbone structure for our children to resolve their own conflicts, we are guiding and instructing them in constructive alternatives to fight, flight, or freeze.

TV AND THE PLAN

A typical scene in many homes goes like this: Two kids are fighting over a TV program.

"It's my turn to watch my show."

"No, it isn't."

"Yes, it is."

"Mom!" (about ten decibels above what is allowed by the city noise ordinance)

A brick-wall parent storms in, angrily turns the set off, and yells, "Stop it, right now. Nobody's going to watch TV." The message is that the kids can't solve their own problem and that an adult has to take care of it for them.

A jellyfish parent runs in to rescue; "Oh, come on, kids. Can't you love one another? Fighting will get you nowhere. Why don't we all sit down and watch a show together?" No tools are given to the kids for solving their conflict. In fact there is no acknowledgment of the value of the conflict, just the desire to have the appearance of peace and to keep the peace at all cost.

Neither jellyfish nor brick-wall parents give their children any help in resolving conflict. They both in their own ways just try to stop it. Brick-wall and jellyfish parents' unspoken message is "You need *me* to resolve your conflicts."

Backbone parents, on the other hand, have the patience to provide the necessary tools for handling conflict nonviolently.

When kids are fighting, it's important to recognize that the slower you walk and the quieter you are, the better the chances that the conflict will be over before you get there. (One exception: If one of the kids is physically hurting the other, get there as fast as you can.) If when you get there, the conflict is still going on, stand a moment without saying a word. Silence is one of your most powerful tools—use it. Walk over to the TV and *gently* turn it off. You are modeling calm and patience for your kids. As you turn it off, they will probably complain, "But, Dad ... but, Dad!"

Just turn to them and say, "You're both fighting. You may turn the TV back on as soon as you both have a plan. Now, what do you need?"

They will probably answer in a whiny voice, "A plan." They rarely respond nicely when they are upset, so don't count on it. All that is necessary is that they understand what they need to do to be able to watch TV: to come up with some kind of plan they can both accept. Your mission is to provide the structure and environment necessary to enable them to solve the problem.

When given the proper tools, kids can and do come up with a productive plan to solve their own conflict. With young children you may have to give them options they can choose from. As they grow older, one of three things will likely happen:

1. They will share—but don't count on it; it's rare. We often say to kids, "Share, share, share." Did you ever watch adults share? We don't always do it well. We are more than willing to share the things we don't mind sharing. It's the things we'd rather not share that we're not very excited about sharing. Kids are people too. They will tend to follow the behavior we model for them. (In one of my parenting workshops a woman said, "I asked my son for a taste of his ice cream; he said no. Don't you think the next time he would like a taste of my ice cream, I should say no?" I responded, "It all depends; if you want to teach your kid that you can be as selfish as he is, don't share. But if you would like to teach him another way, share.") We need to be our children's mentors, demonstrating for them the behavior we feel is decent, caring, and responsible. Some kids take longer to learn, but we can't give up. We don't become like them; we treat them in the way we ourselves would like to be treated.

2. They will both get up and leave, finding something else to do. This happens a lot if we encourage them to solve the problem themselves instead of solving it for them.

3. One of them will come up with a plan they both agree to. As long as the one who came up with the plan doesn't use brute force or intimidation to get her way, let it go. One may say, "I'll beat you over the head if you don't let me watch my program." It is a plan of sorts, but it's not one that you can live with: "Not a good plan, try another one." If the older suggests to the younger, "If you let me watch my program today, you can have two programs tomorrow," keep your mouth shut, even

though you and the older one know that tomorrow is Sunday and there is not much on. The next day, when the younger kid complains to you that the plan's not fair because today there is nothing on TV, a good response is "I notice you have been giving in a lot to your big brother. Would you like to learn a few good techniques for standing up to him?" Now's a good time to teach him assertive responses such as "I'm willing to let you have this program today if I can have the special on Monday and the special on Wednesday, and I'd like that in writing." If you teach a passive kid that kind of assertive line, nobody is going to walk all over him.

As parents we have a tendency to rescue our younger (or weaker, or less creative) children. ("Quit picking on your little sister. Let her watch her program today. She's younger than you.") If one of your children is always deferring to an older, quicker, or more creative sibling, even if the sibling is not using brute force or intimidation (she's just good at weaseling things out of her younger sister), it is important to teach the other sibling to stand up for herself and express her own wants and needs. ("I want to watch my program today. You watched yours yesterday and the day before. I feel that I am always giving in to you. I'm willing to sit here and not watch any program rather than give in to you again.") You can practice the lines until she can say them with pizzazz, firmly and with conviction. Both older and younger kids need to give and take, but the younger ones have been "taken" a lot of times; they need to learn to do a bit of taking themselves, or they will end up as adults who say "When I say no, I feel guilty."

Note that in this situation I asked the two kids to come up with a plan. I didn't ask them to give their own versions of what happened. The best storyteller would probably win, I would be left to make a judgment, and the problem wouldn't be really solved. When the issue is simply the conflict of two wants— one child wants to watch one show, the other child another show—two different stories won't make a lot of difference in the outcome. Each will try to convince you that some grave injustice has been done, and with the wisdom of Solomon you are to pass judgment on the case. The reality is that it is simply a matter of compromise.

On the other hand, if the conflict involves more than an issue of wants, getting two sides of a story can be helpful for both children. Dana wanted her bear back from her younger brother, Matt. Both were in a tug-of-war, and the bear in the middle was at risk of losing an arm and a leg. Dana didn't mind if Matt played with any of her other toys, but the bear was a special gift from Grandma. Matt didn't want any of the other toys. He wanted (said he *needed*) this bear to take on a Smokey the Bear adventure; none of the other toys would do. As a parent you ·can listen, help them listen to each other, and guide them toward a resolution. Don't give them an answer, but do help them come up with options for solving the problem and assure them that you believe they can handle it. The goal here is a peaceful solution. *Shalom*, a Hebrew greeting of peace, also means "fitting together," in a sense creating a harmonious whole. The two children learn to create their own harmony.

Notepad, Pencil, One Story

Two kids run into the house, screen door slamming behind them:
  "Mom, he pushed me off the swing."
  "No, I didn't. She fell off."
  "But he pulled the swing back."
  "But you did...
  "But he did... "
  "But it's my turn..."
Quick-thinking Mom hands one child a notepad and the other a pencil, asking both to come up with one story. The two sit there trying to agree on one story:
  "Okay, you write that I was on the swing."
  "I'm not gonna write that. You pushed me off first."
  "I'm not letting you write that on the notepad."
After a bit of haggling, they agree upon a story starting with "Once there was a swing..." As they work, they learn to look at more than one side of a story and to understand the difference between an editorial and a news story. They realize that no matter where they were both coming from, they both need to end up at the same place: a story they can both live with.
  When I used this technique while I was teaching, two of my

more creative and angry students took the notepad, tore it in half, broke the pencil in two, gnawed the broken end to a working point, then handed me two different stories. I read both and asked them to swap stories and come back with an ending they both agreed upon. During the time it took them to come up with their individual stories, read each other's, and find a creative ending, their anger dissipated, and they ended up laughing with each other, using their energy to come up with not one but several zany endings.

Being able to see the other person's point of view is one of the most useful skills in resolving conflict. When we tell or read stories to our kids, we can begin to teach them this skill by having them look at the other side of the story. We have to be creative with this, since most stories are told from only one point of view. Have you ever thought of "Jack and the Beanstalk" from the giant's point of view? How would you feel if every time you woke up, something else of yours was missing? Try telling the story minus the ending and ask your kids to come up with an ending both the giant and Jack could handle. One of my kids described Jack teaching the giant to look at little things from a different point of view; about the giant helping Jack reach heights he could never achieve on his own; and about Jack's mom teaching both of them that gold isn't all it's cracked up to be.

Sometimes looking at a story from a different perspective, not just the other person's point of view, is helpful. Cinderella is one of the oldest fairy tales, dating back to the ninth century in China. In all of the versions, up to Walt Disney's heroine, Cinderella was the dutiful daughter and the stepmother the "evil" parent. (Stepdads are lucky; they don't exist in fairy tales. Stepmoms, on the other hand, really get a bad rap. They send kids out into the forest with nothing to eat, throw them in ovens, make them eat poisoned apples, and don't let them go to dances. And then we tell kids, "You are really going to like your stepmom.") Cinderella didn't tell you why she didn't get to go to the dance. She had been grounded for what she had done at the last dance. And the reason she was in rags was that her stepmother, a backbone parent, had very lovingly said, "If you put your clothes in the laundry basket, I'll wash them; if you don't, I won't." And she didn't. The only thing in her wardrobe that wasn't in a pile on the floor was her rags, so that is what she wore. Definitely a different perspective; and that perspective can definitely color the way we view a situation.

When two children are in conflict, if I view one of the children as a "good kid" and the other as a "bad kid," my response to the situation will be very different than if I look at the situation as a challenge and an opportunity for both children. In the former there will be a winner and a loser. In the latter, there is the potential for both kids to grow.

Jane Smith, in *Play It Again, Cinderella: A New View of Old Tales,* goes beyond a different perspective to an entirely new view and invites Cinderella "to be more introspective, accept responsibility for yourself and not wait around to be rescued." Giving children the tools they need to resolve conflict will enable them to go beyond one another's perspective and create a whole new view; a solution that is more than a sum of the parts.

USING GOOD SENSE MAKES GOOD SENSE

When we teach our children to look at more than one side of a story, come up with a plan, and speak assertive lines at home, they are better equipped to handle conflict at school and on the streets. Once one of my seventh-grade students got beaten up by three neighborhood thugs. He was a bloody mess. When he came back to school, he exclaimed, "I had every right to be in that block. They had no right to beat me up. Boy, am I going to get them!" Here's this little kid on the fifth percentile in height ready to beat up three thugs.

I put my arm around him and said, "You know what? You had every right to be in that block. They had no right to beat you up. But use your head. When you see three thugs coming down the street, look the situation over very carefully. If you think you can get past them in one piece, go for it. But if it looks shaky, don't get aggressive; you will lose." We didn't have to discuss the losing part at any great length, since he had firsthand experience. But I also warned him not to be passive. "Don't walk past them with your head down and your shoulders slumped, because aggressive people sometimes attack passive people for no reason."

"What else can I do?"

"Use your head and then your feet, in that order, and think

to yourself, 'Hmm, I'm outnumbered three to one and about six to one in weight. This is not a good place to be, good-bye'—and get yourself out of there as quickly as you can."

We have to help kids see that in situations like this they are using good sense, not being chicken. The lesson will pay off in the teen years when their friends suggest they try some fantastic drug.

"No way."

"Chicken."

"Nope, smart!"

Or your daughter's boyfriend suggests they have intercourse to prove she really loves him.

"No way."

"Chicken."

"Nope, smart!"

Or someone invites your teen to drive home with a drinking driver.

"No way."

"Chicken."

"Nope, smart!"

The key here is to teach your children to handle their own conflicts. However, it does not mean that as parents we stand idly by and watch a child steal another child's mitten. If I saw the injustice, I would deal with what I saw. "John, you took Sara's mitten. You have a problem and I know you know how to solve it." (A shorthand version might be "John—the mitten." My tone of voice and facial expression say the rest.) If Sara came running to me complaining that John had taken her mitten, rather than rescue Sara, I would want to give her the assertive tools to handle the situation herself. I would be there to support her and back her up. And if Sara's friend told me that John had taken Sara's mitten, it would be a great opportunity to teach her the difference between telling and tattling.

TELLING OR TATTLING?

Jamie is having a great time swinging on the tire swing. She knew she wasn't supposed to be on the swing today. She had hogged it yesterday, wouldn't let anyone else on it, and wrapped it around a tree branch so that no one else could use it when she was finished. The self-appointed playground monitor comes running up to you to announce Jamie's transgression. If you want to reinforce tattling, just be sure to thank the child for telling you, run out to the swing, and publicly berate Jamie for being on the swing after she had been told not to play on it today. If you'd rather not reinforce the tattling, you can teach the children the difference between tattling and telling:

> *Tattling:* If it will only get another child in trouble, don't tell me.
>
> *Telling:* If it will get another child out of trouble, tell me. If it is both, I want to know.

If Jamie isn't supposed to be on the swing because she hogged it yesterday, don't tell me; it will only get her in trouble. If there is no problem with Jamie being on the swing, and she has her fingers caught in the chain, tell me; it will help get her out of trouble. If she isn't supposed to be on the swing and she has her fingers caught, tell me; it is both an issue of in trouble and out of trouble, and I need to know.

Five-year-olds will need help in making the distinction. Occasionally one will run up to me and I ask the simple question, "In trouble or out of trouble?" He might think for a moment, shrug his shoulders, say "In trouble," and walk away; or he might say, "I don't know." Then I say, "Tell me, and we'll try to figure it out together."

"Mary is sucking her thumb again." Telling me will only get her in trouble; don't tell. "Mary's front tooth fell out when she was sucking her thumb and her mouth is a bloody mess." "Thanks for telling me."

If the distinction is taught to children when they are young, it can pay off in the teen years. Adolescents will understand that it is not tattling (or squealing, as they say) to tell you that their friend is giving his possessions away and saying subtle good-byes to classmates. Telling may help get the troubled teen out of trouble. A friend is five months' pregnant and binding herself up in an attempt to hide her pregnancy. Telling might get her in trouble with some people, but it will certainly get her and her baby out of trouble. There is going to be a fight after school, and an arsenal of weapons has been hidden in the lockers of rival teens;

telling will get kids in trouble in the short term but out of big trouble and serious regret in the long term. A friend is drunk and driving on a stretch of a major highway. Telling will get the friend in trouble and possibly keep him out of bigger trouble.

Here's my suggestion on what to do when asked to play the role of courtroom judge: Don't do it! I get actively involved only with what I actually see or hear, unless what I didn't see or hear resulted in bloodshed or serious damage; in that case I will deal with the problem, whether I saw what happened or not. No blood or serious damage? I let the kids themselves work out a way to solve the problem they created. When I worked with kids who were identified as troubled and disruptive, I found that if they were within ten feet of a fight, they were usually blamed for it, whether they had anything to do with it or not. I would rather not accuse a kid at all than falsely accuse one. One false accusation can destroy months of self-esteem building. (That I don't accuse, though, doesn't mean that I'm not terribly observant. My students used to call me Mrs. C, and it wasn't because my name started with a C; it's because they thought I *saw* everything.)

The Game and the Sit

Two kids are playing a game.
"You didn't turn the spinner right."
"Yes, I did."
"No, you didn't."
"Dad!!"
You are in the other room and didn't see what happened. You can walk into the room and say, "You both seem really angry. Come over here and sit together on the couch. You can both get up as soon as you give each other permission to get up. What is it you need to do?"
"Do we have to say we're sorry?"
"No, you may both get up as soon as you give each other permission to get up."
Don't demand an apology. "I'm sorry" has to come from the heart, not the head. If you demand an apology, you'll probably get one of two kinds: (a) a whiny "I'm sorry" (real heartfelt!?!); or (b) "I'm sorry" followed by the apologizer slugging the other

kid again, followed by another "I'm sorry, I said I was sorry." The kid learns that as long as he says he's sorry, he can hit again.

Apology is not the key here, cooperation is. The two kids sit there, angry with each other.

"I'm not letting you get up."

"I'm not letting you get up either."

"Dad, when can we get up?"

"You may both get up as soon as you both give each other permission to get up."

Neither can move. They both have power over the other, but that power is connected to the other person's power. Kids begin to see that they are not dependent or independent but truly interdependent—not controlled or controlling but rather influencing and influenced. Soon one says,

"You can get up."

"But I'm not going to let you get up."

"Dad, I said she could get up and she's not letting me get up."

"You may both get up as soon as you give each other permission to get up."

Finally they both get the message that *together* they have the power to control this situation.

"I'll let you get up."

"You can get up too."

They both get up. Notice that they haven't been punished. The goal is not to punish them. It's to discipline them:

1. Show them what they have done wrong
2. Give them ownership of the problem
3. Help them find ways of solving the problem
4. Leave their dignity intact

But they haven't been disciplined yet. The reason you ask them to sit down and give each other permission to get up is to get them to cool off. They cannot effectively deal with the problem if they are screaming at each other. No kid will give another kid permission to get up if she is still angry with him. You're not going to hear her angrily tell her brother that he can get up; it just doesn't happen. The permission to get up comes when they are cooled off. When they have calmed down enough to let each other up willingly, then they can go back to the game and do one of three things:

1. Share
2. Both leave the game
3. One of them can come up with a plan they can both live with

What happens if one has cooled off but the other is bound and determined to keep the first child sitting all day? This is the time to use the flexibility of the backbone and as a wise and caring parent intervene.

"Joe, you've given Maria permission to get up. Maria is still angry and needs some more time to cool off. You're ready to get up and find something else to do. Maria, you may get up as soon as you feel that you are cooled off." If Maria hangs on to the anger for a long time, you might want to sit down with her, give her a hug, and tell her you are there to listen if she'd like to talk. The original incident is probably not what is really upsetting her; it was probably just an excuse to vent some anger she has been carrying around.

How old do your kids have to be before you can begin using the sitting technique? When both kids are at least at the level of a normally developing two-and-a-half-year-old. Some will be more verbal earlier, some later. Younger children will often run to the couch, quickly give one another permission to get up, and get back to solving the original problem. Older children may be so angry that they balk at sitting anywhere near one another. You can invite each of them to take a few moments alone to come to grips with their anger before they sit together. Or you may need to sit between the two to keep fists from flying.

Remember, this is only a tool to help kids calm down and begin to dialogue. If one or both of the parties refuse to sit together, don't force the issue. It's not control or compliance that you are looking for; it's calm and cooperation.

If it is a three-year-old who is very angry with a five-year-old, you may need to hold the three-year-old on your lap and rock him while the five-year-old sits close by. The older child will probably complain: "How come he gets to sit on your lap?" To which you can respond, "I'm so glad you can sit by yourself to calm down. Sam needs some help to learn to do it himself. Sam, let me know when you think you can sit by yourself to calm down." You have complimented the older child on his ability to be responsible and you have encouraged the younger one to learn from his brother. If the five-year-old wants to sit on your lap as well—why not?

You Hit, You Sit

Conflict is inevitable—violence is not.
—ELIZABETH LOESCHER

Remember Dana, Matt, and the teddy bear? Instead of playing tug-of-war with the bear, Dana grabs her bear from her brother and pummels him with it. It's time to step in. Dana needs to learn that hitting is not an appropriate way of handling her anger. But she's certainly not ready to listen to her brother's side of the story or come up with a compromise they both can accept. She needs to cool off, deal with the results of her violence toward her brother, then go through the other two steps.

Violence is one of the most obvious and destructive forms of aggressive behavior. Our culture is deeply rooted in a win-lose, victim-victor, adversarial approach to conflict, with violence being the tool of choice to try to end (not resolve) all kinds of conflict. It seems to be condoned at every level of our society, from the government down, and it is encouraged in the media, from the news to police shows to children's cartoons. Constantly, from nearly every direction, kids (and adults) get the message "You got a problem? Hit (or shoot or bomb) someone." Myriam Miedzian, in her book *Boys Will Be Boys: Breaking the Link Between Masculinity and Violence*, writes:

Modeling and reinforcement by the family play an important role in causing aggression, but research indicates that the highest rates of aggressive behavior are found in surroundings where aggressive models are numerous and where aggression is highly valued.... From an early age, young

children internalize the social pressures and role models
they are presented with and develop a concept of the kind
of behavior that is expected of them. A pattern of behavior
can be stored cognitively and only acted on at a much later
date when external conditions are conducive. Behavior
learned in the family, from peers, or from the media may
not manifest itself until years later.

Instead of "bombarding" children with the message that aggression is the way to resolve conflict, we as adults can teach,
through example, guidance, and instruction, that violence is an
immature, irresponsible, and unproductive technique to resolve
conflict and that using nonviolent tools to resolve conflict is a
mature and courageous act.

From the time my own children were quite young, they
learned that if you hit, you sit. Hitting is not an appropriate
way to handle conflict at any age. It doesn't solve anything, and
it only invites more hitting. In our home if you hit somebody, you
sit in the rocker or in your room. If you are a neighbor, you sit in
the rocker or you go home. One day a neighbor child smacked
another kid in our family room. When he saw me coming, he
said, "I'm going to the rocker, Mrs. C." It hadn't taken him long
to figure out the structure in our home.

Sometimes, with older children who have begun to understand their anger, offering a choice between sitting and walking is
a good idea. Some people, kids included, can calm themselves
more easily if they are moving about. The purpose and the intended result are the same: to calm down and then deal with
the original situation.

How long does he sit? Telling him to sit for five minutes, ten
minutes, or half an hour is punishment; it doesn't give him the
message that he can handle his own anger. (Try telling your
spouse that she can be angry for ten minutes—it just doesn't
work.) The child needs to sit quietly until he feels ready to go
back with the other kids and handle the situation responsibly. If
he says he's ready to go back, I just ask him what he's going to do,
what is his plan. If he says he's not going to hit, we aren't quite
there yet—that's not a positive plan; it's what he's *not* going to do.
I want to know what he's planning to do *instead* of hitting when
he wants the same toy his friend is playing with. If the toy

has been broken, part of the plan may be to fix it. Some parents demand an apology. An apology might help, but demanding one will almost never help, because it will almost never be sincere. Parents can teach and demonstrate ways to apologize. Sometimes just offering a hug or a handshake says more than words can.

What if he goes back and slugs his friend again? He sits again. From this he's going to learn one of two things: how to sit or how to play without hitting. The key is to handle it each time with a sit—not letting it go sometimes, threatening other times, and following through once in a while—or worse, hitting him to show him not to hit! It is not the severity of the consequence that has impact, it's the certainty of it that's important. A kid begins to understand that if he resorts to hitting to express his anger, he sits, gets an opportunity to calm down, and come up with another way of handling his feelings.

Occasionally a child will continue to use aggression, growing more and more destructive. Parents often react by imposing stiff punishments that serve only to cement the defiance and destructiveness. Instead of punishing the child, we need to recognize that the behavior is probably a symptom of a deeper, bigger hurt or anger and that she needs help to deal with *that* hurt or anger. She doesn't need punishment; she needs help, and depending upon the situation, it may be more than you can give and you will need to seek professional help. She can't of course continue to beat up on her little brother because she has an unidentified anger or hurt. You may have to be vigilant while she's working through her problem, helping her to understand that it's okay to be angry, but it's not okay to hit her brother.

DOUBLE TROUBLE

Sometimes what you have on your hands is not just one kid hitting another but a genuine fist fight. If two siblings are duking it out, I don't suggest that they go outside and finish it out of my sight. Some parents do exactly that. Our culture often equates masculinity with violence. It's not only acceptable for boys to hit; it's considered part of a virtual rite of passage to prove their masculinity. Too often the culture insists that if they don't hit, they will grow up to be wimps. This message needs to change; and to accomplish that, we as messengers must not allow, condone, or encourage violence as a way of solving problems.

If two kids are hitting each other, I ask them to sit together, with me in between if necessary, or I ask them if they want to go away from each other to cool off. When they have calmed down, they can talk with each other about the feelings that led to the fight. Sharing their feelings will help them learn to be less quick to judge and more able to be compassionate.

A simple format kids can learn is:

When I heard (or saw)...	**not** When you said (or did)...
I felt ...	**not** You made me angry
because I ...	**not** I couldn't help it
I need (or want) ...	**not** You'd better, or else

After both children have shared their feelings, guide them through the four steps of discipline:

1. Show them what they have done wrong

2. Give them ownership of the problem

3. Help them find ways of solving it

4. Leave their dignity intact

Then together they can come up with a plan for handling the conflict next time. And it will be a plan formed with a greater understanding of each other's wants, needs, feelings, and perceptions.

This and all the other techniques we've looked at in this chapter take time and energy—yes, the dishes will have to wait—but what an opportunity! Conflict has become a challenge and opportunity to grow. You have the opportunity, instead of punishing, to *discipline*, to give life to your children's learning.

I believe that if we are to survive as a planet, we must teach this next generation to handle their own conflicts assertively and nonviolently. If in their early years our children learn to listen to all sides of the story, use their heads and then their mouths, and come up with a plan and share, then, when they become our leaders, and some of them will, they will have the tools to handle global problems and conflicts. (Can you imagine two angry

national leaders sitting down together, giving each other permission to get up, actively listening to all sides of the story, and
coming up with a plan they can both live with?)

It's going to take example, guidance, and instruction from us
to impart to our children the wisdom of peacemakers: Violence is
"the knot of bondage"; aggression only begets more aggression;
passivity invites it; and assertion can dissipate it. Peace is not the
absence of conflict. It is the embracing of conflict as a challenge
and an opportunity to grow.

> Are we as parents called to be revolutionaries? Do we want
> our children to grow to be competitive adults, out only for
> all the world can give them? Or do we dance to a different
> drum? The music of my dream is one of love, trust,
> compassion, one of justice and peace—at home and on our
> common planet earth.
> —ELIZABETH LOESCHER, *HOW TO AVOID WORLD WAR THREE AT HOME*

Chapter 9

The Big C and the Three Rs: Chores, Relaxation, Recreation, and Rebellion

Becoming responsible adults is no longer a matter of
whether children hang up their pajamas or put dirty towels
in the hamper, but whether they care about themselves
and others—and whether they see everyday chores as
related to how we treat this planet.

—EDA LESHAN

The time to relax is when you don't have time for it.

—SIDNEY J. HARRIS

Chores and leisure activity are the yin and yang of a strong personal and family backbone. The two cannot be viewed separately from each other, since the interplay between them creates a whole. In Western thought the Chinese opposites of yin and yang are often considered as the male and the female, distinct and separate from one another. In traditional Chinese teachings they are seen as extreme poles of a single whole, a dynamic balance between the two being necessary for harmony and order.

A strong backbone that is at once stable and flexible cannot be developed by emphasizing one or the other. A brick-wall family tends to view work as positive and necessary, and play, unless highly structured and organized, as frivolous and unnecessary. The jellyfish family tends to view work as a necessary evil, doing only what has to be done, and play as the key to contentment. The backbone family seeks harmony and order individually and collectively through a dynamic balance of the two, viewing neither as superior to the other.

THE BIG C

The highest reward for a person's toil is not what they get for it, but what they become by it.

—JOHN RUSKIN

Getting kids to do household chores can be a chore in itself. Kids are more likely to do chores willingly if they feel that we truly need and welcome their help, that we are not simply giving them chores to teach them lessons or because we don't want to do the work ourselves. That means we have to present ordinary chores in such a way that they are meaningful to a child, useful for the family, and part of the harmonious order of our home—no easy task unless we ourselves begin to see ordinary chores in a different light. If we find household chores onerous and complain about having to do them, our children will probably develop a similar attitude and response to the chores we ask them to do. If we do our chores with a sense of commitment, patience, and humor, our children will have a model to do likewise. In *Tom Sawyer* Mark Twain showed how Tom Sawyer made the job of whitewashing a fence look like so much fun that he got other boys to pay him to let them do some of the work. But what is usually forgotten about this story is that the other boys actually did have fun.

Fritjof Capra, a renowned physicist and philosopher, explained, in his book *The Turning Point*, the dilemma faced by adults in our culture as they try to impart to children the value of everyday, *ordinary* chores:

As far as the status of different kinds of work is concerned, there is an interesting hierarchy in our culture. Work with the lowest status tends to be that work which is most "entropic," i.e., where the tangible evidence of the effort is most easily destroyed. This is work that has to be done over and over again without leaving a lasting impact—cooking meals which are immediately eaten, sweeping factory floors which will soon be dirty again, cutting hedges and lawns which keep growing. In our society, as in all industrial cultures, jobs that involve highly entropic work—housework, services, agriculture—are given the lowest value and receive the lowest pay, although they are essential to our daily existence. These jobs are generally delegated to minority groups and to women. High-status jobs involve work that creates something lasting—skyscrapers, supersonic planes, space rockets, nuclear warheads, and all the other products of high technology. High status is also granted to all administrative work connected with high technology, however dull it may be.

This hierarchy of work is exactly opposite in spiritual traditions. There high-entropy work is highly valued and plays a significant role in the daily ritual of spiritual practice. Buddhist monks consider cooking, gardening, or house-cleaning part of their meditative activities, and Christian monks and nuns have a long tradition of agriculture, nursing, and other services. It seems that the high spiritual value accorded to entropic work in those traditions comes from a profound ecological awareness. Doing work that has to be done over and over again helps us recognize the natural cycles of growth and decay, of birth and death, and thus become aware of the dynamic order of the universe. "Ordinary" work, as the root meaning of the term indicates, is work that is in harmony with the order we perceive in the natural environment.

Not only can ordinary chores help children recognize the natural cycles, they can help kids

- Develop the ability to organize their own resources

- Experience closure on tasks

- Organize themselves

- Set goals and build skills necessary to work through more complex physical and mental tasks

As well, chores are a great way to say to kids, "You are important members of our family; we need you, and we are counting on you to help out." Children need to believe that they can make a contribution, can make a difference in their families.

GETTING STARTED

The best time to start assigning chores is when it is least efficient for the parent: when the child *wants* to help, usually around age two. At that age she wants to do everything "by myself." In our home, at two you got to make your own bed (with a comforter and a bit of help). At three you got to help unload the dishwasher (you were climbing into it anyway). At four you got to help set the table, now that you could reach it, and at five you could dust and help push the real vacuum cleaner around. At six kids realize the difference between work and play, but it's too late; they are already hooked into the family routine. As our kids grew older, responsibilities and decision-making opportunities were increased. Hopefully by the time they are ready to leave home, they will be able to manage the many chores necessary to keep a home running smoothly.

Parents sometimes bribe kids to get them to do chores. "If you do the dishes tonight, I'll give you a dollar." You didn't get paid for doing the dishes last night, so why should you pay your kid to do them tonight? Because it's the real world? No, let them do work for the neighbors for pay. I'd like kids to understand that we are counting on them to help make our home a comfortable, safe, fun place to be.

Bribing kids to do chores gives them the false messages that:

All good deeds are financially rewarded. Not true. All good deeds aren't even recognized or acknowledged, let alone financially rewarded.

If it's not rewarded, it's not worth doing. A lot of things worth doing in life are not financially rewarded. Most of us receive no financial compensation for parenting; does that mean it's not worth doing? Some young adults have begun to say raising a child costs too much; they'd rather spend their hard-earned money on something "more productive and enriching" than parenting. Parenting is certainly not time-efficient or cost-efficient.

The bigger the reward, the more worthy the deed. The worth of a deed often has no connection to the amount of money assigned to it. You can knock an opponent out, pummel him to the ground, and make more money in ninety-one seconds of boxing than most of us will make in our lifelong careers. Oscar Wilde stated it simply: "It is possible to know the price of everything and the value of nothing."

But if you don't pay them, will they do the chores? Paying kids to do ordinary, everyday chores can give them the message that they should expect a payoff for any accomplishment. Growing up with such bribery can result in adults who are overly dependent on others for approval and recognition, lacking their own self-confidence and sense of responsibility.

Bribing your children to do chores can also get you into a bind. When you say, "I'll give you a dollar for taking out the trash," your eleven-year-old may respond, "I already have enough money to go to the movies. Grandma gave me ten dollars." Now what are you going to do? Bribes don't work once a child can get the reward from sources other than the parent.

A young boy had been on a token system at school. Supposedly every time he did something "good" or didn't do something "bad," he was given a token. He carried the process home. His mom asked him to get the milk from the milk box outside, and the boy responded, "It will cost you a quarter." The quick-thinking mom said, "Two can play that game. Dinner is seven dollars." The boy leaped up from his chair and said, "What was that you wanted? I'm on my way."

How can you get your kids to take out the trash if you are not going to pay them? A typical scene in many homes: The kid's sitting in a chair, watching TV, and we yell from three rooms away, "Chris, take out the trash." No response. Then we raise our voice, but not to the danger zone. (Every kid knows every parent's danger zone and responds accordingly. It's like the kindergarten kid whose teacher asked, "How come I had to tell you five times to do it?" The kid looked up and said, "But when my mother means it, she says it five times.") "Christopher Stanley!" Now we get louder and more formal. Still no response. (It's amazing how we spend nine months coming up with beautiful names for our children, and the only time we call them by that name is when we are angry.)

Exasperated, we stomp into the family room, glare at the kid, and yell, "Christopher, you irresponsible kid. Get your eyes off the TV right now. And by the way, young man, you did not put your clothes away. And I told you if these weren't put away, I wasn't washing your next load of laundry. And how many times do I have to tell you to put the lid on the peanut butter jar in the kitchen? I don't know what I am going to do with you." Christopher looks up and says, "Huh, what?" Kids have selective hearing—they hear what they want to hear. Meanwhile we are bordering on a coronary, and the trash is still in the kitchen.

How is the trash going to get taken out? First of all, don't yell from three rooms away. Parenting is not an efficient profession; it takes time. That means dropping what you're doing and walking to where the kid is; kids don't have remote controls. You get Christopher's attention, then say, don't scream, "Christopher, I need you to take out the trash before dinnertime; now, what do I need?"

"I know, Mom, you need me to take out the trash before dinner." (It's important to remember that the statement is "before dinner," and not "right now!")

Many of us have a tendency to run our homes as if it is *my* home: we are going to run it in *my* way and on *my* timetable. Here we are, trying to teach our children to share and yet robbing them of a perfect opportunity to do just that and share in the responsibilities of running a household. It is important to remember that it is *our* home: we can run it in *our* time and in *our* way. You want the trash to be taken out before dinner so that the dinner trash will fit in the can. Christopher is watching a program and wants to finish watching it before he takes out the trash. He knows you need it before dinner and can plan accordingly.

Your response is: "You got it, kid."

What you said is not nearly as important as what Christopher said. "You need me to take out the trash before dinner."

Yet some of us will own Christopher's problem all afternoon. ("Chris, don't forget to take out the trash." "Christopher, isn't there something you're supposed to do before dinner?" "Christopher Stanley, you don't take out the trash, you're not going to eat." "Christopher, have you taken out the trash yet?"—a really crazy question, because the trash is sitting right in front of us.) No, let him show up for dinner to find on his plate a note with the word **TRASH** in bold letters. You won't have to *say* a word. Kids have fantastic memories when they need them. "Oh, yes, the trash!" Nagging makes it my problem. Silence and the note keeps it his.

I didn't say he couldn't eat; that would be punishment. I said that the trash needed to be taken out before dinner. It makes sense, since there is no room for the dinner trash until the full can is emptied. A brick-wall parent might be inclined to put the contents of the trash on the plate to teach the kid a lesson. A jellyfish parent would take out the trash and tell Christopher, "Next time you take it out." A backbone parent simply leaves a note on Christopher's plate as a straightforward reminder of a chore to be done before supper.

Not every technique will work for all of us. Nor will one technique work for every kid in the family. You may have bribed your children with food, and anything around dinnertime may appear as a bribe, or you may not be able to use the note on the plate because your kid, like many adolescents, doesn't show up for dinner. What may work for a toddler may not work for a nine-year-old; what works for the nine-year-old may not work for her twin brother.

If you have a teenager who is not going to show up for dinner, an alternative might be, "Suzanne, the trash collectors will be around at two in the morning. Remember, you and I have discussed that you would get the trash taken out before you went to bed. And we have agreed that if it's not done, I will wake you to get it done." Don't say another word. Let her go to bed. At eleven-thirty you go into her room and gently shake her. (Not forcefully, nor with sarcasm, ridicule, or embarrassment. These control tools have no place in the home. Also, no minilecture:

"If you had taken out the trash before, I wouldn't be waking you." She knows that.) You gently shake her until it is more comfortable for her to get out of bed than to have this pleasant parent keeping her awake. You do that twice, and I promise you, your teenager won't think about going to bed before the chores are done. It is not the severity of the consequence that has impact, it is the certainty of it, the fact that the kid knows "If I go to bed before the trash is taken out, Mom or Dad is going to wake me." You say it, you mean it, and you do it.

Waking your teenager may be something you don't want to do—perhaps you are in bed before her, or the two of you have decided it's not a reasonable consequence. Another possible reasonable consequence might be her calling up for an extra pickup, paying the trash company out of her own money, or actually driving the trash to the dump herself. There are any number of options. You and your child have to come up with consequences that make sense and that you can both live with. Consequences need to be reasonable, simple, valuable, and practical. (That's why I marvel that any parent would ground a teenager for a month. I say, can you handle it? I don't want my teenager home for a month! Besides, it wouldn't teach him anything constructive.)

Children who experience reasonable consequences learn that they have positive control over their lives. Our children are counting on us to provide two things: consistency and structure. Children need parents who say what they mean, mean what they say, and do what they said they were going to do. These parents provide a basic backbone structure for children to function with.

When my own children were younger, they all had to make their beds before school. I couldn't say, "If you don't get it made, you can't go to school." I'd have been in trouble with the truant officer. Besides, I could see a ten-year-old thinking, "Oh, I have an exam. If I don't make my bed, I can stay home." We simply had an agreement that they got their beds made before they went to school. If they made them before they went to school, they checked it off their chore list. When they came home from school, they could have a snack and go out to play. If they didn't have their beds made, they could go out *after* they got their beds made. Note that it wasn't that they *couldn't* go out until they got their beds made—that's control. They *could* go out after they got their beds made—that's power. It is a subtle difference but a very important one. Saying they can go after they get their beds made is encouraging and inviting instead of threatening, negative, and intimidating. The effect on the child of the power message instead of the control message is significant.

If you cannot stand an unmade bed (it calls to you all day long, "Make me, make me, make me,"), recognize that it is your problem, not your child's. You will have to come up with a different consequence that you can live with. Perhaps, "Kid, I can't stand an unmade bed. If you do not get it made before you go to school, I'll make it for you. But before you go to school, you must tell me which of my chores you're going to do for me this evening." All you have to do is let him know it's Mom's turn to do the supper dishes and we're having spaghetti; he will probably get his bed made. If he doesn't, refrain from saying to him at the dinner table, "If you'd made your bed this morning, you wouldn't be doing the supper dishes tonight." Your kid knows that and might just say, "I wish I had made my bed this morning" as he's plowing through the supper dishes, but he might not. Just getting to school early to be with friends might have been worth suffering through the supper dishes. You have given your son a choice, allowed him to make the choice and to live with the reasonable consequences for that choice.

The Three Cons

When facing reasonable consequences, kids will often try three con games to get us to back down, give in, or change our minds. They seem to have practiced them in the womb; they know them long before we are aware they are playing games with us. If you can get good at not giving in to these three cons, you'll find you have a lot more energy left for parenting.

(But it is important to realize that not all children's emotional upsets, whether tears or anger, are con games. Sadness and hurt are not cons, though the tears and angry words may appear the same on the surface. There are no rules to tell the difference, but a strong clue is if the feeling message is being expressed through all five channels—body, face, eyes, tone of voice, and what is actually being said—it is not a con. If the message coming through the five channels is mixed, it is probably a con. Reasonably intuitive and caring parents can almost always distinguish them and address the true issues with their kids.)

CON ONE: BEGGING, BRIBING, WEEPING, WAILING, AND GNASHING OF TEETH

"Oh, please, Mom, please let me go out. I promise I'll get my bed made tomorrow. I'll make everybody's on Friday. Oh, please!"

The problem with Con One is that if we give in, it affects the kid's ego. We say, "Okay, go out and play, but tomorrow you get your bed made before you go to school." What we have just said is, "I don't believe in you, I don't trust you, and you're not big enough to handle the consequences everybody else in this household can handle. I'll take care of you." We often do this to kids with special needs. ("Here are the rules for everyone else, but not for you.") We end up giving her a second chance. In other words, we give in to her Con One—a typical jellyfish response. With a second chance she never has to experience the consequences of her own irresponsibility.

As I have said before, I believe in second chances; but I like to save them for life-threatening situations. Your son threatens to run across the freeway on his way to freedom because he "hates" you. You don't stand there and say, "Go ahead and experience the real-world consequence. We'll discuss it when you're back, if you make it." No, you pull him back and give him a second chance at life. The rest of the time, I like to give kids a second *opportunity*:

1. Give them a responsibility
2. Give them a reasonable consequence
3. When they blow it—and kids will...
4. Give them a second opportunity to try the first responsibility, *after* they have experienced the consequence of blowing it the first time

It is really hard not to give in to a Con One around three particular groups of people. If you get good at not giving in around these three groups, you've got it made. The first group is the general public. When we are in restaurants, grocery stores, the mall, and on field trips and our kids are whining "Please, please, please," we tend to give in. We also tend to give in when the second group, our neighbors, are standing around watching the show. The third is the hardest group. If you resist giving in around this group, you really have it made: grandparents.

How do you avoid giving in? You be assertive. And I'm not talking that "assertive aggressiveness" where you attend assertiveness workshops and aggress all over everybody because you have a right. True assertion is your ability as an adult to recognize your own rights, your own needs, and your own wants for the three very different things that they are and to recognize the rights, needs, and wants of the child; and in your wisdom to see all six of those in relationship to the whole. Anna *wants* to go out and play, she *needs* to get her bed made, and she has a *right* to be treated with dignity and respect. She doesn't have a right to go out and play; she has a far greater right—that is, as a human being, to be treated with dignity and respect. You may *want* and *need* your child to make the bed, but you don't ever have the *right* to use brute force, ridicule, threats, or embarrassment to *make* her make the bed.

Just be assertive. But how? With tears rolling down her face, Anna is pleading, "Please, please, please." You just calmly say, "You may go out as soon as you get your bed made." As she pleads more, you calmly repeat, "You may go out as soon as you get your bed made." Your child begins to learn that begging, bribing, weeping, wailing, and gnashing of teeth won't get you to give in or change your mind about a reasonable consequence.

If a Con One doesn't work, kids will try a Con Two.

CON TWO: ANGER AND AGGRESSION

"You mean old mom. Nobody else on the block has to make the bed. I hate you. This is dumb. This is stupid. How come Maria doesn't have to make hers? And Joey puts his pillow in the middle of the bed." Stepparents will recognize this one: "You're not my real father. Wait till I go see my dad this weekend—he doesn't make me do it." You could just strangle the kid. Don't.

If we give in to Con One, it affects the kid's ego. If we hook in to Con Two, it affects our heart. We get angry back. ("Don't you talk to me like that, don't you ever talk to your mother like that.") Aggression only begets more aggression. If she gets angry and you get angry, she'll get angrier, and you'll get angrier. You're going to lose it. Have you ever said something you wished you hadn't said, done something you wished you hadn't done when you were angry? When you get angry, the adrenaline rises and shuts off the thinking portion of your brain, not hers.

If aggression begets aggression, then passivity invites it, so you don't want to be passive either. "Oh, please don't talk to me like that. Wait until your mother gets home."

Another mistake we make when a kid is using a Con Two is to argue. ("I don't care what any other parent on the block says, in this house you are going to make your bed. Maria didn't make hers because she got sick. Joey puts his pillow in the middle of the bed because he's little and he doesn't need the pillow at the top of the bed; he sleeps in the middle.")

I refuse to argue with anyone over two and a half. Their language skills are too well developed, and I'll lose. Remember that the next time you start to argue with a twelve-year-old, they have more energy, will outlast you, and you'll lose.

Still another thing we do is let the conflict with one child affect the way we treat our other children. We are screaming at the child who did not make her bed when another comes up and asks, "Would you tie my shoe?" "Tie it yourself, and by the way, young man, if you had gotten sneakers with Velcro straps like I told you to, you wouldn't be needing to tie those bows. I don't know what I am going to do with you kids. You are driving me crazy."

If you are raising adolescents, you are in a high-risk category for a coronary. You're up against someone dealing with a major hormone attack: feet are too big, hands are too big, bodies are too big or too small, voices are up, voices are down, zits are coming out all over their faces. They come in the front door, all smiles; two minutes later they are in the bathroom crying. You ask what happened. "She used my comb." "He wore my shirt." "She didn't call like she said she would." Are we going to make it through this? Yes, but we can't keep hooking in to our kids' adrenaline.

Aggression begets aggression. Passivity invites it. So what's left? Assertion. The beauty and power of assertion is that it can dissipate another person's aggression. I would caution you, though—as powerful as assertion is, aggression is more fun, and we tend to do things that are more fun. You are at a family get-together; you're just waiting for your sister-in-law to make a comment so you can leap in with the one you've been saving for six weeks. That's a lot more fun but a lot less productive.

It's not easy to deal with your kid screaming at you, perhaps insulting you. Remember that you as a parent and as a human being also have the right to be treated with dignity and respect, just as your child does. Your child may want (temporarily) but does not have the right to use brute force (not unheard of with adolescents), ridicule, threats, or embarrassment against you. You have a responsibility to yourself not to put up with it and a responsibility to your child to teach her better ways of dealing with the situation.

You need, first, to center your energy and calm yourself down. You will then have the opportunity to redirect the child's energy and give life to her learning:

1. Show her what she has done wrong

2. Give her ownership of her problem

3. Help her find ways of solving it

4. Most important, leave her dignity intact

You soften your voice and say, "You may go out as soon as you get your bed made." The same line you started with; you don't even have to get creative. Just say it again softly, "You may go out as soon as you get your bed made."

What if she runs? If she's little, catch her; not just because you can, but because if she is angry and out of control, she might run into the street and get hurt or do something else that's crazy. But when you catch her, don't grab and shake her. (The brick-wall parent, grabbing a kid by the arm, screams, "Don't you ever run away from me, just wait until you get home!") Enfold her in a hug and rock her. I know it looks a bit strange, but it sure beats grabbing and screaming at the kid. Besides, hugging and rocking the child helps keep your adrenaline down and helps lower hers. As you rock her, softly say, "You're angry, you're upset. It's okay." You are not even dealing with the issue of the unmade bed; you are de-escalating a potential temper tantrum or raging fit. After the child has calmed down, you turn her around to face you, smile at her, and say "You may go out as soon as you get your bed made." Consistent.

If the child is older, don't chase him. I don't know about you, but I am not going to chase an eleven-year-old down the street screaming as I run, "You wait until I get a hold of you, young man." Not only are the chances slim that I could even catch him, there is a slimmer chance that he will learn anything from the experience except that he can outrun his mom. It will appear that he has won and his exhausted mother has lost. In reality we will both have lost.

If your eleven-year-old starts to storm out the door, give him permission to go. He'll hate it. Just say, "When you have cooled off, come on back." He can't storm out against you; you gave him permission to do what he said he was going to do. There is no contest. You can't lose, and neither can he. The conflict ends up being not a contest but a challenge and an opportunity. Hasn't he won? After all, he got to run outside and the bed still isn't made. If it was a contest, it would appear that he had won, but as an opportunity to grow, it's not over yet. Sometimes the best thing we can do when we are angry is to walk away from the situation. When he comes back—and trust me, he will—smile (a real smile) as you put your arm around him and say, "You know, kid, sometimes we think we can run away from our problems, but we can't; they are still here when we get back. Another time, not now, but later, let's talk about ways to handle situations without running from them. Meanwhile you may go out as soon as you get your bed made." Hopefully at that point you can both laugh, he will make his bed, and you can both move on to other challenges and opportunities to grow.

When you don't hook in to a Con Two, kids learn that it is acceptable to be angry, but what they do with the anger should be responsible; and name-calling, yelling, and threats simply don't work when trying to get out of having to experience the reasonable consequences of their own irresponsibility. In a moment of calm you can also talk to your child about the abusive language he used when he was angry, and possible alternatives to such language. (Be careful what you model here. If you are accustomed to letting go of a stream of four-letter words, it will be hard for you to chastise your child.)

If a Con Two doesn't work, kids will try a Con Three.

CON THREE: THE SULK

It is the most powerful con kids have because no one can make them do something they choose not to do. ("I'm not going to do it. You can't make me do it. I didn't want to go out anyway; it's starting to rain. Spank me; it won't hurt. Send me to my room; I'll listen to my stereo.") Normal, healthy kids will sulk for five minutes, gifted kids for ten. You say you have an awful lot of severely gifted kids at your house. No, what you have are a lot of kids who have learned how powerful this con is in dealing with their parents.

Con One we give in to; Con Two we hook in to; but Con Three can throw *us* into a One or Two: "Oh, come on, let me help you; we can get that bed made real quick, and you won't be late for your game," or "Wipe that smirk off your face, or I'm going to wipe it off for you!" And they have us.

How do you deal with a Con Three? The same way you dealt with the other two cons: "You may go out as soon as you get your bed made." Assertion. Don't be surprised at that point if the kid says sarcastically, "I know, I can go out as soon as I get my bed made." He mocks you beautifully. Bite your tongue—it is his way of saving face. I don't mean that you should ignore his comment; what you don't do is empower his comment through your own reaction to it. There is a difference. The way you avoid empowering the way the comment was made is by immediately empowering the message of the comment. When your kid is mocking you, calm yourself down, and say, "Yes, that's right, you may go out as soon as you get your bed made." What your kid sees is that none of his antics are working; you have stuck with the original message, have not given in to begging or bribing, not hooked in to his anger, not been thrown by his mocking tone of voice. One of two things usually happens: (a) Your son gets his bed made and goes on out to play; or (b) he storms into his room, slams the door, and throws himself on the unmade bed.

If he chooses to do option (b), let him go, say nothing, and get on with something more constructive for yourself. When it gets to be suppertime, invite him to join you. You may be tempted to threaten him: "Since you didn't make your bed, you get no supper!" When logical and realistic consequences don't seem to work right away, it is not uncommon for parents to use threats and punishment. But give the consequences time to work. Resorting to threats can put you into a power struggle with your son, a struggle one of you is going to lose. His reply to your threat can easily be "That's all right. I've got enough food in my room to last me at least a week!" You fire back with a more extreme threat: "You're grounded for six weeks!" Now you have a kid home for six weeks because he didn't make his bed. Instead of threats, stick with the original statement: "You may go out as soon as you get your bed made." Dinner has nothing to do with making the bed. Invite your son to join you for dinner and start over— don't even bring up the bed. Pretty soon he will realize this is not a big issue with anyone else, and if he'd like to go out and play tomorrow, he will have to get his bed made first.

What if he goes to bed that evening in an unmade bed? Have you ever slept in an unmade bed? The fact he has gone to bed in an unmade bed may be irritating to you, but it's not life-threatening, it's not morally threatening, and it's not unhealthy, so just let it go. Your son, will begin to understand that if he would like to be able to go out and play right after school, it would behoove him to get his bed made in the morning. No nagging, no threats, no reminders, just reasonable consequences.

By your not giving in to the three cons, your kids will begin to understand that you say what you mean, you mean what you say, and you do what you said you were going to do. Your kids are counting on that consistency and structure.

Have I ever given in or hooked in to a con? You bet I have, and even after you know what they are, you probably will too. We all slip once in a while, especially when we are exhausted. Be patient with yourself and your children as you all grow in your ability to relate honestly and fairly with one another. Recognize which con gets to you. Perhaps it is the tears, and you give in every time. Perhaps it's the anger—your mother's words roll off your tongue, and you swore you'd never talk like her. For me, it's the sulk. It drives me crazy, so when it comes, I have to take an extra-deep breath, calm myself down, and make the effort not to respond with the same sarcastic tone my child has just spoken in. The effort is worth it.

SETTING STANDARDS: SLOPPY VERSUS TASTEFULLY SIMPLE (NEAT)

So what if the kid does the job but deliberately doesn't do it well? What if you walk into the bedroom and the bed is very interestingly made? The comforter is spread out on the top of the bed all right, but the undersheet is trailing three feet off the bed, and the pillow is nowhere to be found.

The brick-wall parent, grabbing the comforter, ripping it off the bed, screams, "Do you call this a made bed?" (Crazy question, he just unmade it!)

The jellyfish parent, remaking the bed, shaking her head, wonders out loud if the kid will ever learn.

The backbone parent, walking into the room and looking at the bed, calmly says to the kid, "Your bed's not finished yet."

"But what's wrong with it?"

Don't tell him; if you've taught him, he knows. "Your bed's not finished yet."

"Oh, please." (*Con One*)

"Your bed's not finished yet."

"It's not my fault. Maria jumped on it." (*Con Two*)

"Your bed's not finished yet."

"I'm not doing this stupid bed over!" (*Con Three*)

"Your bed's not finished yet."

"I know, my bed's not finished yet." (*mocking tone*)

Just keep telling him what you need from him. Pretty soon he gets the message that it does no good to beg, argue, or sulk, and it's easier all the way around to get the bed made properly the first time.

As with all chores, we first need to teach our children how to make the bed. Then we need to make it with them and let them see us making our beds. And we need to let them know what our standards are in making a bed. The standards you set should not be rigid brick-wall bounce-a-quarter-off-the-bed type of standards nor jellyfish anything-goes type of nonstandards. There needs to be some backbone structure and flexibility.

We have three very different children. If you walked into their bedrooms, you would see three very different bed-making styles. Anna has her bed very streamlined and simply made. Maria, who layers her clothes, also layers her bed; one coverlet on top of another, pillows piled in the corner, and an array of favorite stuffed animals on the top. Joe puts his pillow in the middle of the bed, something he started doing after reading about the snake and the elephant in *The Little Prince*. Besides, I think he got great satisfaction out of knowing it drove his grandma crazy; for her a pillow in the middle of the bed was not proper. Joe sleeps in the middle of his bed, and it makes sense to have his pillow there. Yet all three know to straighten the bottom sheet, put the top sheet over it, and the comforter on top of those two, with the edges coming somewhere close to meeting. Pillows go on top of all of that and—presto—made bed.

Before you set too many standards for your children's rooms, check your own. If you can't find a clear path to your bed, if the clothes are strewn all over the room and the bed hasn't been made in a week, clean up your own act before you expect as much of your children. If you want your children to learn a skill, do it yourself. Demonstrate for them first, then teach them. Guide them through it, and then let them do it on their own.

When your children are toddlers, they can help you keep their rooms in order. They can help make the bed, help put toys in the box or on a shelf, help fold their clothes and put them away, help dust, and help make the room a pleasant place to be in. In the early childhood years (five to ten), kids can increasingly take over those chores themselves. Then by the time they are teenagers, you can turn their rooms over to them as their first experience in apartment living. You have taught them to make their bed every day; to clean their closets; to vacuum, sweep, or dust-mop; to dust the furniture, pick up toys and books and clothes. They've had a lot of practice, now let them assert their own independence in regard to their rooms.

Dr. Peter Marshall, in his book, *Now I Know Why Tigers Eat Their Young: How to Survive Your Teenagers with Humor*, explains how he avoids becoming involved in the Battle of the Bedroom:

> I recommend one of those hydraulic hinges that ensures the door is always shut (to be bought by the teenager in question). I also suggest that the parents no longer take any responsibility whatsoever for their son's or daughter's laundry. If they would rather throw a clean item of clothing in the general vicinity of the laundry basket than take the trouble to put it away for future use, let them rewash it... They can have their privacy and establish a territory all of their own; they can also have full responsibility for the consequences of not managing their territory efficiently.

Efficient is one thing, environmentally responsible is another. Odors from decaying food wafting through the air when the door is opened, colorful mold growing between a wet gym uniform and the damp carpet underneath, and the complete supply of bath towels scattered throughout the bedroom can become wonderful opportunities to help your teenager learn once again that the art of living in a community requires compromise, negotiation, and consensus. A solution to the problem can be found if all family members affected are willing to find a solution that is acceptable to each of them. ("Yes, you can eat in your room. Bring the leftovers and the dirty dishes back to the kitchen once a day—morning or evening, take your pick." "I'll hang one of those mesh grocery bags on my closet door, and put my sweaty gym uniform in it." "If I had a bathrobe that fit, I would dry off in the bathroom and hang my towel on a hook. Also, if Mary didn't pound on the bathroom door as soon as she hears the shower turned off, I could take the time to get dried off in there. Yes, I would wear your old robe, Dad; and yes, I can take a shorter shower, if Mary promises to quit banging on the door.")

Over the years, there has been a lot of compromise, negotiation, and consensus seeking with our own teenagers. We have arrived at a few simple guidelines we could all live with:

- They can express themselves in their own rooms through furnishings and wall decorations. (Yes, that includes writing and drawing on the walls.)

- They must knock and ask permission to enter one another's rooms. The same applies to us. (One bought and installed her own lock and gave us the spare key.)

- We do not nag them to clean their rooms—a hard one for Don and me to follow through on. Maria said it best when she told us she would do a better job of keeping her room up when it was her problem, not ours; she was right.

As part of the negotiations they agreed that once a week they would:

- Change the bedsheets so that the body oils don't leave a lasting imprint
- Vacuum the floor, which means they have to be able to find it
- Dust the furniture, which may involve moving a bit of clutter around

In order to change the sheets, unless they have had nurses' training, everything will have to be off the bed; to vacuum, off the floor; and to dust, off the furniture. So basically they have a bug-free room.

One day Anna commented that she thought she should spend some time on Saturday cleaning her drawers. I couldn't believe it: My adolescent wants to clean her drawers! She said, "Yeah, I can't get them open." Kids will use the skills we have taught them when they need them. The key is to teach the skills, let them get into the habit of using the skills we've taught them, and then give them freedom within limits to use those skills.

Remember, there are lots of ways to do chores. It doesn't always have to be my way. Be willing to give a bit. This is *our* home. We can do it in *our* way and in *our* time. Figuring out how to do this will mean communicating with one another, making our expectations clear, and listening carefully to one another. Sometimes what is said is not what is heard. A friend showed me two notes she had written to her teenage son and his written response.

Matthew,
A messy room is not life-threatening. A "dirty" room (TV?

your room? laundry room?) is a place for bacteria to grow and bugs to reproduce. Please clear, vacuum, and dust today.

Thank you,
Love,
Mom

Matthew,
My request was serious! I am concerned about bacteria and insect reproduction in your room! Please vacuum.

Love,
Mom

(Matthew's response:)
Excuse me!? Are you telling me I WASTED valuable time on Sunday!? Your ingrateful attitude is FRUSTRATING!!! Where are the notes saying THANK YOU for spending what little time was available Sunday to clean the shower ... vacuum the downstairs ... and bring in wood! I thought that was what the note was all about ... that I could have a messy room ... but my other house duties were more important! NEXT time try to be more specific.

Love,
Matt

Mom and Matt met in the kitchen and, over a cup of hot chocolate, talked about the misunderstanding. They were open to each other and willing to listen. Both were comfortable using humor to get across their own needs and concerns. In a brick-wall home Matthew would never have been able to express his own frustration or believe his mom would listen or care. In a jellyfish home either Mom in a fit of anger would clean the room herself (type A) or the bacteria would have had free rein to grow, with both parent and kid being oblivious to the greening of the bedroom (type B).

Madras T-shirts, Pink Underwear, and Other Mishaps

As kids learn new skills, mistakes will happen. Sorting laundry into whites, light-colored, permanent press, and dark-colored was something Jean, at age ten, had been doing for almost a year with no major mistakes. So it shocked her when she opened the washer to find, not a clean load of whites, but a clean load of pink-tainted underwear, towels, and socks. Protesting that she had not put any colored clothes in with the whites, she emptied out the washer, only to find tucked inside a pink-tainted T-shirt, her brother's favorite red Michael Jordan shirt, now a madras Michael Jordan shirt! When her brother took off both shirts together, the red shirt ended up inside the white T-shirt. Jean had two problems: a load of pink underwear and a ruined shirt. After several washings most of the pink was out of the whites. And after trying unsuccessfully to convince her brother that madras was now in, Jean paid half the cost of replacing the ruined one with a new one. Jean has learned to double-check the T-shirts, and James has learned to separate a colored and a white shirt before putting them in the laundry basket. Jean lives in a backbone home where mistakes are for learning. Had she lived in a brick-wall or jellyfish home, the results would have been very different.

The brick-wall parent: "You did what? How could you? You stupid kid, can't you ever do anything right? Look at all these ruined clothes. What do you think, money grows on trees? I'll never trust you with the clothes again. If I want anything done right around here, I have to do it myself. Just wait until your brother gets a hold of you!" Rather than solve the problems of the colored laundry and bleached shirt, a kid might be inclined to hide the problems for fear of what can happen to her for making a mistake. Or she will blame the problem on someone else. Mistakes are not for learning in this family; they create only another opportunity for blame and punishment.

The jellyfish parent: "Honey, don't worry about it. I'll take care of it. You're too young to do the laundry anyway. Hey, look, who cares what color the underwear is? I'll replace the shirt before your brother even finds out." The kid gets the message that she can't handle her own problems, that she is not responsible for her own mistakes, and that mistakes aren't problems to be solved but shameful errors to be covered up.

Remembering that mistakes are for learning, a backbone parent lends support, guidance, and encouragement when a child makes a mistake. "That's too bad, Jean. I know you can handle this. Rewashing the white clothes in some bleach right away can help. What do you think you can do about your brother's shirt?" Jean gets the message that mistakes happen, that the problems that come with the mistakes are solvable, and that she is capable of solving those problems.

How mistakes are viewed and handled often has a lot to do with a parent's point of view. When all three of my kids were toddlers, I taught them to make chocolate chip cookies. They were on the floor (safer than chairs at that point), a plastic mat spread out, bowl of dough on the mat, and cookie dough from here to forever. My neighbor came in and said, "My goodness, they are making a mess." I said, "No, they're making cookies." It all depends on your point of view. The kids learned at a very young age that if you eat all of the chips that are in the cookie mix, no matter what the picture on the box looks like, the cookies coming out of the oven don't have any chips in them. If your outlook is upbeat and positive, you help your children be upbeat and positive when it comes to learning new skills and solving problems that can come in the process.

DIVVYING UP CHORES

It is important that chores not be gender-biased. Boys and girls can and need to learn to mow the lawn, take out the trash, do the dishes, clean their rooms, do the laundry, cook, sew, use yard and shop tools, baby-sit, scrub the bathroom, pull weeds, plant a garden. For too long, housecleaning and cooking have been seen as feminine chores, outdoor and repair work (anything involving machines and tools, as if vacuum cleaners and skillets aren't machines and tools) as masculine. With these stereotypes we risk raising girls who think that the woman's place is in the kitchen and boys who think that certain types of work are beneath them—as well as men who couldn't sew on a button competently if their life depended on it. There are no biological imperatives where chores are concerned, except possibly those requiring great physical strength. Kids don't need lectures on gender roles, though. They just need to see their parents doing all kinds of chores, and to have the opportunity themselves to do them.

There will always be chores that one child enjoys and another hates, or a chore everyone hates but that must get done. I hate to cook, so I taught my children to cook when they were very young. I will often say to them, "If you cook, I'll clean up the mess." They know how to clean up and I know how to cook, but it's more fun occasionally for all of us to divide and conquer the task at hand. Cleaning the bathroom is a chore we all reluctantly take our turn doing.

Look around your home and see which chores you regularly do that your kids can and should be doing. See what chores are not getting done by anybody, which ones are getting done in a half-baked fashion, which ones can be shared by the whole family, and which you need to keep for yourself. Set up a backbone structure and routine you can all live with, remembering to build into that structure some flexibility that allows for creativity and growth. This is not a onetime, sit-down, and get-it-all-laid-out-in-detail procedure (brick wall), nor a "I know we need to do it, maybe we can look at it next week, if we can find the time" dream (jellyfish). It is an ongoing process of living in a community in a creative, constructive, responsible way. Some of the areas that can be considered are Inside Chores, Outside Chores, Individual Chores, Family Chores, and Seasonal Chores. There's no formula. Every family is different, and every family will divide up the chores differently.

RELAXATION, RECREATION, AND REBELLION

If chores are one side of the yin and yang of a harmonious family structure, the three Rs are the other. Relaxation, recreation, and rebellion may seem easier to deal with than chores, but for many people in our culture, "working" is actually a lot easier than "playing." In fact they may not even know how to enjoy leisure, and import the stresses and strains of their working style into their playtime. This is neither healthy for the adults nor good modeling for kids.

RELAXATION—THE ART OF MEDITATION

Productive work, love and thought are possible only if the person can be, when necessary, quiet and alone. To be able to listen to oneself is the necessary condition for relating oneself to others.

—ERICH FROMM

Take time to be alone with myself? No way. I need to be with other people.

Sit and be quiet with nothing to do? That's crazy. There isn't enough time in the day, as it is, to finish what I need to get done.

I have to be doing something or I don't feel like my day was worthwhile. It's a waste to do nothing.

Drive the car with the radio broken? Are you kidding? We have radio controls in the front and back so we can listen to our music and our kids can listen to theirs.

I can't stand quiet. I have to have noise, any kind of noise. I turn the TV on as soon as I walk in the door.

We as adults are often uncomfortable being alone, quiet, and reflective, and we project those uneasy feelings onto our children. If a child is daydreaming, she is encouraged to go out and play, to find *something* to do with *someone*. If a child is quiet, he is prodded to talk more, speak up, say something, anything. If a child likes to go for long walks alone, she is encouraged to invite a friend along so she has someone to talk to. If a teenager wants to spend time away from the family in the safe harbor of his room, he is called antisocial. From morning to night we bombard ourselves with noise, talk, music, activity, constant movement, as our bodies and our minds cry out for rest and quiet.

Quiet is not often encouraged or celebrated. When asked in an interview, Robert Redford, actor, director, and artist, said he felt that in today's information age, we probably talk too much:

"It's important to have those moments of silence, time to find out things by ourselves, be guided a little more by our guts." Our guts, the intuition Clarissa Pinkola Estés called "lightning-fast inner seeing, inner hearing, inner sensing, and inner knowing," is not easily tapped unless we are willing to be still with ourselves. And so it is with our children. For them to grow in the sense of inner discipline, they need time to be alone and be still. Fritjof Capra, a renowned physicist, said, "What is required for this subtle form of self-regulation is not control, but on the contrary, a meditative state of deep relaxation in which all control is relinquished." Dr. Larry Dossey in his book *Healing Words*, spoke of this quiet, inner-directed action as "the highest form of activity in which humans can engage . . . Prayerfulness . . . is accepting without being passive, is grateful without giving up. It is more willing to stand in the mystery, to tolerate ambiguity and the unknown." And what could be more mysterious, ambiguous, and unknown than your toddler or your teenager!

In a brick-wall family, silence is imposed or forced, not invited or modeled. Rigid rituals are followed and rote prayers are recited, often without a sense of prayerfulness. One of the worst examples that I have seen was a woman slapping her very talkative and bored son at a religious service. As she slapped him, she said in a most controlled and controlling voice: "Shut up, son, we are praying." So much for prayerfulness.

In a jellyfish family, constant activity and chaos leaves little time or space for quiet and reflection. Both the parents and children experience loneliness in a crowd, unable to tap into their own rich resources for comfort.

As a backbone parent, taking the time every day to be still yourself will give you the opportunity to "be guided a little more by your gut." By encouraging your children to "sit down, be quiet, and get to like yourself" you will be giving them the opportunity to tap into their own intuition. Not that it will be easy for a teenager who has just broken up with her boyfriend to sit down, be quiet, and get to like herself; or for you to sit in that silent space with her, caring, loving, and listening while letting her find her own answers to her pain. In the quiet she comes to learn, as Veronica Shoffstall said, "that you really can endure, that you really are strong, and you really do have worth, and you learn and learn . . . with every goodbye you learn!"

Go placidly amid the noise and haste, and remember what peace there may be in silence.

—DESIDERATA

RECREATING OURSELVES THROUGH PLAY

It's more than the shoes, the racquet or bike
It's more than your swing, the fish, or the hike
It's more than the skis, the skates, or the snow
It's ignoring the work and deciding to go.

—KRISTEN SHELDON

With a prayerful spirit comes a playful spirit. To see that spirit, watch a young child at play, spontaneously enjoying the moment without a worry about deadlines, rules, winners or losers, paychecks or bills. Play is more than the absence of work or the reward for work well done. It is not something that has to be earned. It is an opportunity to re-create and renew ourselves, and connect with others in the spirit of cooperation and acceptance. In his *Cooperative Sports and Games Book*, Terry Orlick speaks of the magic realm of play as "the child's natural medium for personal growth and positive learning. Children who are free to develop their creativity not only get a great deal of personal satisfaction but also gain experience in working out solutions to their own problems.... The concept behind cooperative games is simple: People play with one another rather than against one another; they play to overcome challenges, not to overcome other people; and they are freed by the very structure of the games to enjoy the play experience itself. Children play for common ends rather than against one another for mutually exclusive ends. In the end they learn in a fun way how to become more considerate of one another, more aware of how other people are feeling, and more willing to operate in one another's best interest."

Adults can and do turn child's play into rigid, judgmental, highly organized, and goal-oriented endeavors. Five-year-olds are suited up, lined up, and offered up to adult audiences in organized hockey, baseball, gymnastics, basketball, soccer, and other competitive activities disguised as children's games. These games of elimination eventually result in many kids giving up, becoming sports rejects and dropouts.

The argument that we must teach them to compete in order to survive in the real world would be valid if the world we want them to survive in is one of dog-eat-dog competition. If our goal is to raise them up to survive in the real world and make it a better place, it would serve us well to examine our cultural attitudes toward play, games, and organized sports. We can choose to raise our children to be competent, cooperative, and decisive individuals, who, if they want to, or have to compete, will do so with a moral sense. Cooperative games can provide one avenue of play to help develop those skills, all the while inviting children to have fun. Cooperative games are fairly new to Western culture, and I have no illusions about how difficult it will be to effect change away from competitive activities toward more individual and cooperative endeavors in our schools and our homes. Sir Herbert Read summed up the necessity of effecting that change when he said: "To create is to construct, and to construct cooperatively is to lay the foundation of a peaceful community."

Cooperative games are but one avenue for genuine play. Encourage your children to develop hobbies that they can get "lost in," go for hikes in the city or the mountains, swing on swings, run together, share a good movie, and, most of all, laugh together. Let the chores and your work go for the time being. Get out with your kids for no other reason than to delight in one another's company. You will find that play can renew and refresh and reconnect each one of you.

> If play is to be genuine it must be lighthearted and
> pursued without purpose. That is why we usually fail
> if we try to have fun.
>
> —LARRY DOSSEY, M.D.

REBELLION —THE ART OF RESISTANCE

Cowardice asks the question: is it safe?
Expediency asks the question: is it politic?
Vanity asks the question: is it popular?
But conscience asks the question: is it right? And there

comes a time when one must take a position that is neither safe, nor politic, nor popular—but one must take it because it's right.

—MARTIN LUTHER KING, JR.

Just as chores and the three Rs are the yin and yang in the formation of a strong personal and family backbone, relaxation and rebellion are both necessary to achieving a peaceful attitude. It is not enough to practice the art of meditation—to be alone and quiet, reflective and silent, cooperative and seeking harmony in relationships. To be wholly human is to balance this inner journey with the art of resistance.

Our children need to be able to see us take a stand *for* a value and *against* injustices, be those values and injustices in the family room, the boardroom, the classroom, or on the city streets.

Much to their dismay, the art of resistance you model for your children may be your refusal to go along with other parents who provide chocolate doughnuts for breakfast every morning; let six-year-olds ride their bikes without wearing a helmet; find nothing wrong with allowing unsupervised parties for their fifteen-year-olds.

Sometimes it is not enough simply to say no; it's necessary to go beyond resistance to rebellion—that is, actively working toward changing a convention, tradition, or general practice. A group of parents of graduating seniors, concerned about the common practice of some parents arranging for hotel rooms for their teenagers to have private all-night parties, decided to create with their teens a "night to remember," full of fun activities, good food, wonderful entertainment, and a slide show from the past. This is creative and constructive rebellion against a potentially destructive tradition.

We don't have to accept the status quo. We can make a difference, if we are willing to acknowledge what M.C. Richards describes as "passionate priorities"—actively witnessing for the values we believe in, be they expressed in small deeds, simple gestures, or protest marches. The art of resistance involves both taking a stand and taking an action.

When Rosa Parks refused to give up her seat on the bus that hot day in Montgomery, Alabama, she was resisting a law that was

created by one group of people at the expense of the basic
human rights of another group. Her taking a stand helped create
the momentum for the monumental civil rights movement in
the United States. It was a small, courageous act that gave witness
to a "passionate priority" and changed the course of history.

Brick-wall parents don't model or tolerate rebellion or
resistance to the status quo. They follow rules and social mores,
even if the rules make no sense and the social mores hinder
growth. If the sign says "Don't walk on the grass," they won't
walk on the grass, even if it means abandoning a fifteen-dollar kite
that landed by the sign.

Brick-wall parents demand that their children toe the line,
and forbid them to challenge parental authority or deviate from
the "norm," even in little things. "If the shoes came with laces,
there is no way my kid is getting out of this house without those
laces in his shoes!"

Jellyfish parents, as in so many other areas of life, are
consistently inconsistent. They may run a stop sign, explaining
to their kid that it's a stupid place to put a stop sign, then later
punish the kid for violating a rule at school and tell the kid to shut
up when she says that it's a stupid rule. They may sometimes
rebel against a norm simply because they're having a bad day.
They may tolerate blatantly racist or sexist jokes at a party but
swear a blue streak and refuse to cooperate when the city wants
to widen the street in front of their house. Kids get the message
that all rules, authority, and even values are arbitrary.

Backbone parents know what their values are, even if those
values fly in the face of conventional wisdom or the latest trend.
It might be as small a thing as recycling newspapers and cans
when their neighbors on both sides think it's silly. Or it might be
taking the time to go to a city council meeting to protest an
ordinance they feel is unjust to the poor and disadvantaged.
When we do more than give lip service to our "passionate
priorities," when we walk our talk, we model for our children ways
to rebel and resist creatively, constructively, and responsibly.

Children do not magically learn morality, kindness and
decency any more than they learn math, English, or science.
They mature into decent and responsible people by

emulating adults who are examples and models for them, especially courageous parents with principles and values who stand up for what they believe.

—NEIL KURSHAN, *RAISING YOUR CHILD TO BE A MENSCH*

The greatest part of each day, each year, each lifetime is made up of small, seemingly insignificant moments. Those moments may be cooking dinner, taking out the trash, stopping at a stop sign, relaxing on the porch with your own thoughts after the kids are in bed, playing catch with a child before dinner, speaking out against a distasteful joke, driving to the recycling center with a week's newspapers. But they are not insignificant, especially when these moments are models for kids. And every time a child organizes and completes a chore, spends some time alone without feeling lonely, loses herself in play for an hour, or refuses to go along with her peers in some activity she feels is wrong, she will be building meaning and a sense of worth for herself and harmony in her family.

Each small task of everyday life is part of the total harmony of the universe.

—SAINT TERESA OF LISIEUX

Chapter 10

Money Matters

The important thing is attitude, to be pure in giving or
receiving something,

—ROBERT AITKEN ROSHI

Since my children are not paid for everyday chores, I am often
asked if I ever give my children money. Yes, I do give them an
allowance for three reasons: to learn how to handle money, to
make decisions about their own money, and to set financial
priorities. And yes, the money is given to them without their
working *for* it. The job children have with their allowance is to
work *with* it. Teaching kids to work with money first will help
them successfully handle the money they will eventually earn.
Some parents would argue that it is unrealistic to give children
money they have not worked for. I think it is unrealistic to teach
children that the harder they work, the more money they will
earn. It's just not true. We all know people who work half as
hard as we do and make twice as much money, and some do no
work at all and have lots of money. How hard you work is in
reality only a minor factor in how much money you make. The
type of job, who you know, your gender, your race, luck, the
state and trend of the economy, and many other factors are all
important in determining how much money you earn for the
work you do. All of us have at one time or another received
money we did not earn: birthday money, holiday money, lottery
money, an inheritance. To this list I would add allowance. What

is important for kids to learn is that no matter how much money they have, earn, win, or inherit, they need to know how to spend it, how to save it, and how to give it to others in need.

This is what handling money is about, and this is why we give kids an allowance.

READY, SET, GO!

The best time to start giving your children money is when they will no longer eat it. For some this will be when they are two years old; for others it may be when they are four. Basically, when they don't put it in their mouths, they can start putting it in their own bank. They can also begin to identify different coins and combinations of coins, start counting, and keep track of their allowance. They can make slash marks in a small spiral notebook, recording pennies, nickels, dimes, and quarters. (A second child often learns the difference between a nickel and a dime more quickly than the first child because the older child teaches the younger: "If you let me have all the little thin ones, you can have all the big fat ones." It doesn't take long for her to catch on to that scam!)

In deciding how much allowance to give our kids, we need to ask ourselves four questions:

1. How much can I afford?
2. How much do I want to give?
3. How much can my child handle? It needs to be enough not to frustrate the child but not so much that no responsible choices need to be made or priorities set.
4. What does my child need the money for? Obviously the adolescent who buys all of her extracurricular-activity tickets, lunch tickets, schools supplies, and clothing needs more than a younger sibling who needs money only for activity tickets, or an even younger one who only wants to buy toys.

The three kinds of families all give their children money but in different ways with different messages attached to the allowance.

The Brick-wall Allowance

A brick-wall parent gives a child an allowance and then dictates how she spends it, saves it, and gives it. The message is "I'll give you money for your allowance, but I'll control it. I know how to think about money; you don't." She gets a dollar in coins, but 50¢ is taken back. ("I'll put 25¢ in the bank for you. Since you keep opening your bank and playing with the money, I can't trust you to save your money. And I'll give you the other 25¢ when we get to church. If I give it to you before, you might forget to bring it or lose it on the way. The other 50¢ you may spend on toys but not on candy.)"

Some brick-wall parents will insist on controlling *all* the money. And the kid must begin earning money at an early age and risk losing it if his behavior is not perfect. ("If you don't put your clothes in the laundry basket, you lose 50¢ of your allowance.") Comparisons to other kids are common. ("The reason you don't have any money this week is that you've been bad. Look at your sister. She's behaved herself, so she has money to spend.") Minilectures are used to force approved behavior. ("If you don't save that money, you won't be able to go to the movies next weekend with the other kids.")

Kids of brick-wall parents get the following additional messages:

- Money is a status symbol. ("You're worth less than your sister because you have less money.")
- Money is a form of security. ("If you don't save that money, you'll be lonely and left out next weekend.")
- Money is a reward and a punishment. ("If your grades improve, you'll get a dollar more. If they don't, you'll lose a dollar.")

THE JELLYFISH ALLOWANCE

Once in a while jellyfish parents will throw some money at the kid. She never knows how much to expect or when to expect it. Since there is no structure in the family as a whole, there is no structure around spending, saving, and giving. Often the parents' money habits are in total disarray—compulsive overspending, credit card abuse, late payments, little or no savings. Jellyfish parents are quick to blame or minilecture the child for having the same foolish spending habits they themselves practice. ("If you hadn't spent your money on these little toys, you would have had money for this big one. "If you had put some money away, you'd have money for the movie.") There is no bank for the child to put money into, no consistent money-management modeling by the parents.

Kids of jellyfish parents get the following messages when it comes to allowances:

- Money is important but completely unpredictable.
- Certain things are expected of you, but you'll have to figure them out for yourself. You can't expect any help from me.
- Do as I say, not as I do.

THE BACKBONE ALLOWANCE

A backbone parent hands a kid a dollar and reminds him that some of it must go into savings, some to charity, and the rest may be spent on whatever he wants (with the provision that they are not life-threatening, morally threatening, or unhealthy). The backbone structure is that they must save, spend, and give. The backbone flexibility is that *they decide* how to do all three and how much to devote to each. Backbone parents give advice and guidance, not orders and lectures.

Kids of backbone parents get the following messages:

- I believe in you and trust you to make your own decisions.
- I know you can handle life's situations.
- I care for you. You are very important to me. And you can count on me for help when you need it.

Wants and Needs

Enough is a fearless place. A trusting place. An honest and self-observant place. It's appreciating and fully enjoying what money brings into your life and yet never purchasing anything that isn't needed and wanted.
—JOE DOMINGUEZ AND VICKI ROBIN, *YOUR MONEY OR YOUR LIFE*

Given the choice, children who don't want for anything will not save. And many children today don't want for anything. They don't get attached to a little teddy bear anymore; they've got the whole Care-Bear collection. They don't have one Cabbage Patch Kid; they have five—one for the front pack, one for the back, twins on the side, and infant in the carryall! We have an obligation as parents to give our children *what they need*. What they want we can give them as a special gift, or they can save their money for it.

Just beginning grade one and feeling very independent about choosing her own clothes, Maria announced she did not want her plain socks anymore, she *needed* fluorescent socks. We agreed either to buy her the regular socks or to give her the money the regular socks would cost and she could save for the difference. In a matter of weeks she had saved enough money to buy not one pair but two pairs, fluorescent green and fluorescent orange, to layer, of course, one on top of the other.

Occasionally wants and needs are mixed. Anna needed a bigger bike. She'd outgrown the ones that she had gotten as hand-me-downs. But she wanted a *new* one. This was both a want and a need, so we told her that we would go half with her and she could pick out the bike. So she did— a $350 bike. My bike and my husband's bike together aren't worth $350. We choked and realized that we should have put some additional structure into the bike choice—such as limits. We hesitated. Anna threw one of my lines back at me: "But you always say that you say what you mean, mean what you say, and do what you said you were going to do." We suggested that she figure out her budget and we would try to figure out ours. She quickly realized that she would probably have her driver's license before she could afford her half. She decided to look for a cheaper bike or one that was not brand-new. One of her friends had had a sudden growth spurt shortly after buying a very expensive bike and was willing to sell her the almost-new bike for a lot less than the original price. Anna put most of her money into savings, did a few odd jobs for neighbors, and suggested to her grandma that money to put toward the bike would make an excellent birthday present. We kicked in our half, and she got the bike that she needed and that she wanted. When needs and wants are mixed, you can share the burden of the cost.

Giving

How do kids learn to give some of their money to those who have less? As an aspect of the backbone structure, they must give some money to a charitable group or a person in need. When the child is a toddler, you determine the charity, but she gets to decide how much. When she is older, she can determine both. When all the "give-to" letters arrive in the mail, you can hand some of these to her, help her understand what each one is about, and let her choose which one to give to.

Another way kids learn, as in all aspects of behavior, is by their parents' modeling. But in this case the modeling may not be obvious or natural. A lot of us may contribute regularly to a religious organization or charitable causes we believe in without our kids even being aware of it. So when you are sitting down to that wonderful activity of paying bills, call your kid over and let her know what you are doing. "I'm paying for the telephone here, for the heat and electricity here. And here I'm giving some money to a cause I care about a lot." Tell her about why you believe in the cause and why they need your help, whether it's a children's relief fund, an environmental organization, or a religious group. (If it's a political party, she probably won't understand, but you can try.) If the child is too young to understand what checks are, you can make sure she sees you occasionally giving a little cash to someone at a shopping mall collecting donations for a charitable cause.

When charitable giving in the form of money becomes a habit, kids can then become aware of giving of their time and their talents as well.

> Let us not be satisfied with just giving money. Money is not enough, money can be got, but they need your hearts to love them.
>
> — MOTHER TERESA.

SAVING AND BUDGETING

Again, a little work at conscious modeling can be important here. Otherwise kids may not be aware of it. When you're paying those bills, explain that a certain amount of the money is going into savings, so that the family can take a vacation, or remodel the house, or have a financial cushion in case the car breaks down.

A child needs to have a bank from an early age, but let him choose it, whether it's the classic piggy bank, the even more classic old sock, the jar the gerbil food comes in, or one he makes himself out of Legos. He gets to choose how much of his allowance he puts into it every week. Don't worry if he puts in ten cents on the dollar at first. As he gets in the habit of saving and learns more about why we do it, he will adjust the amount of his own accord.

When children start earning money for "out of the ordinary jobs" at home or for work in the neighborhood, they can start contributing to their long-term as well as short-term savings. Short-term savings they have full access to. Long-term savings usually need to have some form of structure: two signatures, for example, yours and theirs, so they don't spend all their university money after an argument with you. And as your kids approach the teen years, you can begin sharing the household budget with them so that they can begin to understand what it takes to run a household. If your budget, or lack of one, is such a nightmare that it would only scare your kids, seek outside help to get a handle on it, then tell them about your experience, the mistakes you made, and how you are fixing those mistakes. In times of serious financial struggle, the charity your teenagers may be able to give to is their own family.

Spending

There must be more to life than having everything.
—MAURICE SENDAK

After giving and saving, the rest of the money may be spent on things that are not life-threatening, morally threatening, or unhealthy. You can allow a lot of freedom to a young kid to buy what is meaningful to her. She will begin to develop her own backbone in understanding and using money.

The toddler learns how not to buy on impulse. She may go to the store with money, if and only if she knows what she's going there to buy; if not, she leaves the money at home. (It wouldn't hurt some adults to practice this too.) As early as five or six years old, she begins to learn that all sales are not bargains and that all bargains are not sales. She then learns to budget for bigger items and begins to recognize the difference between needs and wants, bare necessities, amenities, and luxuries. The structure for responsible money habits is being developed.

Family Savings and Loan Company—We Have Your Interest in Mind and on Paper.

Do you lend your kids money?

- The brick-wall parent: "Never, never, never. Let them feel the pain for their own dumb choices; it will teach them responsibility." "Forcing them to live with what they are given and no more will teach them good money management."

- The jellyfish parent: "Of course, I lend them money for whatever they want. They can pay it back, but they don't have to. After all, a parent has to help out her kids."

- The backbone parent: "I will lend them money in certain situations when they have a plan to pay it back. And they are expected to pay it back."

The backbone parent does not lend money frivolously and for every occasion but recognizes that there are times when any of us may need to take out a loan and repay it later. Your teenager has misspent a good portion of the money she earned at her summer job. She recognizes the mistakes she has made, and is working on improving her spending habits. She has the opportunity to go on a wonderful, exciting, and educational trip but needs to borrow money for the deposit so that she won't lose the opportunity. She works out a payment plan with you, takes out the loan, makes the deposit, and has figured out how to pay back the loan and earn enough money for the trip.

WHEN IS BIGGER BETTER?

When do you increase the allowance? Simple—when your kids can convince you that they *need* a bigger allowance.

Anna asked me for more allowance.

"Convince me."

"Well, I'm older than my brother and sister."

"That doesn't convince me that you need a bigger allowance."

"I need more school supplies than I did last year. I'm in adult shoes, which cost more. I have more activities...."

She wrote out a budget and convinced us that she needed a larger allowance. She also asked if she could get it once a month instead of once a week. She got a bigger allowance once a month and is handling it well.

Maria decided that if her sister could convince us she needed a bigger allowance, so could she. She used her sister's format and convinced us she also needed more. And she, too, asked for it once a month. She has a wonderful facility with money. We could give here a yearly allowance on January 1 (if we could afford it), and she would have it budgeted through December 31, have money to spare, lend some to us, keep good records, and perhaps collect interest on some of the loans.

Joe was impressed with his sisters' success at increasing their allowances and made a super effort to convince us that he, too, needed that size allowance. He even got down to the detail that he could not wear his sisters' shirts as hand-me-downs because boys' shirts button on the opposite side. He got a bigger allowance, not the size he initially requested, but one we could agree on.

He tried getting it once a month but has now gone to twice a month. It works better for him. You and your children may need to experiment with what works best for each child.

As your teenager begins to make larger sums of money from a job or from "out of the ordinary" work around the house, you need to decide *together* if the allowance should cease or if you will turn over increasing responsibilities to the teenager so that he can begin to take care of most of his own financial needs—clothes, entertainment, car insurance, school fees.

My own children are like night and day—and afternoon. They all handle money differently, but they are all learning to spend their own money responsibly and constructively, to save their own money, have a goal for saving, and to give to those who have less than they have and are needy.

THE DESIGNER-SHIRT DILEMMA

We can see the fruits of our money management labors in the three types of family structures by the time our children reach puberty. Your teenager wants a designer shirt, he just has to have a designer shirt:

- Brick-wall parent: "Absolutely not. I'm not letting you waste your money on a designer shirt. It's a fad, it will pass. NO. I don't care if it is your own money, you are not wasting it on a stupid shirt." (Message: I know how to think about money; you don't. I'll let you have money, but I will control what you do with it.)

- Jellyfish parent: "You want a designer shirt, buy a designer shirt, see if I care. But just remember, when you waste all your money on a designer shirt, don't come asking me for money three weeks from now when you don't have any left."

- Jellyfish parent (alternate response): "What a neat shirt! I'll buy one for myself too, even though we both have a closet full of shirts." (Message: Neither of us knows how to think about money.)

- Backbone parent: *Not a word.* (Message: I believe in you and trust that you can handle this situation.)

Your teenager doesn't even have to ask if he can buy a designer shirt. He might discuss it with you, asking your advice or opinion but not your permission. From the time he was young, you let him make mistakes. You let him choose different outfits within limits, and you expanded those limits as his decision-making abilities grew. You taught him that not all sales are bargains, not all bargains are sales. You taught him about quality and quantity. You modeled responsible spending habits. The kid decides he wants a designer shirt, saves his money for it, and purchases it.

All three teenagers attend the same high school. The school booster club is selling T-shirts with the school logo on them—and all three teens feel they have to have a T-shirt:

- Brick-wall parent: "Aren't you glad we didn't let you waste your money on a designer shirt?" (Message: I know how to think about money; you don't.)

- Jellyfish parent: "If you hadn't spent your money on the designer shirt, you'd have money for the T-shirt." (Message:

I have so little trust in you that I need to give you information you already have.) Jellyfish parents are not only good at minilectures, they are very good at lending money with long emotional—not financial—strings attached. Some of you can hear your parents saying, "You're going where for the holidays? You're not coming home?" And every emotional string they have ever attached pulls you guess where? Home, their home, which hasn't been your home for years.

• Backbone parent: Doesn't even bring up the designer shirt, because it's not an issue. You put your arm around your teenager and say, "Sometimes it hurts when we don't have money for things we'd like." He might say, "I wish I hadn't spent my money on that designer shirt." But he also might not say that. The designer shirt may have meant so much to him that he would forgo ten T-shirts and six movies just to be able to have it. Within limits he is making decisions and choices and living with the consequences.

An Unusual Situation: Too Much Money

You have a special problem if you have a wealthy relative who wants to be sure that you receive not a dime of inheritance and instead sends large sums of money to your children, or if you have a noncustodial parent who tries to buy the affection of the children with large sums of money as gifts. This can undermine all the effort you put into teaching kids to handle money.

You, as a backbone parent, can send a note to the relative or parent along with deposit slips for your child's long-term savings account and suggest, for the children's sake, that they send a small amount of money to the children and put the rest in the long-term account. Or they could set up their own long-term savings account for your children. Either way, as a backbone parent, you establish a structure that is flexible and provides an environment that is conducive to creative, constructive, and responsible money management.

By constantly increasing the responsibilities and decisions our children have with their own money from the time they are toddlers, we can help make sure that by the time they leave home, they will be able to spend, save, and give in a caring, creative, and responsible way. It behooves us as parents to teach them well. Who knows, they might be managing *our* money someday!

> Financial integrity is achieved by learning the true impact of your earning and spending, both on your immediate family and on the planet. It is knowing what is enough money and material goods to keep you at the peak of fulfillment—and what is just excess and clutter. It is having all aspects of your financial life in alignment with your values.
> —JOE DOMINGUEZ AND VICKI ROBIN, *YOUR MONEY OR YOUR LIFE*

Chapter 11

Mealtime

I don't care how busy you are—you can take that time
with your children. You can talk about your dreams; you
can talk about your day; you can talk about your
frustrations. The busier you are, the more valuable
mealtime is for your child. If we don't spend this time with
our youngsters, they are not going to develop healthy
attitudes toward family life.

—DR. LEE SALK

If we want kids to learn to break bread with their neighbors,
we must first teach them to break bread at home.

BREAKING BREAD

There is something profoundly satisfying about sharing a meal.
Eating together, breaking bread together, is one of the oldest
and most fundamentally unifying of human experiences. From
prehistory it has signified peace and safety. In ancient Greek,
Germanic, and many other cultures, when strangers showed up at
your door, you first served them a meal. Only then would you ask
them who they were and where they came from and what their
business was. Sharing food was so sacred that one of the worst
crimes in those cultures was to do violence to someone from
whom you had accepted a meal. Even today, though the true

meaning is mostly unconscious, eating together symbolizes peace and harmony. An essential part of every meeting between heads of state, every summit conference, is a banquet where everyone sits down at the table together.

As food nourishes the body, food eaten in company also nourishes the individual spirit, the family, the community, and the world. The harmony of a meal eaten together spreads far beyond the table and far beyond mealtime. Or so it would in an ideal world. But discord has a way of intruding even when harmony is desired, for mealtime is a major disaster area in many families. What is yours like? ("Get your elbows off the table." "Stop that!" "Quit chewing with your mouth open." "No, you can't have that." "You will sit here until you have eaten all your food.") Negative, negative, negative. And kids wonder, "This is a celebration? We're suppose to enjoy this?"

In some families mealtime is not an event at all. It doesn't even exist. Kids put together something that resembles a meal and plop down in front of the TV. There is no opportunity to share anything about themselves, no chance to learn manners, no interaction with other family members. What little structure that exists is determined by the TV: If they are not totally mesmerized by the commercials, they may use the break to get up for more food. This is feeding time, not mealtime.

We need to take time in our busy lives today to celebrate mealtime with our children. It would be wonderful if an adult in a kid's life shared at least one meal a day with her. It can be done. You say that your teenage daughter hates breakfast and with her crazy schedule you never see her for supper. No problem; just tell her you will join her for lunch at high school. She'll find a way to have breakfast with you; it's guaranteed!

Even more exciting would be if the whole family could find a special time each day to come together and share food, good thoughts, and lively discussion. It doesn't have to be around the dining-room table every time. You can have a celebration at a picnic or in a fast-food restaurant; the point is that we take the time to eat and talk together. (This is a bit harder to do in a drive-through, though.) If you can get your young children to talk with you at meals, they will still talk to you when they reach the teen years, since they will have learned that mealtime is a safe time for sharing.

When our kids were toddlers, my husband and I learned very

quickly that we could not talk with each other at mealtime. Having spent a few years before the children were born enjoying leisurely conversations at dinner, we tried to continue afterward, and it didn't work. We quickly realized that we need to talk with our kids. If we tried to talk with each other, the kids would manage to get our attention with spaghetti in their hair or milk in the salad.

We also learned that we got more out of the kids if we didn't ask questions. If we asked, "What did you do in school?" the typical response was "Nothing." Rather, we talked about ourselves or made comments about events of the day. Pretty soon the kids were asking, "You know what I did today?" We were off and running with exciting conversation spiced with a few tips on manners. ("French fries are finger food; creamed corn is not." "Did you see the kind of ice cream the astronauts took on their space flight?" "Why two forks?")

BRICK-WALL BREAK THE FAST

Not surprisingly, brick-wall families have rigid rules for every aspect of mealtime:

1. Where ("Eat in the kitchen. Don't take that into the living room.")

2. When ("You can't have a snack. It will spoil your dinner." "It's not time to nurse her. She'll just have to cry.")

3. What ("You will eat everything I put on your plate." "I don't care if you hate peas; they are good and you will sit here until you finish all of them." "Our family doesn't eat that kind of food.")

4. How much ("You can't be full; your plates aren't empty." "Drink all of your milk.")

These rigid rules are enforced by threats and bribes ("You will sit here all night if it takes that long for you to eat your supper." "If you eat five carrots, three carrots, just two carrots, you can have this luscious chocolate cake.")

Mealtime is not a celebration. It is just a time to consume food and follow rigid rituals. Brick-wall parents have life-time membership in the Clean Plate Club and insist that their children join too. Control issues around food tend to reach a crisis in the teen years, with parents losing the battle when the teen shuts his mouth, refuses to talk, and refuses to eat what's put in front of him. He goes on fast-food binges or uses food as a powerful weapon against his parents (and I don't mean peas flipped from a spoon). It should come as no surprise that the majority of teenagers with severe food disorders such as bulimia or anorexia come from brick-wall homes where self-concept and self-worth are dependent on conformity to external standards and dictates. ("You're such a good girl to eat everything on your plate." "You don't want to be fat like him, do you?" "You will do as I say.")

A La Jellyfish

Jellyfish parents, on the other hand, have little if any structure around mealtime. In their families meals are rarely planned and are often eaten on the run, with little concern for the nutritional value, quality, or amount of food. If it's fast, easy to fix, and easy to eat, it will be on the jellyfish family's shopping list.

Jellyfish parents often use food as a substitute for dealing with emotions. A child cries and is immediately given a cookie in an attempt to stop the crying. Mom may eat when she's sad; Dad may gulp down a beer to avoid dealing with the reality of a layoff. It's no wonder the child comes home from school and eats a whole bag of chips because no one will play with her.

Good manners are rarely modeled by the parents, because the parents themselves have rarely been taught good manners. In the case of parent growing up in a brick-wall family and swearing never to raise his children with such strictness, manners are simply discarded along with the rigid ritual and threats. ("I'll never make my child eat anything he doesn't want to try. My parents made me sit at the table for hours looking at that plate of spinach." "I never eat breakfast, and it doesn't matter if my daughter eats it. My mother forced me to eat breakfast every day, and the day I left home, I quit. I refuse to eat until noon, just because of her." "It's all right if he gets popcorn all over the couch. We couldn't even eat in the living room when I was a kid.")

In jellyfish families kids learn early to fend for themselves when it comes to food. They eat what they want to eat, when they want to eat it, and where they want to eat it. They often develop poor nutrition habits, living mostly on fast foods, sweets, and junk foods. They also learn to keep their thoughts to themselves, because there is little opportunity and no forum in which to express themselves in the family.

BACKBONE BASICS

Backbone parents provide a healthy and flexible structure for mealtime. It is a celebration, an occasion to come together as a family to nourish the body, mind, and soul. It is also a time to teach children about nutrition, food preparation, manners, and conversation or dialogue—the mutual exchange of ideas, opinions, and feelings. This doesn't mean that there won't be disagreements, as there are in any family, about what to eat, where to eat, how to eat. It's just that these disagreements are handled in a framework of reason and dialogue.

When my children were infants, I nursed each one on demand and found that they developed their own different but fairly predictable schedule. I marveled at the parents who bottle-fed their babies and forced the not-yet-empty bottle into the resisting mouths of their children because if it wasn't all gone how could they be full? I could never tell how much milk my babies had drunk; when they were done, there were done. However, once my children started eating food, I, too, fell into the same trap: If it wasn't gone from their plates, how could they be full?

Some of you were raised the way I was: "If you don't eat everything on your plate, all the kids in China are going to starve." Some of you were raised the way my husband was: "If you don't eat everything on your plate, you don't love me." Some of you got both of these injunctions: "If you don't eat everything on your plate, you don't love me, *and* all the kids in China are going to starve. So you did what I did. When you grew up, you finished your plate, your spouse's plate, your kid's plate, the platter, and the contents of the cookie jar because "if it's not gone how could you be full?"

Kids learn to listen to their own bodies at an early age, know when they are full, and try to tell us; we just don't always listen. The baby spits the bottle out of his mouth; you push it back in. The two-year-old pushes her plate away; you play airplane to get her to open her mouth (and all she has to do is shut the hangar door and you're stuck).

Not only is this adult insensitivity an affront to the child, but it can have serious complications for a later age. How older kids respond to the three grave threats of the teen years—sexual promiscuity, drug abuse, and suicide—is related to how they regard themselves, how well they listen to their own bodies, and how well they are able to communicate to others what their bodies tell them. The impulses to indulge in inappropriate sex, drugs, and self-harm, though they are all physical acts, come from the mind, not the body. A person in the habit of listening to her own body will resist unwanted sexual acts, self-destruction, and the ingestion of harmful substances (unless it has reached the stage of addiction). A kid in the habit of listening to her own body will hear self-affirming messages loud and clear and will communicate them to others if, from a young age, she had the experience of being listened to and respected.

Forcing kids to eat when their bodies tell them they are full gives the message "What your own body tells you doesn't count. I know what you do and don't need. You don't." When a kid trained this way is fourteen and peer pressure tells her to have sex or take drugs, she will hear the message she has always heard: "What you feel doesn't count. I (we) know what you need. You don't." She has learned from experience that what she feels in her own body doesn't matter and that her expression of those feelings is discounted and ignored. So she is much more likely to have the sex, take the drugs, or even hurt herself. When kids say they are full, believe them. When they push the food away, don't push it back. Much more than nutrition and table manners are at stake.

At mealtime give choices but make sure they are practical and ones you can live with. You could say, "Do you want half a sandwich or a whole?" not "What do you want to eat for lunch?"

If she says sausage, what are you going to do if the sausage is for supper? Give her options with limits. If she says she wants a whole sandwich, don't remind her that yesterday she ate only a half. Why did you ask her if you already knew what you wanted her to say? Besides, how would you feel if you went to a restaurant, ordered the deluxe salad, and was told, "Last week you needed a doggie bag for that; maybe you ought to order the mini this time!"

After I asked my son if he wanted a half or a whole, he said he wanted a whole sandwich, so I gave him the whole sandwich. But after eating only half, he said, "I'm full." If I had used my old tools, I probably would have had him sit there and eat the whole thing, since he had asked for it, even though his body had already told him he was full. I want Joe to listen to his own body, not someone else's idea of what full is to him. So I said, "No problem, Joe. Put the other half in the refrigerator; if you get hungry before your next meal, you may eat the half sandwich first." I didn't let it stay in the refrigerator until it looked like some kind of biology experiment gone wild, and I didn't serve it as the first course of the next meal. My goal was to let my kid know that he can listen to his own body and that I will respect what it tells him. At the same time I recognized that he can make a mistake in the amount of food he takes and can have a responsible way of dealing with the mistake.

The most effective use of this tool is at suppertime. Your kid doesn't want the second helping of potatoes she put on her plate? No problem; it goes into the refrigerator. She goes out to play. At eight o'clock, when she says, "Oh, Mom, I'm so hungry," you can say, "Oh good; there are some potatoes in the refrigerator." "Potatoes?!" If she's really hungry, she'll eat them. If not, she's not going to starve before morning.

But don't serve the potatoes for breakfast. That's punishment. Remember, you're just helping her make sensible choices about food and quantity. You're not out to control or punish her for making a mistake about how much food she put on her plate. The brick-wall parent will "make" her eat the potatoes before she eats anything else—ever.

The jellyfish parent will throw away the potatoes or give them to the cat. When the child says he's hungry at eight o'clock, the parent minilectures ("If you had eaten all of your potatoes, you wouldn't be hungry") but then gives in to the child's pleas and gives him a bowl of cereal. The kid learns, if I can put up with the minilectures, I eventually get what I want without being responsible for the mistakes I make.

Have a toddler who doesn't like cooked vegetables? Give her frozen corn, frozen carrots, and frozen peas for a snack. You'll probably find that she will eat lots of them. Frozen corn, frozen carrots, frozen peas do not taste like corn, carrots, or peas; they taste like frozen.

Have a kid who dawdles with his food? Don't nag at him. Just say, "We'd love to eat with you. We'll be here for ten more minutes. If you're not finished, no problem; we'll let you eat with some peace and quiet." Let him finish eating by himself and load his own dishes into the dishwasher. If the dishes need to be hand-washed and dried, he can do that himself if the other dishes are already done by the time he's finished eating. This is a reasonable consequence for eating slowly. Avoid nagging, begging, and bribing; they make the problem yours. In reality, eating slowly is probably healthier than wolfing down a meal in three minutes.

Have a child who, if given the opportunity, would eat only macaroni and cheese every meal, every day? You can make up a meal calendar and let her mark five meals that week when she can fix (or help fix) her favorite food. It could be five meals straight in a row, or five lunches, or two lunches and three dinners, or any other combination of five meals during that week. Who said macaroni and cheese wouldn't taste good for breakfast? You can take this opportunity to show your child how to vary the recipe, the method of cooking it, and the ways to serve it, all the while celebrating with her her love of two basic food staples combined. Sure beats the alternative of refusing to let her have any macaroni and cheese and her refusing to eat any food you put in front of her.

Picky eaters, for the most part, come from panicky parents. Most kids would not have a problem with their food if we didn't worry so much about it. But we worry, worry, worry, and they quickly figure out that they have a powerful tool to use to engage us in conflict. (If you have a picky eater, don't serve a casserole to him. He knows that you put *something* in there that he doesn't like and he's bound and determined to find it.)

Food conflicts can be reduced by following a few simple guidelines:

- *Have a variety of good foods in the house and eat those foods yourself.* If you are addicted to chocolates, don't keep them around to tempt the kids. Make a midnight run on the 7-Eleven after they are asleep. Or better yet, reduce your intake of chocolates and model good eating habits for your children. If you sit in front of the TV and munch on a candy bar and sip on a pop, don't be surprised if your child turns down the offer of a bagel and juice. Brick-wall parents say, "No chocolates at all"; jellyfish parents say, "All the time, with chocolate-covered chocolate doughnuts for breakfast as well." Forbidding candy makes it more attractive to your child; candy in excess can cause serious health problems, as well as lost opportunities to eat nutritious foods. Backbone parents say, "Chocolates once in a while and in moderation." They have nutritious snacks readily available: carrots peeled, celery cut, fruit washed, juice in an easy-to-pour container, yogurt on the bottom shelf of the refrigerator.

- *Teach your children about the food they are eating.* "Spaghetti is a carbohydrate, beef is a protein, bran is a laxative, bananas are not." And, yes, you can use the word *carbohydrate* with your toddler. We often underestimate our children's ability to use and understand "big" words. Studying labels on prepackaged food can be like reading a cookbook, novel, mystery, adventure story, and math book all at the same time. Why does an apple a day keep the doctor away, and are carrots really good for your eyes? The U.S. Department of Agriculture, U.S. Department of Health and Human Services, has developed the *Food Guide Pyramid: A Guide to Daily Food Choices.* It makes it easy for you and your children to plan a balanced diet from the food groups.

- *Let your children help plan and prepare well-balanced meals and nutritious snacks.* Using the food triangle as a guide, your children can help you plan and prepare meals and snacks for the whole family. They are more likely to eat what they have helped make themselves. Also they can begin to see that snacks are not extra foods, foods that don't count and aren't important, but are necessary parts of a healthy diet.

The Food Guide Pyramid
A Guide to Daily Food Choices

These symbols show fats
and added sugars in foods.
KEY
☐ Fat (naturally occurring and added)
▽ Sugars (added)

Fats, Oils, & Sweets
USE SPARINGLY

Milk, Yogurt,
& Cheese Group
2-3 SERVINGS

Meat, Poultry, Fish
Dry Beans, Eggs, &
Nuts Group
2-3 SERVINGS

Vegetable
Group
3-5 SERVINGS

Fruit Group
2-4 SERVINGS

Bread, Cereal
Rice, & Pasta
Group
6-11
SERVINGS

SOURCE U.S.
Department of
Agiculture. U.S.
Department of
Health and
Human
Services.

In preschool Maria learned to make "bumps on a log" (celery stuffed with peanut butter, with raisins on top). For months after, anytime it was her turn to help with the menu, we could count on "bumps on a log" to be a part of that meal. We had it frozen, baked, chilled, dipped, for an appetizer, main course, and dessert!

- *Eat a variety of meals served a variety of ways.* Once in a while have a homemade smorgasbord, so that if your children ever get to a real one, they don't overload their circuits—"Oh, look at all of this food!"—and think they need to eat everything in sight. They will have had opportunities at home to select from a variety of foods and know they can take a little of everything. Have a family-style meal and teach your kids to pass the food around without turning the tabletop into a tasty work of art, to figure out how much food to put on their plates, and when not to ask for seconds. Have a picnic and teach them the fine art of balancing paper plates on the knee, as well as how to avoid food poisoning in the tuna salad and live ants as a condiment on their sandwiches. Have a formal meal, so if your children ever get invited to one, they don't say (loudly), "Look, someone made a mistake; they gave me two forks."

- *At least once a month have a formal celebration with your children.* Being Irish myself and being married to an Italian Catholic, and having three kids, we are not at a loss for opportunities to celebrate—birthdays, holidays, holy days, Sundays, anniversaries, the first day of school. At least once a month we put out our best placemats, music, candles, and food for ourselves, because we are worth it, and it is fun to celebrate as a family.

  After one of my lectures a man came up to me, pulling his wife behind him, and asked if I would tell his wife again about "using the good stuff at least once a month." His wife moaned, "But they are family heirlooms; those dishes have been in the family for generations. They might get broken." My comment was not what she wanted to hear. "If you celebrate using the heirloom dishes and many of them get chipped or broken, when you die, your children may have only a single sugar bowl from the antique set to pass around on holidays, but they will have many good memories. That's better than your children looking at a whole china cupboard full of never-used heirloom dishes and commenting, 'Do you remember dusting these twice a year?' Memories are easier to truck around than dishes. Don't collect dishes. Make memories."

- *Teach your children cultural or religious customs that have been in your families for years.* And if you don't have any, create some of your own. In times of celebration or crisis these customs can create a wonderful collective memory. When my husband's grandmother died at 104 years of age, we had a family gathering of three generations. Joe, the youngest of the great-grandchildren, grabbed his fork and large spoon and said, "Let's roll some for Gram!" And three generations grabbed their forks and spoons and rolled some spaghetti for Gram, the way she had patiently taught each one of them to do throughout the years. There wasn't a dry eye in the house.

  Years ago someone gave our family a special red plate, part of a European custom to recognize someone in a

special way at the dinner table. That red plate has become
an important part of our family customs for birthdays, wel-
come-home meals, thank-you lunches, and surprise
breakfasts.

The extended family knows, for weddings, funerals,
and big family get-togethers, to count on my making the one
(and only) dish I take great pleasure in making: English
trifle.

Talk to relatives about customs that created a bond in
their family, ask about traditional dishes handed down
through the generations. Maybe it will be Grandma's
chicken soup, Great-grandpa's molasses, or a cousin's holiday
cookies. If you can't find any relatives to ask, or find any
customs from your family of origin you'd like to pass down
to your children—if your family meals were an absolute
disaster or brought terror into your heart—ask your friends
and neighbors or create some with your own children that
they in turn can pass down to their children.

- *Teach your kids manners, not etiquette.* Manners are social
  graces that enable people to eat comfortably around one
  another; etiquette is adhering to rigid social rules and cod-
  ified courtesies that often get in the way of people breaking
  bread together. Mashed potatoes in the hair is not manners,
  but a young child using a spoon to eat peas could be
  manners. Is it proper etiquette? Probably not. In the movie
  Greystoke the primitive Tarzan sat down as a guest at a
  formal meal and lifted his soup bowl to his mouth. All
  those around him were obviously annoyed by his lack of
  social grace and lack of etiquette; all those, that is, except
  one, the host. In his splendid formal attire and with the
  utmost of grace, the host lifted his bowl to his lips and
  drank his soup too. He had manners.

- *Teach your children how to shop for groceries.* You don't have to
  take them to the grocery store every time you go. You
  would have to be crazy to do that if you could avoid it.
  Give yourself a break. Occasionally take them so that they
  can learn to shop intelligently. When Anna first started
  helping with the shopping, she got to pick out her own
  cereal as long as the first three ingredients weren't sugar.
  Picture a four-year-old looking for the word sugar on the

side panel and her excitement at finding one that had no sugar—shredded wheat! Oh, well, we tried. Still, today she looks at the side panel of the cereal boxes before she buys one. I'm not so sure, with all the information our children are getting at school and through the media, that they won't be teaching us how to shop intelligently. "Mom, that soap isn't biodegradable. Did you know these pears are grown without the use of pesticides? You don't really want that chocolate with wax in it, do you?"

- *Teach your children to cook.* I hate to cook. When I was a nun, we had to try out for choir. If you didn't make choir, you cooked and did dishes for 150 women every night. I cooked and did dishes for 150 women every night. I still can't sing, and no one taught me how to break those recipes down for a family of five. So as soon as they were able to roll cookie dough, I taught my children to cook. Often it is more efficient for you to cook the meal yourself, but in the long run, teaching your children to cook for themselves and others means that when they are on their own, they probably won't buy a case of canned stew and call it dinner for the month. And maybe in your old age they might bring you a few good meals.

Life is meant to be a celebration! It shouldn't be necessary to set aside special times to remind us of this fact. Wise is the person who finds a reason to make every day a special one.

—LEO BUSCAGLIA, *BUS 9 TO PARADISE*

Chapter 12

Bedtime Doesn't Have to Be a Nightmare

... the innocent sleep,
Sleep that knits up the raveled sleave of care,
The death of each day's life, sore labor's bath,
Balm of hurt minds, great nature's second course,
Chief nourisher in life's feast.
                    —WILLIAM SHAKESPEARE, *MACBETH*

Don't lie to your children. Don't tell them they need their sleep. Be honest with them: You need their sleep, and often you need more sleep than they seem to. You have to decide whether you want them to bed early and up early or to bed late and up late. As much as you might like it, you probably can't have them to bed early at night and up late in the morning.

As a family you have to look together at what works best in your home. Because of work commitments and your own body clock, you may prefer to have your young children have a late nap, be up with you later in the evening, and all of you sleep in later in the morning. I'm a morning person. I didn't know there was such a thing as the ten-o'clock news until I married a night person. When our kids were young, I liked to spend time with them in the early morning, so it was early to bed and early to rise for us. You have to do what you can live with, set what works for your family, and be open and flexible to the changing sleep needs and routines of the members of your family.

Even the best-intentioned bedtime routines can turn into bedtime disasters. You announce, "Kids, time to go to bed," and they give the obligatory complaints. ("Aw, can't we stay up just a little bit longer? Just one more show? Why do we have to go to bed so early? None of our friends have to go to bed before ten o'clock.") Finally they get into their beds. You tuck them in, read a story, give them a kiss and a hug, and, smiling, go downstairs to have some quiet time for yourself or with your spouse.

Three minutes later one kid comes down the stairs:

"Mom, I can't sleep. Would you stay with me?"

"Jamie, I've been with you all day. Come on, I'll tuck you in one more time."

You tuck him in. You're sitting in your chair, ready for some peace and quiet, and another kid comes down the stairs:

"Mommy, I have to go potty."

"What do you mean you have to go potty? You said you didn't have to go five minutes ago. If you'd gone before, you wouldn't need to go now." (The interesting thing about young bodies is that they can run around for hours and not feel a need to urinate, but they lie down in bed for five minutes and you start to read a good book and with impeccable timing their bladder signals "full.")

Now the second one is back in bed, and a third appears around the corner:

"Mommy, there's a monster under my bed."

"David, there are no monsters under your bed."

You go look under his bed, and your kid thinks, *Why is she looking if she says there are no monsters under my bed?*

Now you've had it. Your formerly peaceful self starts ranting and raving, "If any of you come down one more time, you are all going to bed two hours earlier tomorrow night. The next one out of bed gets a good spanking. I don't want to see any of you until the sun rises in the west!"

They run and throw themselves on their beds and cry themselves to sleep. Minutes later you tiptoe in and see them sleeping on their tear-stained pillows, and guilt sets in. The rest of your "peaceful and quiet evening" is spent moaning about what a wretched parent you are. There's got to be a better way.

When our kids were babies, I had no trouble putting them to bed. I simply nursed them until they fell asleep. When they were toddlers, however, it became apparent that some sort of routine was necessary. One friend advised that we let them cry themselves to sleep. Another suggested letting them stay up until they fell asleep. And others with older children just shook their heads and said, "This too will pass." Some experts said to just let them cry; some said that the family bed is the cure; and others said that it depends on the individual child. Great help!

Don and I decided that we weren't going to just let them cry themselves to sleep. We had already been doing the family-bed routine with the nursing babies, and all three children had individual sleeping patterns. So during the toddler years, one of us would put the kids to bed and the other would do the supper dishes and the laundry. One of us supposedly got a break, and at times, as we both collapsed on the couch after the three kids were asleep and the dishes were done and the laundry folded, it was a real toss-up as to who really got the break.

Brick-wall Bedtime

Bedtime in a brick-wall family is not so much a routine as a prescribed ritual. The brick-wall obsession with order, control, and obedience is seldom so much in evidence as it is now. Having been told by experts that a baby may want to be rocked to sleep but really needs to learn to fall asleep on his own, parents put their infant in the crib at a set time, turn the lights out, and go into the next room, turn the TV volume up, and let the neighbors listen to the baby's cries for the next hour. The baby's feelings are ignored or negated, and yes, he eventually learns to fall asleep by himself and, if he wakes up, to readily get himself back to sleep with no help from his parents. It is no surprise that often both the infant and the parent become increasingly desensitized to pain and crying. ("After a month of letting him cry himself to sleep, he's become such a good baby. We hardly hear a sound out of him. It worked.")

Rigid bedroom separatism is the rule. Children sleep in their own beds in their own bedrooms at all times, no exceptions. The belief is that if you ever let them sleep in your bed, you'll never get them out of it.

Bedtime is set by the parents from the time the kids are infants and continues through their teen years with little or no input from the kids. ("It is eight o'clock, and you will be in your bed and asleep by eight-fifteen.") No bending of the rules for special occasions or when friends are over is allowed. ("I don't care if the movie isn't finished. You should have thought of that before you started watching it. Eight o'clock is bedtime, and you need your sleep.")

Threats and bribes are used to enforce compliance. ("If you two don't stop talking, I'm never going to let you have another friend over." "If you go to bed at eight o'clock, without any trouble for the baby-sitter, I'll bring home a treat for you.")

JELLYFISH BEDTIME

Bedtime in jellyfish homes is either bedlam, or parents and kids simply fall asleep wherever and whenever they will. There is no routine around teeth brushing, putting on pajamas, bedtime stories, and getting into a bed. The jellyfish parent raised in a brick-wall home will often refuse to establish a routine for her children. She has rejected the rigidity of her parents but does not have her own backbone structure, so she doesn't know how to create a constructive routine for her children. ("We have no hassles with bedtime. I just let them fall asleep in the living room. It's okay with me if they sleep in their clothes; I often fall asleep on the couch myself.") This works for a while, but eventually, when poor sleeping habits begin to wear on both parent and children, she reverts to the brick-wall messages from her childhood. ("Get to your bed right now; I'm tired of you being up so late and falling asleep on the couch; you're getting too big to carry upstairs." "If you get out of your bed one more time, you are going to get a good spanking." "Get those teeth brushed. I'm tired of paying such huge dental bills.")

Another kind of jellyfish parent, himself raised in a jellyfish home, has no concept of the need for bedtime routine for young children. His kids run around the neighborhood at all hours of the night and are late for school because they all overslept. Often the oldest child will attempt to create some kind of order in the younger children's lives, trying to get the younger ones to school on time and to sleep at night, but in the chaos of the home it is an almost impossible task unless some caring adult intervenes and provides the support, skills, and resources.

BACKBONE BEDTIME

Backbone parents provide a basic bedtime routine that is flexible enough to adjust to the needs of the individual family members and the family as a whole. Responsibility for establishing the routine rests first with the parents, but then, as the children grow older, responsibilities and decisions about bedtime and bedtime routine are increasingly turned over to them. By the time they leave home, the children have a healthy regard for the need to sleep, an understanding of their own body clock, and respect for the needs of those around them. In the give-and-take of family life they have learned common courtesies and are able to balance their own needs and wants with the needs and wants of those they are living with. Turning the music down so as not to wake up a four-year-old brother can translate into keeping the music down in the room when a college dorm mate is trying to study. Brushing teeth, throwing dirty clothes in the laundry, putting on pajamas, crawling into bed to read awhile before turning the light out are habits, practiced regularly as a child, that don't just disappear when a young adult leaves home.

As a backbone parent you set up a structure that avoids the rigidity of the brick wall and the chaos of the jellyfish. Basically what has to be established is a bed *time*, bed *place*, and bedtime *routine*.

TIME FOR BEDTIME

Bedtime will vary with the age of your children. Infants have their own sleep schedule that you as a parent tune in to. As the baby grows, her sleep routine begins to develop in relationship to her own body clock and the structure you establish for naptime and bedtime. An eighteen-month-old may resist a nap in the afternoon, but skipping it has taught you that without one she takes on the personality of Oscar the Grouch. Often naptime evolves into rest time and is gone by the time most children begin school.

I'm not so sure that it is a good idea to abandon rest time. I rather enjoyed naptime and rest time with my toddlers. Taking a rest in the middle of the day was once a universal custom and is still practiced by two-thirds of the world's population. Taking time to rest and get away from the hustle and bustle of the day is a need the body never outgrows. Instead of fighting the signals from the body and downing more caffeine and sugar via coffee, pills, or chocolate, it might behoove us as adults to learn from our children the need to rest awhile.

It is not necessarily true that as children get older, their bedtime automatically and naturally gets later. Your first-grader may be going to bed before your toddler because the toddler has an afternoon nap. Let the toddler stay up, and you can spend some special time with your first-grader brushing teeth, telling a story, giving a massage, and tucking her in. Once children are old enough to read, give them a reading light. Then, after your usual bedtime routine with them, they can fall asleep when they are ready. You may think that your kid would stay up all night given the chance. Probably not. My oldest had a stack of books by her bed for the first few nights. For three days she dragged herself to school with her eyes half shut. I could have minilectured her, "If you hadn't tried to read so many books, you wouldn't be so tired." But she knew that, and she had to deal with the pain of being so tired. By the fourth day she was reading for a while and falling asleep at a decent time. There are times even now that I look into her room before I go to bed and find her reading light still on and Anna asleep with a novel covering her face.

As your kids reach the teen years, you have to decide, "Do we need the house, or do they get it?" That's a legitimate question. Some people need more sleep than their teenagers. They can say "Kid, when you are done with your homework, turn out all the lights." Others may be the way I was. I said, "I need some time alone at night, so at ten o'clock I'd like you to be in your bedroom, at your desk, or in your bed. The choice is yours, but I need some space here." And I think that's fair.

You might go past their bedroom door at midnight, look in, and find them working on a term paper that is due the next day. Resist saying, "If you had done that three weeks ago, you wouldn't be staying up all night." They know that. A jellyfish parent will attempt to rescue the teenager. "Here, let me finish this term paper for you. It's awfully late; you've got to get to bed." Let them finish their own term paper and feel the pain of going to school dead tired because they procrastinated, thereby experiencing the real-world consequences for waiting until the end to complete an assignment.

Will they learn to organize their time better? They might, they might not. I was one of those people who made the outline for a term paper after I had written the paper, and I tended to write it just before it was due, saying I write better under pressure. One day my husband chided me: "How would you ever know; you've never really tried it any other way." And he's right.

Talk with your teen about reasonable bedtimes. If you get a phone call from the school counselor telling you that your son is disturbing the math class with his loud snores, more sleep is called for. If getting up in the morning is an impossible chore for your daughter, an earlier bedtime may be needed.

From the time your children are born until the time they leave your home, there are going to be nights that they have trouble falling asleep, nights when they just want to talk or need a second hug. That's the beauty of a backbone: The structure is there and so is the flexibility.

Parents who have only infants and toddlers wonder if there will ever again be such a thing as an eight-hour sleep. Anyone who has only ten- and eleven-year-olds will tell them, "This too will pass. Trust us." Sleep deprivation is a common malady of parents of newborns. An encouraging thought from one who has been there is that "it will be gone before you know it."

But sleep deprivation returns during your kids' teen years. The only difference is, as parents of newborns, your babies keep you awake and at home, but as parents of teenagers, you have to try to stay awake as you wait for them to come home. I've been tempted on occasion to set an early curfew, not because our teenagers needed to be in early but because I needed sleep.

BED PLACE

Where to sleep? Much has been written about where children should sleep. The advice ranges from the family bed to their own beds and never anyplace else. The truth is that there isn't only one best way; there isn't one right way and a bunch of wrong ways. Each family needs to explore options it is comfortable with, ones that best enable all family members to get the sleep they need along with balancing the need for cuddling, the need for privacy, children's emotional needs, and parents' need for a spontaneous and satisfying sex life. (Yes, it is possible to have one after your kids are born, even though adolescents are sure their own parents never "do it.")

When our children were infants, they slept with us, older infants were in a crib attached to our bed with the railing down— easy on all of us. When they became toddlers, though, they each had their own bed in a bedroom apart from ours, and we locked our bedroom door—not just once in a while to arouse curiosity but always. We explained to them that parents need time *alone* to kiss, hold each other, and "engage in loving." If they awoke in the night, they only needed to knock, and one of us would get up and lie with them in their own bed.

One night when Maria was about three years old, I woke up to find her trying to climb into the bed. She wanted me to come back to her room and lie down with her. I was puzzled by how she got in the room in the first place and where her dad was. "Oh, he fell asleep on the floor next to my bed. It's your turn now."

Why lock the door? For one, you're less likely to wake up with extra bodies in your bed; two, you'll have some privacy; three, your kids learn to knock before walking into a bedroom; and four, you will be awake when you carry them back to their own beds. And yes, we've opened our bedroom door some mornings and tripped over one of the kids who had pulled a sleeping bag up to the door and camped out in the hallway for the night.

Do we ever make exceptions? Sometimes, when our kids were ill, they slept in our bed or one of us slept next to theirs. On most Saturday mornings when they were little, they would all pile into our bed, and we'd have some quiet reading time or some unquiet tumbling time together. Occasionally after a stressful week we might all camp out in the family room, have munchies, watch a good movie, and fall asleep, sometimes waking in the night to crawl into our own beds, sometimes not.

BEDTIME ROUTINE

Bedtime routines also need to be as individual as the families who create them. Kids count on some kind of consistency and some sort of structure. Basically they need to take care of their personal hygiene (face and hands washed, maybe a bath or shower, teeth brushed, toilet if necessary—usually advisable), change into bedtime wear (nowadays sleepwear can be more than just pajamas), do something calming to relax (singing, storytelling, reading, massage), dim the lights (some kids are like some adults and can sleep in the dark, and some are like other adults and need a small light on), and fall asleep.

If you do the routine with your toddlers, as they grow, they will increasingly be able to do most of the routine themselves, forming good mental and physical habits as they become more independent. When our kids were babies, we swabbed their teeth buds, then their teeth. Around age two they wanted to take over the brushing themselves. "Okay, let me brush them first, then you can finish up." As they got older, it was, "I'll brush mine and you brush yours for three minutes." Then I asked the dentist for the red disclosing tablets so that once a week the kids could check to see if they were doing a good job themselves—any red on the teeth and you've missed a spot.

Teaching kids to brush their teeth is like teaching them to do almost any other skill:

1. Model it
2. Do it with them
3. Teach them to do it themselves
4. Let them do it on their own and be responsible for it

(An added bonus to brushing your teeth while they are brushing theirs: You probably won't be inclined to make a run on the 7-Eleven at midnight for that chocolate fix you were craving.)

Storytelling

Bedtime can be a wonderful time to hook kids on books, to fascinate them with animated sound effects, and to teach them about family history and traditions through storytelling. Our three children loved to have their dad make up wonderful stories for them, with crazy characters they still remember fondly. They liked me to read their favorite stories, acting out each character with its own voice and personality. Grandma shared old stories from her childhood.

When I was traveling, I would often record a story on tape before I left and leave it for the kids; they could choose their dad's tales "live" or mine on the tape. You can create a few tapes of your own. When you leave your children with a baby-sitter, you can record a story in your own voice, sound effects and all, and also leave a few comments concerning bedtime routine for the benefit of sitter and child alike: "And now it's time to cuddle with your bear; the sitter will turn the lights down and sit in the rocker next to your bed until you fall asleep."

Massage, the Nourishing Touch

Touch is the most intimate of our senses and in reaching out to others, the message is clear: I'm here, I'm close, and I care. What a pity that many of us wait a lifetime to discover this miraculous power.

—LEO BUSCAGLIA, *BUS 9 TO PARADISE*

Touch is critical to human bonding. All of us, no matter our age, need to touch and be touched. Stimulation of our skin, or lack of it, can have profound effects on our physical and mental well-being.

Infants thrive on full-body massages, gentle stroking in a circular motion over their entire bodies. Toddlers and older children like having their heads, backs, arms, legs, and feet massaged. If you have a very active child who has trouble calming down at bedtime, try giving him a warm bath, gently dry his skin with a warm towel, carry him into his bed, and firmly rub the bottom of his feet. The Chinese have known the value of foot massage since ancient times and have a proverb that the eyes are the window of the soul, but the feet are the doorway to the body. Firmly rubbing your child's feet does two things: relaxes the child and keeps him in bed.

Touching your child in a caring and loving way also gives her the message that her body is good. Nurturing touches—massage, gentle tickles, or hugs—communicate your acceptance of your child's body. She will learn to accept it herself. And your respect for her personal boundaries—not tickling or hugging her if she isn't in the mood, for example—will help her recognize those boundaries and understand that they are to be respected and that she has an absolute right to her own body. Sometimes it is hardest to give children hugs when they need them the most: when they are upset. If a kid is pitching a fit from frustration or fatigue, often the most calming and helpful thing you can do is to enfold him in a gentle but firm hug. He gets the message of acceptance, through his body, that short-circuits the immediate events of the upset.

Many parents, having been raised either in families where touching was taboo or families where physical boundaries were not respected, are resistant to touching. Sadly they have missed one of the primary forms of nurturing, and touching their children regularly in a natural and healthy manner is something that has to be learned. If we give hugs and bedtime massages and backrubs to our kids, they will grow up to be adults for whom touching is natural. And there is an additional benefit: nourishing touch is mutual, and we ourselves will enjoy the physical contact with our kids.

NIGHTMARES, BOOGIE MEN, AND MONSTERS

Now that they are fast asleep, you can sit down to relax—maybe. When kids have nightmares ("Daddy, Daddy, a bear is chasing me, I'm scared") it's time to begin to teach them how to handle their dreams. Dreams have power in all our lives. When my kids have nightmares, I just give the child a hug and let him know he is safe. Then I say, "You know what? Dreams are fantastic things because in your mind you can do things you can never do when you are awake. One thing you can do is run faster than any bear in the whole world; another is you can create a tree that no bear can climb. And in your dream you can turn around to any bear and say, 'Hi, bear. I'd like to be your friend.' "

The things not to tell kids are that if they don't go to sleep, the boogie man will get them, or that if they get out of bed, the monsters in the closet will grab them, or that their dreams aren't real. The boogie man will not get them, there are no monsters in the closet ready to grab them, and dreams *are* real. Telling kids that dreams are not real is an insult to their intelligence.

A friend's three-year-old was having nightmares. He said to his son, "Joel, I know dreams can be scary. I sometimes have scary dreams, too, but I know that I will always wake up." But that wasn't good enough for Joel. He took matters into his own hands. One day his dad watched him carefully tying and stretching string from the bottom of the stairs up to the landing, around the corner, down the hall, and into his room, where he tied the end to his bed. Finally he asked the kid what he was doing. "It's a dream trap. I'll know when they are coming up the stairs. They can't get me now." His nightmares stopped shortly after that; of course his dreams did not. But he no longer needed his dream trap because most of his dreams weren't so scary anymore.

If we are open to our kids' dreams, fears, and nightmares, just as we are to all of their emotional experiences, and if we treat those experiences with respect and teach our kids how to handle them, that power will serve them well all their lives.

NIGHT TERRORS ARE NOT TERRIBLE NIGHTMARES

Night terrors are a far cry (both literally and figuratively) from nightmares. Around the age of two, after an especially stressful or conflict-ridden day, your child may begin fitfully throwing himself from one side of the bed to the other, screaming uncontrollably, all the while remaining in a deep sleep. The scream is bound to bring you running into your child's bedroom. As you reach the bedroom door, take a deep breath and calm yourself down before going to the child. The last thing your child needs is to be woken up from a night terror only to see a terrorized parent standing by his bed. After you've collected yourself, calmly shake your child awake and assure him he's going to be all right and that you will be there with him until he falls asleep again. He'll probably not remember the incident and you'll probably never forget it.

Bedtime is a special time, a time of transition. It is an opportunity for closure to one day and a preparation for the next. It is a small turning point in the natural rhythm that gives structure and meaning to life. Just as the seasons and their holidays and celebrations mark the great natural movements of the years, so bedtime marks the turning of the days. With care and patience and awareness of our children's needs, each bedtime can be its own celebration of love and life.

For in sleep, we are recreated and renewed.
—LEO BUSCAGLIA

Chapter 13

Ready, Sit, Go—Toilet Training

When you gotta go, you gotta go
—ANNIE, IN *LITTLE ORPHAN ANNIE*

Just about the time your child is moving from babyhood into the terrific twos and asserting selfhood in lots of creative and sometimes not so constructive ways, your neighbors and relatives start asking when you are going to start toilet training her. Just yesterday she wouldn't open her mouth as you tried to fly the airplane spoon full of peas into the hangar; she threw a temper tantrum when you wouldn't let her store her sandwich in the VCR; and she put her teddy bear in the toilet for a swim. Today she got frustrated when she couldn't get her shoes off by herself, insisted on opening the peanut butter jar without any help, and practiced saying no every chance she got, taking great pride in the power she had with that one word. Are you ready to take on the challenge? And more importantly, is she? All the actions I've just described are examples of your child's attempts to take complete control of her body. Toilet training is the first time she will actually have that control.

WHOSE TOILET TRAINING IS IT ANYWAY? BRICK-WALL APPROACH

A brick-wall parent, as in all of the other areas of her children's lives, takes ownership of the process of toilet training. She often wants to start the process before the child is physically ready. The child has learned to please in all other areas of life and will try to gain approval from her parent by being successful on the toilet, but after several accidents will become either frustrated or resistant, feeling like a failure or refusing to sit on the toilet at all. You may hear a proud brick-wall parent boast that his child was trained at ten months of age. He sat her on the toilet every ten minutes. One has to ask who was trained, the parent or the child?

Pressure, in the form of tangible rewards and punishments for mistakes, is put on the child to perform. Rewards include:

"Go potty and you can have an M and M."
"If you stay dry all week, I'll take you to the ice-cream store."

Punishments include:

"You bad boy. I don't like little boys who wet their pants." (*emotional abuse*)
"Big girls don't pee in their pants." (*verbal disapproval*)
"You are going to have to wear diapers like a baby." (*humiliation*)
"Jimmy and Melanie don't wet their pants anymore. Why can't you be a big boy like them?" (*comparing*)
"I don't want to give you a hug—you wet your pants." (*withholding love and affection*)
"You cannot get up until you go. I am going to hold you here until you do something. I am sick and tired of changing your pants. If you don't go or you get off the toilet, I will spank you." (*threats of physical punishment*)

A brick-wall parent sets up a battle of wills, and the child can choose to please or to resist. Either way the child loses and in the end gets the message *I don't have control over my own body functions.* Complications can set in if the parent and child really lock themselves into a full-blown struggle over toilet training. The child can refuse to have a bowel movement and become constipated. And suddenly the child finds her body invaded with enemas, suppositories, and laxatives. The stress of trying to perform perfectly for her parents can make the child more nervous, scared, and fearful, all of which can result in loose bowel movements, which in turn are almost impossible to control, and the cycle of failure, shame, and hurt continues.

Ho-hum Toilet Training—Jellyfish Approach

The jellyfish parent has a laissez-faire attitude about the whole process. She provides little if any instruction on how the body functions. That a child might be ready to learn at two is missed by the parent because she doesn't see the signs, doesn't have the energy or patience to structure the task for the child, or is simply not there to provide the consistency, structure, support, and guidance. It isn't until the director of the preschool tells her that her child can't come to preschool until the child is toilet trained that the parent begins to get concerned. Either not knowing where to begin or not wanting to be bothered, some jellyfish parents turn the process of toilet training over to a day-care provider, diapering the child on weekends and sending a bag of training pants to the day-care provider's home at the beginning of each week.

Inconsistency only prolongs the toilet-training process. The child is reminded to go sometimes and sometimes not, told to hold it until she gets home, or told just to go in her diaper when it's not convenient to find a toilet. The jellyfish-A parent not only is inconsistent, but also gives mixed messages. One day it is all right or even funny that the child tried unsuccessfully to get to the toilet in time; the next day the parent flies into a rage and severely punishes the child for having wet his pants while playing at the park.

Kids of both jellyfish and brick-wall parents will eventually end up toilet trained, but the cost may be high. Kids may feel powerless, unloved, insecure, humiliated, and confused, and these feelings will spill over into other areas of their lives. In neither family do the kids learn that they have control of their own bodies.

THE THREE Ps OF TOILET TRAINING: PREPARE, PRACTICE, PATIENCE— BACKBONE APPROACH

The backbone parent lets the child be in full control of her body functions and master her own toilet training at her own speed. The parent has a flexible routine, is positive and nonchalant about the routine, expects mistakes and sees them as opportunities to learn, has a relaxed attitude, and is available to help. She is not overly concerned about other adults' expectations and comments. The Three Ps are the backbone structure that is used.

PREPARE

Both you and your child need to be ready to take on the task of toilet training. You need to be willing and able to give your child the time, patience, and encouragement she will need from you. And you need to know why you are helping her. Is it because you are tired of changing diapers, or the preschool won't take her unless she is toilet trained, or your neighbors' son sported training pants months ago? If these are the reasons, take a moment to think again. These might influence you, but the real question is, are you ready to help your child because she is ready to be helped?

Three clues to her readiness are:

1. *Physical development.* Most children are physically ready between the ages of eighteen months and two and a half years old, although for some normally developing children it can be as late as three and a half to four years old. The basic signs of being physically ready are that her bowel

movements are fairly regular; she is consciously aware when she is urinating or when she is ready to have a bowel movement; and she is able to stay dry for long periods of time during the day.

2. *Willingness to toilet train.* A child can be physically ready but have no interest in being toilet trained at eighteen months, yet at two and a half develop a great interest in wearing cartoon-character underwear just like her friends. A good sign of willingness is her wanting her diaper changed immediately after urinating or having a bowel movement.

3. *Ability to communicate with you.* Though not necessary for successful toilet training, it is helpful if a child can tell you verbally what her needs are. ("I had a BM." "I am wet." "I need to go.") She can also understand simple directions. Having worked with children who had special needs, I know that nonverbal children and their parents are able to communicate without words whatever is needed for successful toilet training.

If any of these is missing, no amount of coercion, candy, threats, or books on the subject will get her toilet trained. If a child is willing to learn and can verbalize her needs, yet is not physically ready, she could get a lot of practice in "dry runs" (or "wet runs") to the toilet, but until her body is ready, she will not be successful and she could get very frustrated, giving up and refusing to try even when her body is ready. The nerves and muscles that control voluntary elimination may be developed, but if she is upset about her new baby brother taking over her nursery, her crib, and your time, it is probably not a good idea to begin toilet training, even if the preschool you had planned to send her to requires that she be toilet trained.

When the three ingredients are there together, you and your child are ready to embark on the toilet-training adventure. After the ingredients come the tools.

Number one is a potty chair; it is often easier to get on and off and less intimidating than a potty seat placed on the toilet. Your child can enjoy sitting on it in the bathroom as you sit on the larger seat, both of you "reading" your magazine or book. Let her play with her potty chair and get used to it being around.

At first the teddy bear may spend more time sitting on the chair than your toddler.

Number two is a comfortable, easy-to-manage outfit. Plastic-covered cotton training pants with Velcro closures are easy for your child and easy on you when she has had an accident. The new disposable pull-up training pants serve the same purpose. Both are easy for your toddler to pull up and down and easy for you to take apart if you need to help out with cleaning up after an accident.

Number three is lots of toilet paper. For some unknown reason, once kids figure out how to use it, they will often practice wiping all their stuffed toys, as well as the entire bathroom. As they become adept at urinating and having their bowel movements while on the potty chair, you will need to wipe for them at first, then help them, then finally let them do it themselves. It is important to teach little girls to wipe from the front to the back since the bacteria in their bowel movement can cause an infection if it gets into their vagina.

Number four is a stepstool that can be used by them, first to reach the sink so that they can wash their hands, then to rest their feet when they advance from the potty chair to the big toilet.

Number five is a supply of diapers. Yes, a supply of diapers—and you thought they were gone forever once toilet training started. Some older toddlers, once in training pants, never go back into diapers except for nighttime. Other toddlers find that they are not yet ready or able to control their bladders consistently and need to be able to go back into diapers, not as a punishment but as a break from toilet training. There is no hurry; there is always time to try again.

PRACTICE

As with any other skill, it takes practice for a child to learn to control her bladder and her bowels. There is no one right way to toilet train. You and your own toddler can find what works for both of you. The key to remember is that you are helping her learn to take control of her body. The following are some time- and toddler-tested suggestions.

When she is toddling around and taking an interest in

everything you do, bring her with you into the bathroom and tell her what you are doing. (Little boys will take great interest in their father's ability to aim at and hit wads of toilet paper thrown into the toilet and will see it as a big step when they can practice with him.) When changing her diapers, you can begin to give her the words she can later use: "Jamie is wet. Jamie had a bowel movement (or BM)." If she is grunting, straining or pacing, you can comment that it looks like she is trying to have a BM and ask her if she wants to sit on the potty chair. Let her choose to sit or not. Try to remember that it is her body, and she will learn to control it in her own time and in her own way. She just needs your help, guidance, and support.

If you are alert to your child's physical as well as verbal clues, you will see a schedule emerging that can give you advance notice of when she will need to go. Your own body schedule can also be a clue; when you get up in the morning, after lunch, naptime, and before you go for a ride in the car. It is important to take your child seriously when she says she has to go. Toddlers can hold it for a while; younger ones simply can't.

Being around other kids who are already trained and watching them use the potty chair can help a toddler understand the whole process. When accidents happen, your child will see that they can happen to other people too; it's not a big deal; and there is always another pair of dry pants. All children have accidents at some time in their toddlerhood and often beyond, especially when there is a major change in their lives: a new baby, a move, a divorce. Remember, it is a skill they are learning, not a contest they are winning.

Bladder control usually occurs after bowel control, and daytime control usually occurs before sleeping control. Bed-wetting (enuresis) after four or five can be a source of conflict, guilt, and shame on the part of both the parent and the child. The parent may feel a need to punish or reward the child to get him (it is more often a boy than a girl) to stay dry at night. Neither really works and can invite the child to say he doesn't care or to try to hide the wet sheets. Dr. T. Berry Brazelton, a noted pediatrician, in his book *Touchpoints: The Essential Reference*, gives the best advice I have heard on the subject:

> In bedwetting ... a child's need to become independent
> at his own speed is at stake. Though the reasons may be

physiological, such as an immature bladder that empties
frequently, or too-deep sleep (the result of an immature
signaling system), the issue of who will control the situation
is there. As parents and physicians begin to investigate
reasons and institute measures (such as alarms,
punishments, or signal devices that go off when he wets),
the child's autonomy and need for control become lost. He
sees himself as a failure—immature, guilty, and hopeless.
The damage of this self-image to his future will be greater
than that of the symptoms themselves.

There are nighttime shields on the market today that you
can get for your four-or five-years old (or older) child who is still
wetting the bed and wants to spend a night at a friend's but is
afraid to because he would be embarrassed. In fact I see nothing
wrong and everything right with your child wearing them every
night until his bladder has matured. The shields are worn inside
the underwear and have a pad that absorbs the urine; no bulky
diapers, no leaking, no odor, and peace of mind for your child.
Grandma or Grandpa might be willing to explain that in their
older age they, too, rely on Depends.

Contrary to what some popular books claim, toilet training
cannot be learned in a day. If you wait long enough, you may be
able to put "big girl" panties on your older toddler and she will
keep them dry from day one. In reality she has been taking in all
the other steps for months. Second and third children in the
family often take less time than the first, simply because there are
more models for them to imitate.

Modeling, trial and error, imitating, and a good sense of humor
are keys to successful practice. Waving good-bye to the bowel
movement being flushed down the toilet, aiming at toilet-paper
targets in the toilet bowl, and singing toilet tunes can put a bit of
fun into learning a lifelong skill.

PATIENCE

Patience: "The power or capacity to endure without complaint
something difficult." It takes patience to stop in the middle of a
phone call from a long-lost friend to help your child onto the
potty chair, only to have her say, "I guess it's not ready to come

out yet." Even more patience to help her clean up after she wets her pants three minutes after she emphatically told you she didn't need to go before she got in the car. And extra patience to put up with all the knowing adults convinced that your child will go from diapers to Depends because she hasn't been toilet trained by two and a half. But every bit of your patience is worth it.

Once you and your child embark on the toilet-training adventure, thanks to your willingness to establish a backbone structure of preparedness, practice, and patience, your child will be able to begin to see herself as a competent, resourceful, and responsible person who is learning to treat her own body with dignity and regard.

> Relax. Many mothers and fathers are concerned that teaching their children bowel and bladder control is a mysteriously powerful parent-child interaction fraught with all sorts of hidden pitfalls, any one of which can induce crippling neurosis. But in reality, toilet learning is not different from any other early childhood learning experience—learning how to handle a fork, or button a shirt—that requires a combination of mental and muscular coordination.
>
> —ALISON MACK, *TOILET LEARNING*

Chapter 14

Sexuality Is Not a Four-Letter Word

If only we could accept the inherent naturalness of our
sexual system as we do the digestive and elimination
system, we would be well on our way to raising sexually
healthy children.
—LYNN LEIGHT, R.N. *RAISING SEXUALLY HEALTHY CHILDREN*

A seven-year-old came running into the kitchen and asked,
"Mom, where did I come from?" Dropping a dish in the sink,
Mom turned around and asked her son to have a seat at the
kitchen table, she would be right with him to answer his question.
A bit unnerved and somewhat irritated, Mom ran up to the
bedroom and pulled a couple of books from behind the night-
stand. Dad had promised to go through these books with his son
on the last camping trip; now it looked like it would be up to
Mom to break the news to the seven-year-old. As the books
were carefully placed on the kitchen table, the little boy, anxious
to get back out and play, took one look at the covers and shook his
head. "Dad went through these with me on our last camping trip.
I just wanted to know where I came from. I forgot, is it New York
or New Jersey?"

Many of us are uncomfortable talking to our children about
sexuality in general and sex in particular, partly because our
parents did not say anything about it to us, or said very little
and hoped we got the necessary information in our health

class. And you and I know how misinformed we often were. Storks bringing babies? Birds and bees do it—do what? Bad girls do it, good girls don't. Who of us has not had a friend who thought she couldn't get pregnant the "first time," or if she stood up, or if she was menstruating, only to find out she had wrong information, and what a way to find out? Or known a boy who was afraid hair would grow on his hand if he masturbated, then the whole world would know what an ugly thing he had done? A girl convinced she is bleeding to death when she has her first period; a boy afraid he is losing bladder control when he has his first wet dream.

Kids learn about their sexuality even if it is not us doing the teaching. But often what they learn is misinformation and mis-interpretation, exaggerations, and exploitive notions about their own bodies and bodies of people of the opposite sex. By avoiding talking about sexuality, we give our children subtle and not-so-healthy messages: "It's off limits, don't ask, don't question, don't look, find somewhere else to get your information."

If we want to be the primary sexuality educators of our chil-dren, it is critical that we begin an open communication about sexuality early in our kids' lives so that a positive pattern of com-munication is established before the hormonal changes of pu-berty affect our teenagers' thoughts and feelings about their own sexuality. With the understanding that sexuality is much more than sex, as parents we can convey with verbal and nonverbal messages that our sexuality is a wonderful part of our total being, not just what we do with our genitals. Our actions and expres-sions, our emotions, the way we treat our own bodies and our children's bodies, the way we respond to their cries and react to their basic bodily functions—all these help our kids to develop healthy attitudes about their own sexuality, as well as help to create a comfortable environment for our children to get to know their own bodies and ask questions.

The three types of families handle issues around sexuality in predictably different ways.

Thou Shalt Not, You Better Not, Don't You Dare (Brick-Wall Parents' Reproach)

Brick-wall parents communicate mostly "don't" messages, hand down moral absolutes, and instill a sense of shame about sexual activity: "Don't touch. It will fall off." "You messed your pants, you bad boy." "Every month you'll have the curse." "Don't touch it. It's yuck." "Good girls don't do it." "When you're old enough, we'll go to the priest and let him talk to you about it." "Sex is something that's expected of you. You don't have to like it, you just have to put up with it."

Often there is a "holy silence" around sexual issues, and kids get the message that you just don't ask any questions. Rather than gaining an understanding about themselves and members of the opposite sex, they remain fearful and ignorant. One of the problems with withholding knowledge is that instead of keeping kids from sexual activity, it often does just the opposite.

> Current research indicates that children who are well-informed and comfortable in talking with their parents about sexuality are least likely to have sexual intercourse when they are adolescents. Knowledge does not lead to inappropriate behaviour, ignorance does.
> —BARBARA JONES, *THE STORK DIDN'T BRING YOU*

Having worked with many pregnant teenagers, I've yet to see one of them pregnant on information. It just doesn't happen. Kids are less likely to have intercourse in their teen years (and as a result get pregnant and/or contract a sexually transmitted disease) if they are given good information, have open communication with their parents, and see their parents interacting in sexually healthy ways.

I Hope Nothing Bad Happens (Jellyfish Parents' Approach)

Jellyfish parents' laissez-faire attitude about life characterizes their messages about sexuality. They hope the school, friends, TV, books, or the clergy will teach their children what they as parents can't, don't want to, or don't know how to teach. The extreme jellyfish parents have no limits or boundaries on the expression of their own sexuality. They model promiscuity, and they expose young children to abundant sexual information that they are not ready to understand or that is abusive and derogatory: "It won't hurt him to watch this X-rated movie. I've seen lots of them and they haven't hurt me." "Sure, I leave those magazines around. They're a good way to teach kids things they won't talk to us about." "I want her to be popular."

Rather than gain a healthy understanding of their own sexuality, kids in jellyfish homes come to see sex as a tool to use to get something else. The information they have about their bodies is distorted, the boundaries for appropriate, healthy, sexual behavior nonexistent.

In both these types of families kids are unable to ask questions, learn to set their own limits, or explore their own sexuality in a framework of awareness of the worth and dignity of their own and others' bodies. It is easy for these kids to succumb to peer pressure. ("Everybody is doing it." "Prove to me you love me." "Don't believe what your parents tell you. They just don't want you to have fun." "Trust me, I won't get you pregnant.")

It is also easier for them to succumb to something even more devastating than giving in to peer pressure alone.

Too many American teenagers face rising rates of morbidity associated with sexual ignorance, poor decision-making, and inadequate sexuality education. Over one million teenage women become pregnant each year. One in seven teenagers contracts a sexually transmitted disease

annually. One in 500 U.S. college students is infected
with HIV.

—ROBERT WM. BLUM, M.D., PH.D., PRESIDENT,
SOCIETY FOR ADOLESCENT MEDICINE

THE BEGINNINGS OF A WONDERFUL RELATIONSHIP

Backbone parents begin to lay a strong foundation for raising
sexually healthy children even before their children are born,
by coming to understand their own sexuality and how it is an
integral part of their values, morals, emotions, and sexual feelings.
(Easier said than done! And no, it's not too late to start right
now, even if your own children are reaching puberty.) This strong
sense of self enables backbone parents to celebrate the beautiful
qualities of both boys and girls without stereotyping the sexual
roles of their individual children. It also becomes a model for
children to emulate. Treating your own body, your spouse's
body, and your child's body with dignity and respect is the
beginning of a lifelong relationship of trust, caring, and nurturing.

CURIOSITY, COMFORT, AND CORRECT WORDS

As your young children begin to locate and explore all of their
own body parts, you can begin to establish an open and honest
channel of communication by using the proper names for *all* of
the body parts. This is also easier said than done as habit and
poor modeling creep into our vocabulary. ("Here are your eyes,
your ears, your nose, your elbow, your knee, your ankle, and
your wee-wee?!") Amazing, there are 101 slang words for penis
and 125 slang words for breasts—and no slang words for ankle.
That says more about a cultural attitude toward sexuality than it
does about a lack of creativity when it comes to ankles. Slang
terms, rather than the proper names, imply something mysterious,

secretive, unnatural, forbidden, or dirty. Using slang allows us to walk around the subject of sexuality rather than talk directly about sex organs and their functions.

Avoiding the proper names can also result in confusion and alarm: "The baby is growing in Mommy's tummy." Just yesterday you told your four-year-old that the spaghetti he ate went into his tummy. Now he has a picture in his mind of the spaghetti and baby all mixed together. Direct talk is what kids need: "The baby is growing in Mommy's *womb*. A womb is a special place a girl has where a baby can grow until it is ready to be born." And you can be off and running with an opportunity at the dinner table: "No, boys don't have a womb. Would you like to see a picture book that shows the special parts that you have as a boy?" (If he has a sister, he has probably already noticed a few anatomical differences, and this will not be the first time the subject has come up, nor will it be the last.) Four-year-olds need specific information, not a long, drawn-out explanation.

The book my own children enjoyed looking at at an early age and then read on their own for the facts of life without any nonsense and with illustrations was *Where Did I Come From?* Leaving it in the bookcase with the rest of the books gave a message that the information in this book was as important and normal and fun to learn as the information in *The Cat in the Hat*.

A four-year-old girl announced to her mom in the grocery checkout line that her vagina itched. The adults around her gasped. Far better a four-year-old can say her vagina itches than, when she is thirty years old, to be telling her doctor, "It itches down there." Most four-year-olds can tell you Snufalopagus used to be an invisible friend of Big Bird's, and probably tell it to you in two languages. And yet we think that they can't say or understand uterus, or pregnant, or penis, or clitoris.

Teachable moments are simple, ordinary, everyday situations that present opportunities for teaching your young children about sexuality. The neighbors' cat has a litter of kittens; your sister has a new baby; sensitive subjects are raised at the dinner table in front of all of the relatives ("Dad, Billy is self-pleasuring at the dinner table, I thought you told him to 'do it in private, please.'") —all present opportunities to impart knowledge, values, and a moral backbone on which your children can build their own sense of themselves as sexual beings.

Dormant Doesn't Mean Don't Talk

During the later childhood years, sometimes called the dormant period, kids are more interested in the facts. ("Just give me the facts.") They don't want any long, drawn-out explanations about anything they ask you. (Remember the why-period when you felt like your toddler was going to send you to the funny farm with his constant questions. That time has passed.) Usually having little interest in members of the opposite sex, they are now more interested in learning about their own bodies and comparing their bodies with those of members of the same sex. ("You show me yours, and I'll show you mine.") However, it is not a time for you to stop bringing up correct information about sexuality. Keeping the information flowing during this time, although it may seem one-sided, is important for two reasons.

First of all, misinformation is flowing just as fast in the school yard, on the streets, through the media, and sometimes in your kid's head. Don't be lulled into thinking that because you've explained it, the school taught it, or your child saw it on TV, he really got it.

Roy Bonisteel, former commentator for the Canadian Broadcasting Company, tells the story of two six-year-old boys who find a five-dollar bill on the sidewalk.

One boy said, "Wow, let's go get some cookies and candy and ice cream."

The other boy exclaimed, "Oh, no, let's go buy some Tampax."

"Tampax?"

"Yes! With Tampax, we can go horseback riding, hiking, and swimming!"

Just because they heard it doesn't mean they understand it.

The second reason to keep the information flowing, even if it is you asking the questions, is that the channels of communication are more likely to remain open during the next and very critical age of development.

PRETEENS AND THE LONG CAR RIDE (AGES NINE THROUGH ELEVEN)

The dormant period is over, yet the hormones are not yet raging. It is time to capitalize on your preteens' interest in their own bodies and the changes that are occurring that affect their bodies, minds, and emotions. They are receiving a lot of mixed messages about sexuality, sex, love, dating, diseases, and pimples. They want to know what it's all about. Now is the time they need to know the detailed facts about sexuality, intimacy, dating, and sexually transmitted diseases. The more knowledge they have now, the better able they will be to make responsible decisions about the expressions of their sexuality later.

The best way I know to begin sharing this information is to get in the car with your preteens, lock the doors, and head down the freeway to a town about an hour and a half away. You do that for three reasons:

1.   Neither of you can jump out of the car on the freeway.

2.   You don't have to establish eye contact. Staring straight ahead, you can say, "Son, I need to talk to you about sex." "Oh, Dad, I know all about that stuff." "Son, I need to tell you what I know. If I get any of it wrong, tell me. If I leave anything out, let me know." And you just keep talking.

3.   When you get to your destination, you can both get out and share a meal. The conversation is over; you can both take a deep breath and know it is really only the beginning of many in-depth conversations on the topic.

If your own information is scanty, and for many of us it is, go scour the library and bookstores for books and films that not only impart accurate information but present it in a way that mirrors the values you would like to share with your children. And look at some that don't. They could be helpful in letting you know what other information is out there and also allow you to examine your own values to reaffirm them or challenge old messages that are not serving you or your children well now.

THE UN AGE—UNABLE TO BE AN ADULT, UNABLE TO BE A CHILD, AND WANTING TO BE BOTH (AGES TWELVE THROUGH FIFTEEN)

The drive to separate from their parents is taken up in earnest during these next few years. At the same time adolescents are looking for your approval, support, and guidance. Wanting to be treated like an adult and upset if they are expected to act like one, they try the patience of the best of the adults around them. All three of our kids were "lippy" at this age, but after we survived Anna's going through it, we resigned ourselves to the fact it would happen with Maria and Joe and that this, too, would pass.

This age is punctuated with raging hormones and simple questions that have complicated answers. Your daughter comes in the front door all smiles. Next minute she is in the bathroom crying. Your son answers the phone in a deep tenor voice, only to have it reach a high soprano note two seconds later. He wonders if the squeak will ever go away.

The big question asked by both girls and boys is "Am I normal?" Looking around, they see their friends' body shapes changing. Their own bodies are changing, but not at the same rate as their friends'. The only thing that seems normal is that everyone looks and sounds different. It will help your teens if you talk to them about the stages of development *before* their bodies begin the radical changes they will undergo in the next few years. And while you are at it, tell them about the changes the members of the opposite sex will be going through as well. They will be noticing; you might as well help them along with *factual* information.

Your teen will probably be wondering about falling in love, crushes, self-pleasuring, homosexuality, intercourse, and issues related to wet dreams, periods, and pregnancy. Although you have already touched upon all of these with your preteen, now she wants more detailed information: "Is it really love?" "I'm in love with my history teacher, am I normal?" "Do only boys pleasure themselves?" "If I am attracted to my best friend, am I gay?" "Do all boys have wet dreams?" "How come everyone else has had their period and I haven't?" "Can a girl get pregnant the first time she has sex?"

Girls tend to begin their physical and sexual growth spurt at eleven or twelve, boys at fourteen or fifteen, and emotional development for either can occur before, after, or simultaneously with the physical growth spurt. It's no wonder that the most pressing question is "Am I normal?"

CELEBRATE PUBERTY

Celebrate puberty? Why not? We celebrate almost every other milestone in our children's lives: first tooth, first word, first birthday, first time on a bicycle without training wheels, first grade, reaching five feet, first date, first shave, first time driving without a parent in the car. Why not our daughter's first period and our son's first wet dream? Many cultures and religions have celebrations or rites of passage as they welcome teens into a more mature involvement in the community. (I am not talking about initiations or hazing rituals that test young men or women and in the process often strip them of their sense of dignity and self.)

We are our children's parents until they reach puberty. When they reach puberty, it is time for us to move out of the parenting role to become their mentor, a model and a guide. If we mentor them well in the teen years, in adulthood they can become our friends. (Some of you may not yet be friends of your parents. They haven't stopped parenting you yet.)

As our children reach the milestone of their entry into puberty and we begin our journey as mentors, we can start with a celebration. One way is to take your teen out for a special meal, or a special hike, or special bike ride, just the three of you—Mom, Dad, and kid. (If you are divorced and still speaking to each other, come together to celebrate with your teen. If you are not talking to each other, perhaps you can celebrate with your teen individually. Teens need to know that both Mom and Dad know what's happening and are willing to be there to be a mentor.) You can give your teens a special gift as you tell them how exciting and scary it is to have them reach this wonderful milestone in their lives. Remind them that they have a tremendous right and an awesome responsibility. Then assure them you will be there to guide them through their exciting teen years as they begin to more fully understand and explore the richness of their own sexuality.

SEX, VALUES, INTIMACY, AND COMMITMENT (AGES SIXTEEN THROUGH NINETEEN)

It is during this stage that your teens will move toward independence in all areas of their lives. No longer seeing you as their parent, they look to you as a mentor and guide when it comes to issues such as responsible and respectful sexual behavior. Issues that have been touched upon before now command stage front and center:

- Sex—why is something so natural and good so complicated?
- Abstinence—the only sure way to avoid pregnancy and sexually transmitted diseases. Are there other benefits?
- Gynecological exam—what is it and when should I have one?
- AIDS and other sexually transmitted diseases—causes, prevention, signs, and symptoms. Can I trust her if she says I am her first?
- Contraception and safer sex—can the two be mutually exclusive?
- Love and sex—can you be in love without having sexual intercourse?
- Sexual abuse—what is it and how can I avoid it?
- Intimacy and friendship—what's the difference and can I have both?

As they move on into adulthood, they will assume full responsibility for their physical, spiritual, moral, and sexual growth. You will remain a mentor and begin the wonderful process of becoming their friend.

> Children who feel loved and wanted, and have been fortunate to have parents who respect themselves will have the best chance for a healthy sexual development.
> —BARBARA JONES, *THE STORK DIDN'T BRING YOU*

Epilogue

Your children are not your children.
They are the sons and daughters of Life's longing for itself.
They come through you but not from you,
And though they are with you, yet they belong not to you.
You may give them your love but not your thoughts,
For they have their own thoughts...
You may strive to be like them, but seek not to make them
    like you.
For life goes not backward nor tarries with yesterday.
                                —KAHLIL GIBRAN, *THE PROPHET*

Dear Parents,

After you've been caring, and consistent ... firm and fair ... you've said what you meant and meant what you said and did what you said you were going to do ... you've eliminated sarcasm, ridicule, and embarrassment from your talk with your kids ... and you've developed a backbone structure around mealtime, bedtime, chores, allowances, fighting—and you are totally exhausted, there is one more thing you can do. After your kids are asleep this evening (it's easier when they are sleeping), walk into their bedrooms, look down at each one of them, and remind yourself that there is one thing you and I as parents cannot do, nor do we want to do if we really think about it, and that's control our children's will—that spirit that lets them be themselves apart from you and me.

They are not ours to possess, control, manipulate, or even to make mind. What they are is what Kahlil Gibran said they were: "Life longing for itself." They are gifts to us. Now, granted some came in very unique packaging, but they are still gifts to us, and we need to treat them as gifts. We need to encourage members of this next generation to become all that they can become, not try to force them to become what we want them to become. Neither we nor they would benefit from this narrow-mindedness. You and I can't even begin to dream the dreams this next generation is going to dream, or answer the questions that will be put to them.

If you want your kids to make wise choices, give them the opportunity to make lots of choices—including some unwise ones. Unless the unwise ones are life-threatening, morally threatening, or unhealthy (in which case you have to intervene), allow them to experience the real-world consequences of their own mistakes and poor choices, as painful as they may be.

When they fall, don't be standing in front of them to rescue, or over them to punish. Be behind them to support and guide them. Give them the six critical life messages: I believe in you ... I trust in you ... I know you can handle this... you are listened to ... you are cared for ... and you are very important to me.

If you are going to give your kids these six critical life messages, I have an assignment for each one of you. Model these messages for your children. The best way I know to do this is to take at least a half hour out of your day, every day, and give it to the only person who's going to spend the rest of your life with you—and that's you. You're honestly the only person you can count on being there when you need you the most. So, take that half hour and do something that says, *I like me!*

Some of you are probably saying, *Woman, you don't understand—we're talking laundry piled three feet high, dishes stacked in the sink, three kids and one on the way, and you want me to give myself a half hour?* You bet I do, because if you don't, I promise you, nobody else will. You must believe first that you're worth it before you can impress on your kids that they're worth it. So take that half hour and run, pray, read a good book, sit quietly, take a long bath (don't eat a hunk of chocolate cake, or you'll regret it)—do something that says, *I like me.*

When you've done that, you won't find that you're the perfect parent or that you have the best-behaved kids in school or the kids with the highest test scores. No, if you give yourself that half hour, you're going to find something greater—you're going to find the energy and serenity every day to know three things: *I like myself; I can think for myself; and in parenting today there is no problem so great it can't be solved.* You will find yourself winning at parenting, not beating your kids, not controlling them, not making them mind. Rather, you'll be winning by inviting and encouraging your children to become all that they can become. Which is responsible, resourceful, resilient, loving individuals who have the gift of inner discipline.

You're worth it, and so are they. And if that's not enough reason to take the time to develop a strong backbone in your family today, I'd like to leave you with this last reason: old age. Hopefully, you and I are going to have the opportunity to grow much older and share our wisdom with the generation in which we are now investing our time, our energy and I believe, in parenting, our very lives.

If we can raise this next generation to believe that they can love themselves and in loving themselves, they can then extend themselves in a loving way to others.

If we can teach them that they can think for themselves, and in thinking for themselves would never allow others—governments or drug dealers or friends—to manipulate them, nor would they choose to manipulate others for their own gain.

If we can teach them that they don't have to be good-looking, bright, thin, and young (that silly medium of exchange in our culture) in order to have dignity and worth, then they will understand that it is because they are children and for no other reason that they have dignity and worth—simply because they *are*.

If we can teach them to not be so dog-eat-dog competitive, but to be truly competent, cooperative, decisive human beings, who if they need to, want to, have to, or are forced to compete, will do it with a moral sense.

And if we can teach them to solve their own personal, social, and academic problems, then I believe we will have taught them that, in this world, there is no problem so great that it can't be solved.

If we teach our children these things, then, when you and I are old and this next generation starts making decisions for us and for the next generation they will create, we can trust that the time and energy we spent parenting our children and developing a strong backbone was well worth it. Thanks to our time and energy and love this next generation will be able to make responsible, caring, loving decisions.

You're worth it! Your kids are worth it!

Joy!

Barbara Coloroso

Index